John Castell Hopkins

The Sword of Islam, or, Suffering Armenia

Annals of the Turkish power and the Eastern question

John Castell Hopkins

The Sword of Islam, or, Suffering Armenia
Annals of the Turkish power and the Eastern question

ISBN/EAN: 9783744797092

Printed in Europe, USA, Canada, Australia, Japan

Cover: Foto ©Lupo / pixelio.de

More available books at **www.hansebooks.com**

THE
SWORD OF ISLAM
OR
SUFFERING ARMENIA

ANNALS OF TURKISH POWER

AND THE

EASTERN QUESTION

BY
J. CASTELL HOPKINS
Author of "Life of Sir John Thompson," "Life and Work of Mr. Gladstone," Etc., Etc.

WITH A PREFACE BY

Right Reverend A. Sweatman, D.D., D.C.L.
LORD BISHOP OF TORONTO.

THE BRADLEY-GARRETSON CO., LTD,
Brantford and Toronto.
1896

Entered according to Act of Parliament of Canada, in the year one thousand
eight hundred and ninety-six, by the Bradley-Garretson Company,
Limited, in the Office of the Minister of Agriculture.

CONTENTS

CHAPTER I.
THE RISE AND FALL OF TURKISH POWER.

Origin of the Turks—The Ottoman dynasty—Rise and fall of various Mahometan powers—Sweep of Islamism through Asia Minor—Battle of Kassova—Conquest of Constantinople—Establishment of Turkish rule upon the ruins of the Greek Empire—A strong and aggressive Moslem state—Europe trembles before its soldiers—Wars with Christian states—Venice, Austria, Poland, and Hungary feel the force of Turkish arms and reckless bravery—Character and quality of the Mahometan soldier—Cruelty a predominant feature—Great rulers of the Empire—Despotism, debauchery, and corruption undermine the strength of the country and the vigour of the Sultan's rule.................................21-37

CHAPTER II.
THE MAHOMETAN CREED.

Influence of religion upon national characteristics and government—The secret of Turkish power and weakness—Precepts and practices of Mahomet—The Koran and the laws and institutions of Turkey—Mahometanism in Turkey, originally an aggressive, conquering force, now mainly a system for the preservation of a vicious system of government and an immoral code of laws—The fortunes of the Turkish Empire controlled by this fact—Islamism encourages ignorance, promotes domestic slavery, and through the pernicious influence of the harem destroys morality and crushes the better instincts of child-nature—Deception lawful against Christians—Moslem intolerance—Mahometan converts to Christianity condemned to death—Cruelty a characteristic of the Moslem creed 38-53

CHAPTER III.
MODERN TURKEY.

The Sultans of the century—Steady decadence of Turkish power—Corruption, misgovernment, and moral degradation the main reasons—Wars with

Russia, and the influence of that country—Prolonged exertions of Great Britain to obtain reform and melioration of Christian conditions—Natural opposition of Turkish officials—The strong effort of Mahmoud II.—Destruction of the Janizaries—Reigns of Abdul-Medjid and Abdul-Aziz—Mahometanism absolutely antagonistic to free government—The great work of Lord Stratford de Redcliffe—The Magna Charta of Turkey—An excellent but useless document—Midhat and Reschid Pashas—The Grand Vizier inferior to the Kislar Aga or Chief Eunuch—No hope of any real reform—The prophetic utterance of Lord Palmerston—The Berlin Treaty and Cyprus Convention.............. 54-69

CHAPTER IV.
CONSTANTINOPLE—THE CENTRE OF ISLAM.

The shadow of the Sultan—Constantinople—Its beauty and ugliness—The home of secret crime and poisoned pleasure—Annals of a great and historic city—Its place in the world of diplomacy and war—The exquisite scenery of the Bosphorus, and the military importance of the Dardanelles—The strength and weakness of Abdul-Hamid II.—His character, pursuits, and power--His ministers and instruments—His responsibility for Turkish rule and misrule—The personal embodiment of ignorance and historic bigotry—A product of his environment and creed—Some good qualities which only add to the sufferings of the people 70-85

CHAPTER V.
RUSSIA AND TURKEY.

The early relations of these countries—The Muscovite profits by the decline of the Turk—Both are barbarian powers, despite the nominal Christianity of Russia—Treaty of 1774, and large Russian acquisition of territory—Aims of Peter the Great and the Empress Catharine—A maritime outlet demanded by Russia—Constantinople its ultimate goal—Unity and continuity of its aggressive policy, whether in Turkey or the far East, whether striking at Stamboul or Cabool—War of 1828 and Treaty of Adrianople—Russian intrigue, and the Treaty of Unkiar Skelessi—Conquest of the Circassians and of vast countries in Central Asia—The Crimean War—Protection of Christians a mere excuse for intervention in Turkish affairs—Modern intrigues, the War of 1877, and British policy...................................... 86-101

CHAPTER VI.
THE GREEK CHURCH AND EASTERN CHRISTIANITY.

Commencement and early extension of Christianity in the East—Founding of the Greek Church—The Patriarchs of Constantinople take the place in the East which the Popes of Rome held in the West—Severance of the Eastern and Western Churches—Decline and fall of the Greek Empire—Conversion of the Bulgarians and Russians—Government, principles, and practices of the Greek Church in Turkey and Russia—Its relationship to the Eastern Question, the aims of Russia, and the ambition of Greece—Differences between the Greek and other denominations of Eastern Christianity and Roman Catholicism—Eastern Christianity not always a help to Western missions—The Christian and the Moslem..108-115

CHAPTER VII.

A Survey of European Turkey.

A wonderful and perplexing mixture of races and creeds—Hardly any state a unit in nationality or religion—Montenegro an exception to the rule—A grand race of Christian warriors—Prolonged struggles with the Turks—Their mountain homes, history, and customs—Other minor states—The Albanians—A warlike, active race, with marked tendencies to brigandage—Their connection with the Greeks, and antagonism to the Turks—Mixture of races and creeds in Macedonia—Claims to the territory by Bulgaria and Greece—Apparently hopeless rivalry of Bulgarians and Servians, of Greeks and Turks—United action of the Christian states of Turkey apparently impossible—A separate view of the more important countries necessary in order to comprehend the situation...116-131

CHAPTER VIII.

The Struggles of Modern Greece.

Grecian war for independence—Bitter hatred of the Turk—Qualities and character of the people, as compared with those of the ancient Greeks—Prolonged and oppressive rule of Turkey—Atrocities committed during the rebellion—Invasion of Ibrahim Pasha and intervention of France and England—The battle of Navarino and establishment of the Kingdom of Greece—Reign of Otho I.—The Greek Church in Greece—Its constitution and influence—The people in public and private life—Their character, morals, and faculty for self-government—Russian intrigues—The Greeks in other parts of Turkey a constant source of trouble to the Sultan—Memories of Cretan struggle and Turkish outrages—The Ionian Islands—Present position of the country, and the natural ambition to revive the empire of Constantine......................................132-148

CHAPTER IX.
BULGARIA AND THE TURKS.

An ancient, kindly, and prosperous people—Misgovernment and oppression by the Turks since the conquest in the fourteenth century—The mass of the people belong to the Greek Church—The commencement of the terrible troubles of 1876—The people taxed to deat'—Cruelty and corruption of Turkish officials—An uprising, followed by the appearance of the Bashi-Bazouks and a record of barbarity and slaughter unequalled in the annals of Europe—England roused by the nature of the Bulgarian horrors, and by Mr. Gladstone's indignant eloquence—Effect upon British public opinion, and the policy of the Government during the ensuing Russo-Turkish war—The Congress of Berlin, and the practical independence of Bulgaria—Russian intrigues and war with Servia—Possible future of Bulgaria..151-166

CHAPTER X.
SERVIA AND ROUMANIA.

Two important and now independent states—Origin of their people, and the history of their severance from Turkey—Struggles for independence, and present relations with the Sultan—Austrian plots in Servia and Russian intrigues in Roumania—Other religious interests and natural characteristics—Rulers and institutions—The Treaty of Berlin—Their pla^ in the ever-changing Eastern Question—Roumania a well-governed state with an excellent future before it, if not absorbed by Russia—Servia a quarrelsome state, with questionable prospects 169-181

CHAPTER XI.
BOSNIA AND HERZEGOVINA.

Originally a part of Hungary—Conquest by the Turks—Subsequent efforts at independence—Austrian claims and intrigues—Revolt of 1875—Austrian intervention and invasion—Population of the two provinces—Characteristics and religious divisions of the people—Many Mahometans, but few Turks—Memories of Mahometan misgovernment and cruelty—Austrian protection and practical settlement of this branch of the Eastern Question..182-193

CHAPTER XII.
EGYPT AND THE OTTOMAN POWER.

Historical memories—Conquest by the Saracens, and then by the Turks—Invasion by Bonaparte, and first British intervention—The rise of modern

Egypt under Mehemet Ali—Career of Ibrahim Pasha, and invasion of Syria and Greece—The progress of his power and of French intrigues alarms Europe—A second British intervention—Egypt brought into submission again to Turkey—The present position of England and Turkey in the land of the Nile—Its place in the much-vexed Eastern Question, and the problem of establishing a Christian power in Constantinople. 194-209

CHAPTER XIII.
HISTORIC ARMENIA.

In the mists of the past—The supposed site of the Garden of Eden—A very ancient state and people—Curious traditions and records—Conquest by Mithridates and the Parthians—Reign of Tigranes II., and the Armenian victories in Syria—Collision with the Romans—Subjection to Persia—Early Christian conversion, and persecutions—Various dynasties and revolutions—Conquest by Timour and the Saracens—The Moslem wave sweeps over Asia Minor—King Leo visits England—Disappearance of Armenia as a nation—Its survival in a scattered race—Origin, barbarism, and power of the Kurds—Present population, and divisions of ancient Armenia...210-228

CHAPTER XIV.
ARMENIAN RELIGION AND CHARACTERISTICS.

One of the most ancient divisions of the Christian Church—Its history, constitution, and principles—Relationship to the Greek and Roman Catholic churches—King Tiridates of Armenia an earlier convert to Christianity than the Emperor Constantine—Influence of Arminianism in the East—Sacraments, doctrines, and liturgy of the Church—Character and scope of its clergy—Divisions in its ranks—Cleverness, and peaceful, progressive character of the Armenian people—Customs and home life—Entire absence of liberty and tolerance from the country—Turkish outrages—Business aptitude and success of the Armenian under fair conditions—His claim upon the protection of Christian Europe........... 231-244

CHAPTER XV.
A GLANCE OVER ASIATIC TURKEY.

The birthplace of Christianity now the domain of the Moslem—The Holy Land and Syria, Mesopotamia, and the stamping ground of ancient empires sharing in a common state of stagnation—Divisions in Moslemism and Christianity—General condition of the countries and people of Turkish Asia—Russian schemes and Russian conquests—The Berlin

Treaty and British obligations under the Cyprus Convention—No country in Asia Minor fit to take up the falling reins of Ottoman power—Tremendous difficulties in the way of settlement—Oppression and submission characteristic of Eastern governments and peoples—A united Armenia might achieve something, but Russia and Persia stand in the way—Opportunity for development and religious liberty in Asia Minor under British protection—Present neglect of vast natural riches under insupportable taxation and the other evils of Moslem rule.......247-259

CHAPTER XVI.

CHARACTERISTICS OF THE TURK.

In Europe an isolated barbarian; in Asia a despotic tyrant—His place amongst nationalities and countries absolutely unique—By nature, training, and religion, a complete barbarian, he yet holds a place amongst the civilised powers of the world—Much that was energetic and noble in his original character obliterated by the effects of indolence, immorality, and fatalism—The poorer classes somewhat superior to the others in morals and life—As a rule, however, the Turk is enervated by corruption, despotism, and vice—A section still make good soldiers, and can be roused into desperate and dangerous fanaticism—Home life of the people—Customs, amusements, and religious observance—The unspeakable Turk and the immutable Koran—Moslemism to be propagated and preserved by the sword 260-275

CHAPTER XVII.

RELATIONS OF GREAT BRITAIN AND TURKEY.

Natural antagonism of England and the Ottoman power—Modified by ignorance, then by commercial considerations, and finally by the necessities of European peace—The Levant Company and development of English trade with Turkey—Early interventions in Turkish affairs—The independence of Greece—Lord Stratford de Redcliffe's prolonged exertions—Russian aggression and growing power compel still further British support—Intervention against France and Egypt in Syria—Another complication in the existence of 50,000,000 Mahometans in India—Many look to the Sultan as the sacred head of their race—The Suez Canal—Constantinople and the road to India—British policy in Turkey and Armenia not to be judged by surface indications and hastily cabled conclusions—Immense variety of interests to be watched and intrigues to be checkmated 276-293

CHAPTER XVIII.
THE SHADOW OF THE SWORD IN ARMENIA.

The apotheosis of oppression—Long-continued and barbarous misrule—Massacres and maltreatment of Armenians twenty years ago—An Erzeroum incident of the early Seventies—Russian invasion of 1877—Some of the agitators for reform unfortunately give rise to the suspicion of being instigated by Russia—Government of Russian Armenia—Mahometan outrages and Kurdish cruelties apparently encouraged, and certainly permitted, by the Ottoman Government—The way prepared for the atrocities which amazed the civilized world in 1895 294-309

CHAPTER XIX.
THE SWORD OF ISLAM FALLS.

Rumours of horrible massacres, at first disbelieved, then minimised, and finally corroborated in all their sickening details—Worse than the Bulgarian horrors in 1876—The Kurds use their power to slaughter, torture, and outrage great numbers of peaceful Christians in the Sassoon district—Details too horrible for description—As in the case of Bulgaria, every conceivable, and many inconceivable, atrocities committed—Towns and villages desolated—Population of parts of the country absolutely decimated—Turkish denials, and a continuous stream of affirmatory statements from missionaries and others—Sorrow and sympathy in the English-speaking world.........................310-325

CHAPTER XX.
THE EASTERN CRISIS.

British public opinion demands action—Immediate communications pass between the Powers—England now feels that the practical protectorate of 1878 should have been maintained and enforced—Lord Salisbury follows Lord Rosebery in trying to promote the united action of the Great Powers—The Sultan receives the consequent protests, promises much, and does practically nothing—The Commission of Inquiry—The mutual rivalries of the Powers prevent efficient intervention—Great Britain does its best, but the Sultan remains master of the situation—Meantime massacres and the wildest disorder continue—While the Powers talk and protest, the Armenians suffer and die.........................326-342

CHAPTER XXI.
M. GLADSTONE AND ARMENIA.

The aged statesman expected to intervene—Many even hope that he will undertake an active campaign against "the unspeakable Turk"—His views on the many-sided question—For a while he remains in retirement, only writing an occasional brief letter—Finally, he receives a deputation of Armenians, and speaks out in terms of strong and vigorous denunciation—An abstract of his speech—The death of 10,000 inoffensive and defenceless Christians—The Turkish Government declared to be responsible—England has a special right to interfere—Turkish pledges absolutely worthless—Advocates sending an independent Commissioner into Armenia—An admirable but not very useful utterance—The Duke of Westminster and the Duke of Argyll stand by their old leader...345-360

CHAPTER XXII.
RENEWAL OF THE OUTRAGES.

A year passes amid continued rumours of crime and cruelties—Then comes the report of renewed and wholesale slaughters—The massacres at Trebisond—Murders near Baiburt—Massacres at Bitlis, in Erzinjan, at Marash—Terrible details—Buildings of the American mission at Kharput destroyed—Thousands of people homeless and hopeless wanderers—Four thousand Armenians said to have been massacred in the Vilayet of Sivas—Crowds of refugees passing into Russian Armenia—Massacre at Constantinople—Massacres in Erzeroum—The Kurds literally sweep the land with a storm of savage slaughter..........................363-378

CHAPTER XXIII.
THE CHRISTIAN POWERS AND THE MOSLEM.

The Eastern Question in one of its most acute stages—Apparent collapse of the Moslem—The Powers appear as much afraid of the Turk in his decay as they were in his days of greatness—United only in protest; disunited in policy and interests—Afraid of a great European war as the result of any active military intervention—The Sultan denies knowledge of the new outrages, and announces "perfect tranquillity" while the massacres continue—Diplomatic, but futile exertions of the Powers; extra, but useless guardships; vigorous, but valueless protests—Hypocritical attitude of Russia—England's sincere but difficult position—Rendered more difficult by the attitude of the United States in Venezuela—Fall of the Grand Vizier—Promised Armenian reforms................381-396

CHAPTER XXIV.
INTERESTS AND DUTY OF THE UNITED STATES.

The Monroe doctrine should be waived at this crisis—Intervention, with England, in Turkey an American duty and privilege—American sympathies with Russia based upon error—The Poles and the Jews—The interests of the Republic in Turkey very considerable—Sympathy of its people with the Armenians—Resolution of the United States Congress—American missions in the Turkish Empire—Great Britain should be helped in its policy of persuasion, and urged to join with the United States in practical intervention—Probable willingness to do so—Dangers of collision with Russia and France—Let English-speaking fraternity prevail, and the flags of the Empire and the Republic mount guard over Christianity and liberty in the East................. 399-412

CHAPTER XXV.

THE ATTITUDE OF CANADA.

The Dominion stands by England—Effect of the Venezuelan troubles—Contrast between the practical sympathy thus offered by Canada and the hostility of the American Republic—Principal Grant's views—General desire for united action between England and the States in connection with Armenia—Intimate relations, but no annexation, the sentiment of Canada—Meetings throughout the country—Contributions from Toronto, Montreal, Halifax, and St. John—Canadian interests in the East—Mr. Charlton's motion in the House of Commons—Sentiment of intense indignation and general desire for some definite action—Mr. Chamberlain's view of the situation.......... 413-424

CHAPTER XXVI.

WHAT OF THE FUTURE?

The Eastern Question nearing its final settlement—All the roads of diplomacy now lead to Constantinople—The collapse of Turkish power has brought the final, but it may be prolonged, convulsion—The disorders incidental to a dying State—Not easy, however, to anticipate the end—To drive the Turk out of Europe, or conquer him in Asia, a decidedly unpleasant task—All the dormant fanaticism and ferocity in his nature might be aroused—Possible danger to England from the Mahometans of India—The ideal settlement of the question as against present international jealousies and complications—British statesmen on the crisis—The United States might prove an all-potent factor, and turn the scale in favour of British intervention, European peace, and the preservation of the Christians in Turkey........ ... .'..........425-447

LIST OF ILLUSTRATIONS....... 18
INDEX 448-449

PREFACE

It would be difficult to point to any public occurrence that has so thoroughly roused the indignation and evoked the sympathies of all Christendom as the atrocities inflicted upon "suffering Armenia," under the connivance of the Ottoman Power, during the last eighteen months.

The details finding their way, from time to time, into the public press have so revolted the sense of civilization as to unite the Christian nations in determination to make the power of righteous sentiment felt, in compelling resistance to the irresponsible rule of injustice and wrong; the piteous appeal of the homeless, destitute, and starving victims of Moslem persecution has entered into the heart of Christian people; and from all parts of the two great English-speaking countries, on either side of the Atlantic, gifts are flowing in, in a generous stream, for their relief.

The present interest in Armenia is unmistakable and widely spread; but it may be questioned whether the knowledge of its people and their history is at all as definite and general. It is the design of this work to supply such knowledge; and most opportune is its appearance.

With much research, the author has compiled an exhaustive narrative of all that concerns the Armenian question; the history of that ancient country; the rise and fall of Turkish power; the religious conflicts between Mahometanism and Christianity; the political relations of the European Powers with Turkey; and the present aspect of the Eastern Question.

Apart from the strong feeling of sympathy towards the Armenians kindled by the recital of their cruel sufferings, other considerations render them peculiarly interesting as a people, and stimulate curiosity as to their origin and history. The very spot on the globe which they inhabit is that which, perhaps above all others, is invested in our imagination with the romance of early antiquity, as associated with the story of the genesis of our race.

No subject of speculation has invited more conjecture than the locality of the first home of man—the Garden of Eden. And although all such conjecture has been baffled by insuperable discrepancies in every supposed identification that has been investigated in the three continents of the old world, that which has received the greatest support from learned men of all nations, ages, and beliefs is the claim of the high table-lands of Armenia. This region, 7,000 feet above the sea level, lying at the foot of Mount Ararat, and watered by the Tigris and Euphrates, with other streams, is Armenia proper—the home from the earliest ages of this ancient and remarkable race, though its people have become widely scattered, and though the theatre of the recent horrors covers a much larger area.

The Armenians claim for their ancestors a great grandson of Japhet, called Haik, who settled in the country defined, which, in the native language, bears the same name. From that time onward they have preserved their distinct nationality in the same marked and wonderful way as have the Hebrews; and in spite of the vicissitudes of conquest, partition of their territory, and successive raids with wholesale slaughter and depredation by their Kurdish neighbours and foes, have spread and multiplied in almost all the countries of the old world. In their own beautiful and fertile land, leading an industrious pastoral life, amassing wealth in flocks and herds, only to be plundered and driven from their devastated homes by the ruthless Kurds from the mountains, they have carried into other lands the same commercial instincts as the Jew, the same keenness in trade, the same faculty of growing rich; and wherever they are met with they are still Armenians, the ancestral type unchanged; but, at the same time, always peaceable and submissive subjects.

This same feature of persistence of type marks, in a still more interesting way, the history of their religion. No doubt, the strongest plea in the appeal which the sufferings of these poor people make upon our sympathies is that of a common Christianity, that they are one of the very oldest Christian nations in the world, one that has kept its faith and form of worship almost intact from the first century to the present, through the unparalleled persecutions of one thousand years. They claim to have received the Christian faith from the apostle Thaddeus, who, they say, accompanied by Bartholomew and Judas, preached the Gospel and founded a Christian Church in Armenia as early as the year 34. Traces of Christian worship in the country at a very early date go to bear out this story, though it can only be regarded as legendary. But there can be no doubt of the historical fact that St. Gregory "the Illuminator," who converted the King of Armenia and many of his subjects to the faith, through his influence, was consecrated by the Archbishop of Cæsarea to be Bishop of Armenia in 302. And his successors, in unbroken line, under the title, first of Patriarch, and subsequently of " Catholicos," of whom there are now five, have continued to rule that Church to this day.

The ecclesiastical status of the Church of Armenia is that of one of the separated churches of the East, cut off from communion with the orthodox Greek Church. The separation took place in A.D. 491, and was due to the non-acceptance by the Armenian Church of the decrees of the Council of Chalcedon, in that year, which condemned the doctrines of Eutychius. But there appears to have been some misunderstanding as to the effect of the decrees which led to this schism; for although the Church of Armenia is to this day classed as an Eutychian Church, it never adopted or favoured that heresy. In fact, it is almost purely orthodox; and, while in formal heresy, is so far recognized that Greek priests are allowed, under certain circumstances, to communicate individual Armenians.

With the exception of the secessions which took place in the fifteenth and sixteenth centuries, under the agitation of Jesuit missionaries, and which led to the formation of the Armenian Uniat Church, the ancient Church of Armenia has maintained its doctrine and discipline unimpaired with unexampled fidelity; and the constancy of Armenian Christians, even unto martyrdom, has been abundantly illustrated in the present persecutions, when thousands of tortured victims have accepted a cruel death as the alternative of abjuring Christ and professing the Moslem creed.

These are the people on whose behalf the aid and sympathies of Christians everywhere are invoked in their terrible sufferings. Mr. Castell Hopkins' work, setting forth so fully and graphically their eventful story, with its long record of bitter injuries from the most despotic, fanatical, and wily power that ever wielded the sword in the sacred name of the one God, will fulfil a mission of mercy if it succeeds, as it deserves, in intensifying this popular sympathy and quickening the flow of practical relief for "suffering Armenia."

The volume amply sustains the author's well-earned literary reputation, and is presented by its enterprising publishers in a most attractive form.

ARTHUR TORONTO.

LIST OF ILLUSTRATIONS

* * * * * * *

ARMENIANS AT BAY	Frontispiece
MAHOMET THE PROPHET	19
A GROUP OF ARMENIANS WHO ESCAPED FROM THE SASSOUN MASSACRE	311
A BEREAVED ARMENIAN FAMILY	230
A NEWSPAPER CORRESPONDENT INTERVIEWING ARMENIANS IN ERZEROUM	296
CITY OF CONSTANTINOPLE	20
CITY OF ERZEROUM	293
CITY OF ST. PETERSBURG	88
CITY OF TREBIZOND	361
SULTANS OF TURKEY—MAHMOUD II.	39
ABDUL-MEDJID	40
ABDUL-AZIS	71
ABDUL-HAMID II.	72
RULERS OF RUSSIA—PETER THE GREAT	87
CATHARINE II.	103
ALEXANDER I.	104
NICHOLAS I.	140
ALEXANDER II.	167
ALEXANDER III.	183
NICHOLAS II.	184
VIEW OF SUJ BULAK	130
INTERIOR OF ARMENIAN COFFEE HOUSE IN ERZEROUM	360
THE FORTRESS OF BATOUM	308
BURIAL OF ARMENIAN VICTIMS	312
THE ARMENIAN CITY OF SINNA	327
AN ARMENIAN MOUNTAINEER	229
BRITISH AMBASSADORS TO TURKEY—LORD STRATFORD DE REDCLIFFE	277
RT. HON. G. J. GOSCHEN	278
LORD DUFFERIN	380
SIR PHILIP CURRIE	379
TURKISH AND ARMENIAN NOTABLES—THE ARMENIAN PATRIARCH	397
GERVONT SHISHMANIAN	398
KIAMIL PASHA	118
NAZIM PASHA	117
ARMENIAN MONASTERY NEAR VAN	246
AN ENCAMPMENT OF KURDS	245
ARMENIAN PEASANT WOMEN	211
WOUNDED ARMENIAN WOMEN AT STAMBOUL	195
INTERIOR OF A KURDISH TENT	196
ARMENIAN HOUSE IN ERZEROUM WHERE THE MASSACRE BEGAN	212
SOME INFANT ARMENIAN VICTIMS	262
SIR WILLIAM FENWICK WILLIAMS, OF KARS	134
BRITISH LEADERS CONNECTED WITH TURKISH AFFAIRS—	
LORD PALMERSTON	133
THE LATE EARL OF DERBY	36
LORD BEACONSFIELD	55
RT. HON. W. E. GLADSTONE	343
MARQUESS OF SALISBURY	344
ARMENIAN REFUGEES FROM SASSOUN	261
PRINCE GORTSCHAKOFF	168

The Golden Horn, Constantinople.

Mahomet the Prophet.

CHAPTER I.

THE RISE AND FALL OF TURKISH POWER.

Upon a memorable day, some six hundred years ago, when Poland was an important European state, Venice the mistress of a wide maritime supremacy, Constantinople the head of a tottering Greek Empire, and the centre of Eastern Christianity, a small band of four hundred Tartar or Turkish warriors might have been seen with their families wending their way down the banks of the Euphrates. They had come from the distant regions of Central Asia in search of safety from the Mongol invasion, and of some place to settle where they might have a reasonable chance of obtaining power and wealth. For a time, under the leadership of Ertoghrul—" The Right-Hearted Man "—they had rested on the plains of Armenia, but were now again journeying westward.

All at once the little band came in sight of a field of battle on which two large bodies of armed men were struggling for the mastery. One of them, however, was so obviously the weaker, and so clearly getting the worst of it, that Ertoghrul chivalrously decided to help it, and charged upon the larger army so promptly and with such success as to turn the tide and win a signal victory. The leader whom he had thus saved turned out to be Alaeddin, the Mahometan Sultan of Iconium, and his opponents proved to be a wandering host of the hated Mongol. A grant of territory to Ertoghrul was the immediate result—the sweep of the Turk over Asia Minor and up to the walls of Vienna was the ultimate consequence. From such trifling events do great empires rise. This Tartar or Turkish band was, of course, only one of many such from the vast steppes of Central Asia, where the population is more than a third Turk at the present day. Turks are even now to be found in large numbers in Russia, China, and Independent Turkestan; they may be seen and heard in distant Siberia, along the banks of the Lena, and in the Arctic Circle itself. As far back, indeed, as the sixth century the ruler of the Turks to the east and north of the Sea of Aral had sent a deputation to the Emperor Justinian.

But Ertoghrul and his son Othman were the founders of the Ottoman Turks and the Ottoman Empire. Other Turkish bands had migrated to the rich lands of Asia Minor before this, and other empires—notably that of the Seljukian Turks—had been established upon the ruins of Saracen power. Their conquests, however, were limited to Asiatic territory, their dynasties had been comparatively short-lived, their footprints on the sands of Eastern history were not very deep or lasting. With the Ottomans it was very different. Starting with a territory which included the classic ranges of Mount Olympus, Othman gradually increased and extended it—at the expense of the steadily weakening Greek Empire. Under his son, Amurath I., there commenced a period of systematic and continuous conquest. He over-ran many parts of Asia Minor, entered Europe and took Adrianople in 1361, hemmed the Eastern Empire in with a wall of Turkish fire, and soon limited it to Constantinople and a few distant outlying possessions. Under Amurath II. the war with the Christians took a still more serious form.

The separate and independent kingdoms of Bulgaria, Servia, and Bosnia were conquered, and a prolonged conflict between the Crescent and the Cross followed in Hungary and Albania. Huniades in the former country, and Scanderbeg in the latter, upheld the Christian banner for a long time with unrivalled skill and bravery, but had finally to succumb. Meanwhile the great Mongol Empire, which had held Central Asia, and Russia, and Persia under Genghiz Khan, had fallen to pieces, and was replaced late in the fourteenth century by the conquests of Timour, who rose from obscurity somewhere in the centre of the continent, but who seems to have been a Turk rather than a Mongol, and was certainly a Mahometan. He belonged, however, to one of the unorthodox sections of the faith, and therefore came into Western Asia, where he fought and finally conquered the Ottoman Sultan, Bajazet. But he died in 1405, before he could consolidate his dominions or cross into Europe, and the Ottomans, who had elsewhere maintained their ground, soon regained it in Asia.

Then came the long-expected conquest of Constantinople, and the overthrow of Eastern Christendom. At the first battle of Kassova the Turks had defeated the Servian Christians. At the battle of Nicopolis the flower of European chivalry and a Christian crusade had been beaten by the Moslem. At the second battle of Kassova Huniades and the Christian kingdom of Hungary had been overpowered. And now, on the 29th of May, 1453, the capital of the Greek Empire was entered by the conquering Turk after a prolonged and cruel siege.

The story is an old but never to be forgotten one. Of all the two-score sieges endured by the City of the Golden Horn this was the worst, as it was the last. It was the dying struggle of Christian supremacy in these historic lands; the last desperate effort of a weakened and divided Church to uphold the secular power of the Cross against the all-conquering banner of the Crescent. And, to the eternal disgrace of Western Christendom, no help was given the beleaguered Emperor Constantine, who, when he finally saw that all was lost, rushed upon the spears and sabres of the advancing foe, and died exclaiming, "I would rather die than live." Of the fatal break in the walls which caused the downfall of the city, Shelley has written:

> " A chasm,
> As of two mountains, in the walls of Stamboul;
> And in that ghastly breach the Islamites,
> Like giants on the ruins of a world,
> Stand in the light of sunrise. In the dust
> Glimmers a knightly diadem, and one
> Of regal port has cast himself beneath
> The stream of war. Another, proudly clad
> In golden arms, spurs a Tartarian barb
> Into the gap, and, with his iron mace,
> Directs the torrent of that tide of men,
> And seems—he is—Mahomet !"

Amidst the slaughter of thousands of Christians, the plunder of a rich and splendid city, and the slavery of its helpless people, Mahomet now established a great Moslem power. The head of Constantine was embalmed and sent, as a ghastly trophy, round the chief cities of Asia, while the beautiful Christian Church of St. Sophia became the chief of the mosques of Islam. Thus, at the early age of twenty-three, Mahomet II. began a career of conquest which made Turkish power a dread and menace to the whole Christian world. He soon over-ran Greece and the ancient Christian empire of Trebizond. He conquered the Crimea, through his Grand Vizier, and transplanted thousands of its inhabitants to Constantinople, thus striking a tremendous blow at the commerce of Genoa in the Euxine. The prolonged defence of Albania and Bosnia was at last overpowered, and an immense Turkish army was being collected, in 1481, on the Asiatic shores of the Bosphorus, for some purpose then unknown— now believed to have been the invasion of Italy—when the conquering Sultan suddenly and fortunately died. The motto of Mahomet II. seems to have been secrecy and celerity, and, while his methods were those of a barbarian, pure and simple, there was much in his personal character that was both noble and admirable.

Under his successor the Turkish navy was developed, and ships sent to ravage the coast of Spain, in response to appeals from the Moors of Grenada. Bajazet II. had, however, to encounter much internal dissension, and was a very weak ruler. But the power of the Turk was now well established, and even attracted an embassy from the haughty Spaniard—which the Sultan did not return.

Selim I., whose reign ensued, had to face the rivalry of Persia and Egypt. These two powers professed Mahometanism, but, in the case of Persia, it was of the Shiite variety. The Persians followed and recognized Ali, the Prophet's son-in-law, in preference to Abubeker, his father-in-law, who had founded the Saracen Caliphate of Damascus. In 750 the descendants of Abbas, the uncle of Mahomet the Prophet, had overthrown this last-named dynasty, and established themselves at Bagdad in a series of memorable reigns. Upon the collapse of the Saracen power, the headship, or Caliphate, of the orthodox Mahometans was supposed to have nominally passed to certain rulers in Egypt. Persia remained at the head of the unorthodox Moslems.

Selim's great achievement was a campaign against Egypt, the capture of Cairo, the conquest of the country, and assumption of the title of Caliph, or spiritual head of the Mahometan world. He also over-ran Syria, and invaded Persia, making himself master of its capital. Back to Constantinople he brought great spoils of war, and the most skilful artisans from Tabriz and Cairo. But the central feature of his reign was the augmentation of Turkish authority and power by the general Mahometan acceptance of his right, and that of his successors, to the sacred position of Vicar of the Prophet of God, Commander of the Faithful, and Supreme Imam of Islamism. Though a bigot of the cruelest and darkest order—" bloody, bold, and resolute " in character—he possessed high administrative abilities, and his reign further developed that dominating doggedness and courage which is the only redeeming feature in the character of the old-time Turk.

Solyman the Magnificent, who reigned from 1520 to 1566, was almost what one of his titles claimed him to be—the Lord of the Age—and this in a period which boasted Charles V. of Spain, and Francis I. of France. He was merciless in war and pitiless to his foes. Yet his character was sincere and moral, his courage very great, and his military skill approached to genius. His encouragement of art and literature was as liberal as his Court was splendid, and his personal surroundings magnificent. And despite the great power of the Emperor Charles, who ruled Germany and Spain, the Netherlands and the Indies, Portugal and the Austrian States, Naples and Sicily, and South America; despite the strength of Poland, under Sigismund I.; the power of Venice; the revived strength of Persia, under Shah Ismail; and the might of India, under Akbar the Great; Solyman was perhaps the most powerful ruler of his time, and menaced Christianity at every point, shaking

Europe to its very foundations. Belgrade, which had stood out as a bulwark against the Moslem wave, was first taken. The Isle of Rhodes, which had so long braved the might of the Turk, and which was now indispensable for the free communication between Constantinople, and Syria, and Egypt, was besieged by an Ottoman fleet of 300 vessels, whilst Solyman led to the conquest an army of 300,000 men along the western coasts of Asia Minor.

The gallant Knights of St. John, with 5,000 warriors, opposed, for five months, the whole power of the Sultan, but were finally forced to surrender. Four years later Solyman invaded Hungary with an army 100,000 strong, and 300 pieces of artillery; defeated King Louis at the battle of Mohacz; and destroyed, at one blow, the mass of the Hungarian nobles, the king, and 24,000 of his soldiers. Buda and Pesth at once submitted, while Hungary became practically a province of the Ottoman power, and was swept by fire and sword, pillage and outrage. When the conqueror returned home, his army drove before it a hundred thousand wretched Christians, men, women, and children, destined for the Turkish slave markets. The Archduke Ferdinand of Austria, brother of Charles V., then claimed the vacant throne, as did a native prince named Zapolya. Each claimant sent an embassy to Constantinople. They were received with true Moslem arrogance. One of the ambassadors was told by the Grand Vizier that where the hoof of the Sultan's horse once trod became, at once and forever, part of the Sultan's dominions. "We have slain King Louis of Hungary," said he; "his kingdom is now ours, to hold or to give to whom we list. Thy master is no king of Hungary till we make him so. It is not the Crown that makes the king—it is the sword. It is the sword that brings men into subjection; and what the sword has won, the sword must keep."

Finally, a civil war ended in the Turks siding with Zapolya and preparing for the conquest of Vienna, and a proposed victorious march to the banks of the Rhine. Solyman left Constantinople on May 10th, 1529, with 250,000 men and 300 cannon, on a campaign which promised an illimitable future of conquest and power. It was the assault of Asian barbarism upon European Christendom, though neither Charles V. nor Francis I. seemed to so regard it. Had the Sultan succeeded in taking Vienna, as he soon did in over-running Hungary and placing Zapolya upon its coveted throne, he would have been followed by a perfect torrent of Asiatic hordes, and the history of Europe might have been totally altered. With the first of the autumn storms, the terrible irregular cavalry of the Turks—the Bashi-Bazouks and Kurds of an earlier age—swept around the walls of Vienna. These Akindji, as they were called, received no pay for their services, and the rapacity and atrocity of their conduct have seldom been excelled. Austria became one vast riot of ravage and slaughter, and the country, far as the eye could see from the walls of Vienna, was white with Turkish tents.

The city only held some 15,000 defenders, but they were well worthy of being the advance guard and protectors of Christendom. They knew the fate that awaited them and theirs, and for weeks held out in the teeth of the most savage and determined assaults. Then Solyman gave way—not to the Christians, but to the Christians' weather. His eastern soldiery could not endure the inclemency of the climate, and compelled him to raise the siege. Before leaving the scene his soldiers massacred thousands of Christian captives, preserving only a few of the women and boys for purposes of slavery. Three years later Solyman invaded Germany again, and dared Charles V. to meet him in battle. But the latter declined, and what would have been a picturesque and deadly personal conflict between the great potentates of Christendom and Islamism was averted. The war then continued, with intermissions, until, in 1544, Charles and Ferdinand made overtures for peace, and, in 1547, a truce of five years' duration was concluded, which left the Sultan in possession of all Hungary and Transylvania, and bound the ruler of Austria to the payment of a yearly tribute of 30,000 ducats. To this treaty the Emperor of Germany, the King of France, the Pope, and the Republic of Venice were also parties.

Meanwhile, the Turkish navy had carried the flag of the Crescent along the coasts of the Mediterranean, the Red Sea, and the Indian Ocean. The famous Khaireddin Pasha, or Barbarossa, had conquered the piratical states of North Africa, swept the Genoese coast with fire and slaughter, transported 70,000 Moors from Andalusia to his own Algerian dominions, sacked a number of Italian cities, captured Tunis, conquered the Venetian islands in the archipelago, and defeated the combined fleets of the Pope, Venice, and the Emperor Charles at Previssa. While the fleet was gaining these laurels, Solyman was carrying on campaigns against Persia and heterodox Islam, as well as against Austria and "infidel" Christendom. Large territories in Armenia and Mesopotamia, and the strong cities of Erivan, Van, Mosul, and Bagdad, were added to the Turkish dominions. His reign concluded with the famous but futile siege of Malta, in which 25,000 Turks were killed, and all of its gallant defenders but 600 men. Solyman died at the head of a fresh army and in the beginning of a new war with Austria and the Germans.

For seven weeks his great army of 150,000 men struggled and won victories, captured towns and cities, and was led to and fro in the name of a dead man, embalmed, and carried in a litter. And not until the Grand Vizier knew that Selim II. had been enthroned in Constantinople did the hosts hear, amid the stillness of the night and the gloom of a great forest, the Moslem death chant: "All dominion perishes, and the last hour awaits all mankind." With this great ruler the power of the Turk reached its highest point, and from his death, with certain fluctuations, its decline becomes apparent. He had divided his empire into twenty-one governments, which included all the celebrated countries of Biblical or classical times. The dominions of this descendant of Othman—or of his father, the homeless and wandering Ertoghrul—embraced many of the most beautiful and the richest regions of the world, and stretched from the Tigris and Euphrates across the Bosphorus, and through Europe to the borders of Austria proper; over much of Poland and Southern Russia; along the shores of Africa from Tripoli to the banks of the Nile. In the words of Sir Walter Raleigh, the Turks and the Spaniards were at this time the two powers most threatening to the independence of Europe, "the one seeking to root out the Christian Religion altogether, the other the truth and sincere profession thereof; the one to joyne all Europe to Asia, the other the rest of all Europe to Spaine."

From this period, however, dates the decay of Moslem power. Selim II. proved a miserable shadow of his predecessor; the authority of the viziers and the degrading influence of the women and the harem increased; love of luxury, ease, and wealth began to everywhere prevail. The soldiers in succeeding reigns fought more and more for plunder, and less and less for glory or religion; the taxes were farmed out to Greeks and Jews; and, above all, the power of Russia slowly developed on the national horizon. In 1571, and for the first time, the Christian defeated the Turk in pitched battle. The great conflict of Lepanto, between Selim's navy and the fleets of Venice and Spain, mark the commencement of this new epoch. Three hundred years of hostility with the Muscovite also began by the soldiers of Ivan the Terrible compelling the Turks to raise the siege of Astrachan. But as the Crimean Tartars stormed Moscow not long afterwards, honours were about equal.

Meanwhile Cyprus had been taken from the Venetians, its heroic defender, Bragadino, being subjected to the grossest indignities, and at last flayed alive. The action embodied the cruel spirit of the age. At this time, so-called Christian powers seemed as barbarous as the Moslem. The massacre of St. Bartholomew had just taken place. A little later the Russians captured Wittenstien, in Finland, cut the garrison in pieces, and roasted the commandant alive. The sacking of Madgeburg by Tilly, and the invasion of the Netherlands by Alva, are later memories of misguided Christian cruelty. The difference, however, is that with the Turk the manifestation of this spirit was continuous, and not exceptional. And during the ensuing century, and under the rule of various forgotten Sultans, the sword of Islam remained sharp and in constant use, though its glories were departing.

Amurath II., who reigned for seventeen years after 1623, was surnamed "the Imperial manslayer." When he rode abroad, any one crossing his path became liable to immediate death, and he very often shot people down with an arrow from his own bow. Upon one occasion a party of women dancing in a meadow were seized and drowned by his order because their merriment disturbed him. At another time a boat full of women was passing down the Bosphorus, and, as he thought it came too close to the walls of his seraglio, it was sent to the bottom by the batteries. In his old age he used to say, "Vengeance never grows decrepit, though she may grow grey." And he is alleged to have slaughtered by personal command over 100,000 of his subjects. Yet the dominating temper and vigorous administration of Amurath suppressed all violence but his own, and temporarily restored Turkish prestige in the East.

He was the last Sultan to make a personal progress through Asiatic Turkey, and, while doing so, on the way to retake Bagdad from the Persians, pashas and officials from all parts of the empire crowded to kiss the stirrup of the Commander of the Faithful. Woe at that moment to the functionary whose loyalty or activity was suspected. His head would roll under the hoofs of the imperial charger while in the very act of homage. Bagdad was taken after a desperate charge, and by order of the Sultan, some days later, the inhabitants of the city were massacred to the number of 30,000.

The last act of Amurath was to order the execution of his brother and successor, Ibrahim. He was not obeyed. But Ibrahim possessed no redeeming feature to make the historian glad that he survived the command. A selfish voluptuary, debased, mean, and cowardly in character, his reign is chiefly marked by acts of individual cruelty and the growth of a national spirit of savagery. Amidst war with the Venetians, and the Cossacks on the Russian frontier, he was justly and wisely put to death by rebellious Janizaries and Ulemas in 1648. His successor was a child of seven years—Mahomet IV. During the minority which followed, Court intrigue, military insubordination, venality, and oppression grew apace.

But in 1656 Mohammed Kiuprili became Grand Vizier, and must be remembered as the first of a series of ministers whose qualities and abilities counteracted the weakness and vice of the Sultans, and retarded, though they could not avert, the decadence of the Ottoman power.

Unsparing cruelty, however, was usually the basis of their administration; unflinching despotism the secret of their success. The fact is, that under conditions in which corruption was a matter of course, political morality not even a name, barbarism the mainspring of individual and national action, religion a fatalistic and sensual code of life, there was no other way in which to hold Turkish dominions together. During the five years of Mohammed Kiuprili's sway, 36,000 people were put to death by his orders. The chief executioner of Constantinople confessed that he had himself strangled 4,000 persons, and thrown them into the dark and secret depths of the Bosphorus. But Mohammed quelled internal revolt, revived the naval power, fortified the Dardanelles, recovered the islands of Lemnos and Tenedos from the Venetians, and fortified the Dneiper and the Don. On his deathbed he gave the young Sultan four special rules to follow—never to listen to the advice of women, never to permit a subject to grow over-rich, never to allow the treasury to get empty, and never to let his armies lie idle.

Ahmed Kiuprili, who succeeded his father as Vizier, was a really great statesman, and one of a more beneficent type. In civil administration he excelled; in war he had to face Austria and the Christian powers in a new and fierce contest. Bearing the Sacred Standard of the Prophet, with 121,000 men, and immense numbers of camels, mules and cannon, he advanced through Hungary in 1664, and, after taking several Austrian fortresses and cities, and devastating much Austrian territory, met the Christian armies on the banks of the river Raab. The memorable battle of St. Gothard, which followed, was the first occasion on which a direct collision between the military forces of Turks and Christians had taken place with success to the latter—Lepanto having been a naval conflict. The genius of Montecuculi prevailed; more than 10,000 Turks were killed, and forty Moslem standards captured. Nevertheless, the conquests already made were retained, and Ahmed Kiuprili was able to return as a conqueror to Constantinople.

Then followed a victorious campaign against Poland, and the cession of Podolia and the Ukraine to the Sublime Porte. Some years later, however, Sobieski came to the front in Polish affairs, refused to pay the Turkish tribute, and routed Kiuprili with great slaughter. But after a prolonged war the resources of the Ottomans were found too powerful, and their previous conquests were allowed them by a treaty of peace in 1676. Three days after this was concluded, Kiuprili, "the light and and splendour of the nation, the Vicar of the Shadow of God," died, and was replaced by Kara Mustapha, a minister of boundless arrogance and limited ability. An inglorious war, into which he plunged with Russia, was followed by his famous Austrian campaign—the last great aggressive effort of the Ottomans against Christendom. The Grand Vizier's regular army numbered 275,000 men, and with irregular troops and camp-followers must have reached a total of 500,000. This vast Moslem horde moved on toward Vienna—which was garrisoned by only 11,000 men—and surrounded its historic walls on July 15th, 1683. The Emperor Leopold had been unable to obtain help other than a promise of some 60,000 men from Sobieski, of Poland. But the Polish hero was himself equal to a million of men. On the 12th of September he reached the heights above Vienna, and rolled his small army down upon the encamped hosts of Islam with a force and suddenness which carried all before it; swept the Turks out of Austria; relieved the Christian capital; and, in its result, brought the Venetians and Russians upon the now stricken Porte, gave part of Greece and Dalmatia to Venice, Podolia to Poland and Hungary to Austria, and the district of Azof to Russia.

War now succeeded war, and Sultan followed Sultan. To be head of the Moslem world, since the reign of Solyman, had been no light and pleasant task. To hold the position with strength and success required a personal greatness which the education and environment of the Sultan's palace rendered almost impossible. Weak and vicious in character, most of these rulers shadowed the annals of their country with crime and cruelty, and passed away by violent deaths or deposition. Amurath III. killed his five brothers; Mahomet III. strangled all his brothers and drowned his father's wives in the gloomy waters of the Bosphorus. Mustapha I. was deposed by the Janizaries, and ultimately strangled. His successor was strangled by the same dominant organization, as also was Ibrahim. Mahomet IV., Mustapha II., Achmet III., and Selim III. were all deposed by the Janizaries, and died in some unknown fashion. As for the people and the race, after the last siege of Vienna, it was no longer a struggle for conquest; it was a fierce fight for the preservation of Turkish territory.

Success varied from time to time, and much depended on the Chief Minister of the moment. Greece was retained, but, in 1717, Belgrade was lost, and, in 1784, the Crimea was ceded to Russia. In a succeeding war with Austria and the Muscovite—1787-91—the Turks lost over 200,000 men and a vast extent of territory. During this eighteenth century the internal condition of Turkey had been deplorable. Grand Viziers, such as the third and fourth Kiuprili, Ali Coumourgi, Ibrahim (1718-30), Topal Osman, Raghib Pasha, and Hassan Pasha, did their best, amid all the clamour of constant war, the tyranny of local rulers, the insubordination of officials, and the universal corruption, to hold the empire together, and make its administration more bearable. But under such conditions the best of efforts were of only passing benefit.

As the nineteenth century opened, Turkey, under the sultanate of Selim III., had become a festering mass of misery, disaffection, and revolt. The insurgent Wahabites were masters of Arabia. The Mamelukes in Egypt flouted the Sultan's standard and disregarded his orders. Syria was full of warring and really independent tribes. Northern Greece and Montenegro, Moldavia and Wallachia, and the Herzegovina, practically defied the government of the Porte. The Pashas everywhere did as they liked, and ruled their territories with a savage cruelty which justified itself under the Sultan's name, while it defied his authority. The whole empire seethed with the two extremes of cruel rebellion or ruthless local despotism. Money would do a great deal and buy almost anything, so that extortion, bribery, usury, and peculation were the predominant occupations of the people or their rulers. Oppression was the motto of the Pasha; reprisal the instinct of his subject. Torture prevailed widely, persecution of the Christian was a very ordinary matter, and neither life nor honour were of serious import in the general turmoil. The famous Janizaries, which had been first formed by Othman in the fourteenth century, and reorganized by Amurath I., through the tribute of children exacted from conquered Christian states, had gradually changed, as the empire changed, from the indomitable instrument of aggressive conquest into a turbulent band of cruel mercenaries. They now acted, and for a prolonged period served, as the special servants of feeble Sultans, or the instruments of unscrupulous leaders who endeavoured, from time to time, to rise into power upon the familiar bases of corruption and cruelty.

Such was the empire of the Ottomans and the dominance of the Moslem after

"Many a vanished year and age,
And trumpet's breath, and battle's rage,"

had passed over these historic and beautiful countries. And though the picture is a sad and sombre one, it only portrays the inevitable decay and degradation which must come to any nation following a religion which permits fatalism, selfishness, and immorality to become practically embalmed in its creed and embodied in the laws of the state.

CHAPTER II.

THE MAHOMETAN RELIGION.

There is no influence so great in the formation of national life as religion. To a certain extent the one acts and reacts upon the other, but in the end the particular religious principle which predominates must control the expression of the public will, and affect the homes, and customs, and life of the people. It modifies government, makes institutions, and moulds manners. But its influence can be perverted or self-limited. Confucianism, for instance, by compelling the people to look upon the distant past as perfection; by teaching them to look back instead of forward; by claiming that nothing could be better than what had been; made progress in China an impossibility and stagnation the stereotyped condition of the country.

The Greek Church in Russia, by laying too little stress upon priestly dignity and education, has weakened its position and capacity to resist the corruption, or remedy the ignorance, incident to Russian peasant life. The Roman Catholic Church, through many centuries, has made obedience and order a central point of its religious observance, and, in so doing, has unintentionally enabled strong men and despotic minds to sway nations, such as Spain, in the direction of cruelty, despotism, and intolerance. Protestantism, by going to the other extreme, has produced a vast and varied number of sects, and has indirectly influenced more than one country to a point where liberty becomes license, and the popular will a

Mahmoud II.
Sultan and Emperor of the Ottomans, 1808-1839.

Abdul-Medjid
Sultan and Emperor of the Ottomans, 1839-1861.

mere expression of the brute strength of a fleeting majority. Each of these three great divisions of Christendom, however—Greek, and Roman, and Protestant—have the Gospel of Love, the living principles of morality, the elevating hope of a lofty future, as the fundamental subjects of faith and work. And in so far as these principles are carried out by the individual Church is the nation civilized, developed, and liberalized.

But Islam is different from all other great historic religions, in having elevated polygamy into a sacred custom; made a sensual paradise the hope of the faithful; and engrained fatalism in the national and individual character of its devoted followers. Mahomet the Prophet preached, and the Koran embodies, belief in the unity of God, the immortality of the soul, predestination, and a last judgment. He also enjoined circumcision, prayer, alms, and fasting. But he permitted polygamy and concubinage. To the Arabs, and the Eastern races of indifferent idolaters, amongst whom this religion spread, predestination meant the most absolute fatalism—what is to be, must be—and "Kismet" became the characteristic word embodying the very life and thought of the Arab and the Turk. To quote the words traced by the miserable Sultan Abdul-Aziz on the dust of his prison table just before his mysterious death:

> "Man's destiny is Allah's will,
> Sceptres and power are His alone,
> My faith is written on my brows,
> Lowly I bend before His throne."

Like all men really great and capable of achieving great ends—either good or ill—Mahomet was sincere in at least his earlier self-deception. He seems to have really believed his visions, and his apparent inspirations from the Angel Gabriel came upon the Arabs with all the force of personal enthusiasm, and all the power of innate ability and a commanding temperament.

The story or tradition is an interesting one. Born and bred a heathen, Mahomet had the stirrings of a better nature within him, and despite home ties, which seem to have been of a happy character, he spent, as a young man, much of his time in the desert, or in solitude, communing with his thoughts, and groping after something better than the varied idolatry which then constituted the religion of Arabia. The world of the mysterious and supernatural opened to him; he became a mystic, and then a prophet. It was in what afterwards came to be termed the month of Ramadan that Mahomet, while repeating his pious exercises and meditations on Mount Hera, had a vision in which the Angel Gabriel came to him, held out a silken scroll, and compelled him, though he could not read, to recite what stood written on it. The words remained graven on his heart, and constitute a first portion of the Koran:

"Read! in the name of thy Lord, who created man from a drop. Read! for thy Lord is the Most High, who hath taught by the pen, hath taught to man what he knew not. Nay, truly, man walketh in delusion, when he deems that he sufficeth for himself; to thy Lord they must all return."

For a couple of years after this, Mahomet was in great misery. He thought that a Divine call had come to him, and yet he was so worried by doubts that more than once he was on the point of committing suicide. Then he beheld the angel a second time, the revelations began once more, his faith was assured, the Koran was gradually built up, and he became the prophet of a new and, as he claimed, inspired faith. Amid the effete beliefs and decrepit national life of the Arabs, it soon gave him influence and followers ; then local power and position ; and, finally, wide dominion and world-wide greatness.

From about A.D. 610 to 623, he spent his energies in proselytizing and in defying persecution. From the latter date Islamism became a fiercely aggressive religion ; and at the Prophet's death, in 632, had conquered Mecca, and over-run all Arabia. From this time onward, the sword of the Moslem laid ever new countries and peoples under the commands of the Koran. First, the Persians, and then the greater part of Asia Minor and Egypt, acknowledged this religious supremacy, and that of the Caliphs at Medina. Thence it spread through the East into India, and through all the more important parts of Africa.

The Caliphate passed from hand to hand ; was transferred from Medina to Damascus ; and from thence to Bagdad. The Saracens, as the Moslem conquerors were called in cne great stage of their history, rose into a mighty eastern empire, conquered Spain, and were the heroes of the prolonged and picturesque struggle with the Crusaders. And, so long as their religion remained aggressive, it continued powerful. At one time Moslem voyagers might be seen in the China seas, while Moslem caravans from Spain carried European products into the marts of Syria, Arabia, Persia, Turkestan, and India, returning laden with the silks of China, the spices and precious woods of Hindustan, the glass of Syria, or the steel manufactures of Irak and Yemen. Armenia, Egypt, and Tunis contributed also to swell the commerce and wealth of this great dynasty.

But the death of the Saracen power, and the fall of the direct line of Caliphs from Mahomet, came about in 1258, when Genghiz Khan captured Bagdad, and overthrew for a time the dominance of the orthodox Moslem. A scion of the Abbaside dynasty fled to Egypt and established himself there in a comparatively weak position, and one from which his descendant was subsequently ousted by the Turkish Sultan Selim. With the rise of the Turks, some hundred years after the fall of Bagdad, came the revival of Islam and its extension into Europe.

In this religion of Mahomet, the personal element, the national element, and the military element, are all intermixed and interacting. The Prophet, in his latter days, was far from considering a moral code necessary for himself; and he therefore made his precepts in that direction broad enough and lax enough to suit the wildest license of Eastern custom. He gradually became a leader and sovereign, and therefore moulded the Koran into an instrument of law and state government, as well as of religious guidance. He developed into a conqueror, and therefore made his religion more and more an aggressive war-inspiring instrument. Gradually, too, the doctrine of predestination, under Eastern conceptions of the principle, became a cover for every degree of crime and vice, and made the Koran itself the centre of a system in which every man acted according to his own fancy, because he believed his destiny to be outside of, and uncontrolled by, his inherent qualities, or personal action.

If he lived a Moslem, worshipping with due form and ceremony according to the injunction, "There is but one God, and Mahomet is his prophet," Paradise would certainly be his. And should he be so fortunate as to die in defence of the faith, or in its propagation by the sword, a still brighter and fairer spot in a heaven peopled with beautiful houris would be reserved for him. Such a belief explains the character of the Saracen, as it does that of the modern Turk, and illustrates the causes of the spread of Islam in the East, as it does the reasons for the decline of its power in the West. During the vigorous and aggressive period of its history, the fatalistic principle helped greatly in the development of the conquering character by removing fear of death, while the eversharpened sword of war prevented the predominance of the more sensual elements of the religion. Hence the Saracen bravery, and even chivalry, which all Europe once admired. That period, and the reign of Solyman the Magnificent, in Turkish annals, were those in which the military principle most powerfully controlled the Moslem world.

With the decadence of the aggressive spirit came the triumph of the malignant immorality engrained in the system of Mahomet. The life of the harem and the institutions resulting from the moral code of Islam gradually ate into the heart of Moslem power, and prevented its further extension in Europe, as it undermined its influence and authority in Asia. But still the numerical weight remained, and, if the East and the West no longer fear its conquering force, Asia none the less feels the burden of its teachings, and bears the load of its cruel fatalism. To-day, one hundred millions of people pay what they call spiritual allegiance to Allah and Mahomet, and the pressure of such a mass of rigid and intolerant religious sentiment menaces the safety and lives of local Christianity, though it no longer appears to threaten the Powers of Christendom.

The influence of the Koran upon this great body of worshippers is marvellous. To them it is far more of a sacred book than the Bible is to many Christians. Their reverence for it is simply unbounded, and finds expression in the act of kneeling whenever they read its pages; in keeping the volume in the best and most prominent place possible; in the universal belief that, as a direct produc of Divine thought, it is a part of God—eternal and uncreated. They have to be first washed, or legally purified, before even touching its sacred pages; and on the cover is often written the sentence, "Let none touch it but they who are clean." They swear by it, carry it with them in war, write sentences from it on their banners, adorn it with gold or precious stones, and never knowingly allow any one not a Mahometan to possess it. They regard it as a perfect model in style and language, and in itself a miracle, as having proceeded through an ignorant, unlettered man who could not even write.

It is probably the most widely-read book in the world, because the reading of the Koran in Moslem schools and public institutions is not perfunctory, but real and earnest. It controls the place and power of the Caliph, and makes the ruler of the Turk a recognized representative of the Prophet. It permeates every part of the daily life and thought of the Mahometan, affects his institutions, and moulds his manners into that haughty indifference to fate, and profound contempt of "Christian dogs" and other infidels, which is still the most striking characteristic of the Turk. It made the original Mahometan brave in war, indifferent to death, and fanatical in the extreme. It has sunk his modern successor into a condition of prevailing indolence, indifference, and immorality, while preserving within him a profound belief in his own secure and blissful future.

The book itself is remarkable in many ways. In dreaming of a faith which should unite Jew and Christian and idolator in the common worship of one eternal, invisible, and all-powerful God, Mahomet was as sincere as he was afterwards self-deceived regarding his inspirations from the Angel Gabriel. And this conception was all the greater for having been born in the mind of an uncultered, wandering Arab, surrounded by every kind of superstition and ignorant misapprehension of the principles of Christianity. As ultimately developed, the central point of his creed is the unity and oneness of God; the central point of the Koran is the greatness of Mahomet as the last and chiefest of the prophets of God; the central point of his code of laws is the control of the State by the Church—the people by the representatives of their religion.

Islamism is based upon Mohamet's conception of religion—the worship of one God—as being a fact from the beginning of the world. From time to time, as he claims, this religion of Islam was blessed with new dispensations from succeeding prophets, of whom the first was Adam, and the last Mahomet. The intermediate ones—all great men, free from any serious sin—were Noah, Abraham, Moses, and Jesus Christ. Each dispensation abrogated the preceding one; each was Divine in itself; but the last and greatest—the final seal of God's communion with the world—was the Koran. By this last revelation, Mahomet claimed to reform all abuses, and to reduce religion to what he termed its primitive simplicity. By it he divided religion into the two heads of faith and practice. Under the first came the leading and vital principle, "There is no God but the true God, and Mahomet is his prophet," and the belief in angels, in the Koran, in the prophets, in the resurrection and day of judgment, in God's absolute decree and predetermination of both good and evil. Under the second came the fundamental and all-important command of prayer—including the ceremonial washings and purifications—the giving of alms, the observance of certain fasts, and the pilgrimage to Mecca.

The Koran contains many beautiful thoughts, although it seldom rises into the exquisite imagery of the Psalms, or the Epistle to the Romans. There is much of Oriental luxuriance in its language and its ideas, but the absence of Divine inspiration—if shown in no other way—would appear abundantly from the omission of those precepts of self-sacrifice, purity, humility, and brotherly love by which the New Testament has so powerfully appealed to humanity, and in the light of which so much of the modern practice of Christianity appears puerile, hypocritical, and false. The first words of the Koran are, however, absolutely irreproachable, and illustrate one of the many curious phases of this great but unequal book:

"Praise be to God, the Lord of all Creatures; the most merciful, the King of the day of judgment. Thee do we worship, and of Thee do we beg assistance. Direct us in the right way, in the way of those to whom Thou hast been gracious; not of those against whom Thou art incensed, nor of those who go astray."

This is taken from Sale's famous translation, but a more modern and perhaps improved rendering makes the first part read, " In the name of God, the Compassionate Compassioner. Praise be to God, the Lord of the worlds, the Sovereign of the day of judgment." Such a wording brings out more forcibly the Oriental imagery of the work, and, certainly, teachings of this nature, coupled with vigorous denunciation of idolatry of every kind, could not but work for good amongst the susceptible races of the East. Unfortunately, however, the purely material enactments of the Koran soon overpowered in practical action, though not in nominal supremacy, the spiritual code. Worship of the one God was, and always will be, the central *function* of Islamism; but, in effect, the Prophet's conception of an aggressive religious power following upon, and perhaps modelled after, the warpanoplied Hebrew of the Old Testament became and long remained the *practice* of his followers. Similarly, his embodiment in the Koran of the Eastern idea of woman's inferiority and degraded place in the evolution of humanity became the pivot upon which his whole creed and system turned away from possibilities of good into a dark and pervading potentiality for evil.

Through the life and creed of Mahomet, through the history of Islam in its greatness and its degradation, run these two factors of militarism and sensuality. The one built up the Saracen power in Bagdad and the East, the other contributed largely towards its overthrow. The one extended Moslem power into Spain and Sicily; into Sardinia and Corsica; crossed the Pyrenees; and maintained itself for a time in Languedoc and Provence; but was ultimately weakened to the point of dissolution by luxury and indolent immorality. The one built up the Turkish power, while the other has been chiefly responsible for its decline and fall.

By the dictates of the Koran and the developing spirit of Islam warfare against the infidels had become a holy mission, and those dying in defence of their faith, or in action against the unbeliever, were declared and believed to be martyrs. The Mahometan divines proclaimed the sword to be the key of heaven and hell, and accommodated to their own general purposes the specific declaration of Jeremiah: " Cursed be he that keepeth back his sword from blood." All that the Jew possessed of military inspiration and command; all that the Old Testament dispensation revealed of militant and aggressive Judaism in cases of specific selection, were embodied in the new creed as a general and far-reaching religious principle.

In the eighth chapter of the Koran we find the injunction: "O Prophet, stir up the faithful to war—if twenty of you persevere with constancy, they shall overcome two hundred . . . It has not been granted to any Prophet that he should possess captives until he hath made a great slaughter of the infidels in the earth." In the forty-seventh chapter is this still more striking passage:

"Thus God propoundeth unto men their examples. When ye encounter the unbelievers, strike off their heads, until ye have made a great slaughter amongst them; and bind them in bonds; and either give them a free dismission afterwards, or exact a ransom; until the war shall have laid down its arms. This shall ye do. Verily, if God pleased, he could take vengeance on them without your assistance; but he commandeth you to fight his battles that he may prove the one of you by the other. And, as to those who fight in defence of God's true religion, God will not suffer their works to perish; he will guide them, and will dispose their hearts aright; and he will lead them into Paradise. O true believers, if ye assist God by fighting for his religion, he will assist you against your enemies; and will set your feet fast; but, as for the infidels, let them perish."

And, again, Mahometans are told, in the second chapter, to "kill them wherever ye find them, and turn them out of that whereof they have dispossessed you; for temptation to idolatry is more grievous than slaughter. This shall be the reward of infidels. Fight against them until there be no temptation to idolatry, and the religion be God's; but, if they desist, then let there be no hostility, except against the ungodly." And, in using the Koran to denounce the Christians for having worshipped Christ; the Jews for having worshipped Ezra—a supposed tradition he is said to have heard amongst some heretic Israelites; the Roman Catholics, or Western

Christians, for having worshipped Mary; Mahomet appealed to his great fighting principle of One God, while classing all his foes as idolaters in one sweeping and effective charge. Hence the word "infidel" flung by the Saracens at the Crusaders, and returned with interest by the Christian knights.

Intimately connected with this spirit of war, in the days of Moslem aggression as in its period of declining defence, was the Paradise offered by Mahomet as a reward to true believers. To the Eastern mind, the Christian heaven offered few attractions. Neither spiritual instincts nor aspirations were sufficiently potent to enable the masses to comprehend the exaltation of life and hope which is taught by true Christianity. Hence Mahomet's adaptation of existing ideas and more or less debased conceptions in the formation of the Paradise promised to the faithful. Under his system there is a heaven, a hell, and an intermediate place having a partition not too formidable to prevent communication from either side. Paradise is pictured as a place of most exquisite beauty and fertility in every species of pleasure and material delight. Here is the tree called Tûba, which is said to stand in the palace of Mahomet, and to be laden with every sort of fruit—pomegranates, dates, grapes, etc.—every form of food which may be desired at the moment, and every kind of horse to ride or garment to wear. Here are the rivers so often mentioned in the Koran—rivers of water, rivers of milk, rivers of honey, rivers of wine—all coming from the root of the tree Tûba; together with fountains whose pebbles are of rubies and emeralds, whose earth is of camphor, whose beds are of musk, and sides of saffron.

One of the descriptions given in the Koran is very illustrative of the nature of Islamism in this last and highest objective point; and forms a curious combination of Persian traditions and Jewish anti-Christian fables:

"The whole earth will be as one loaf of bread, which God will reach to them like a cake; for meat they will have the ox, Balaam, and the fish, Nun, the lobes of whose livers will suffice 70,000 men. Every believer will have 80,000 servants, and seventy-two girls of Paradise, besides his own former wives, if he should wish for them, and a large tent of pearls, jacinths, and emeralds; 300 dishes of gold shall be set before each guest at once, and the last morsel shall be as grateful as the first. Wine will be permitted, and will flow copiously without inebriating. The righteous will be clothed in the most precious silks and gold, and will be crowned with crowns of the most resplendent pearls and jewels. Besides the ravishing songs of the angel Israfil, and the daughters of Paradise, the very trees will, by the rustling of their boughs, the clanging of bells suspended from them, and the clashing of their fruits, which are pearls and emeralds, make sweetest music."

Such was the Paradise held out to the true Moslem. Such was the embodiment by Mahomet of Eastern sensuality in a conquering Eastern religion. Intimately connected with it, however, was the domestic system which he instituted or allowed. In this, also, he followed, in modified form, the customs of his environment, and thus laid the fatal axe of polygamy at the very root of his tree of faith. With an immoral basis in the homes and high places of his people, and a sensual heaven as the object of their hopes, only one result was possible whenever the wave of conquest should cease or be temporarily checked. At the very heart of the Mahometan domestic system is the principle of inferiority in women. "Men," says the Koran, "shall have the pre-eminence above women, because of those advantages wherein God hath caused the one to excel the other, and for that which they expend of their substance in maintaining their wives."

The true Moslem may chastise his wife or wives when he considers such punishment to be necessary, and Mahomet states that in his glimpse of hell he saw the vast majority of the suffering creatures there to be women. They *may* enter Paradise, but the Koran does not hold its joys before them with directness or certainty. And it does say distinctly that each true believer on earth is entitled to four wives. Out of this view of the relationship between the sexes, combined with the general customs of the East and the injunctions of the Prophet, grew the harem system of the Saracen and the Turk—the evil which has sapped Mahometan vitality and destroyed the supremacy of Islam.

Of course there is much that is good in the Koran, and in Mahomet's original conception of his religion. It made prayer the pillar of the faith; it converted millions from the worst forms of corrupt idolatry; it gave the world much of nobility in character, and performance, and career; it produced a Saladin, and the Moorish civilization of Spain it helped by the very pressure of external force to dev 'op in Christianity some of its grandest phases; it forbade in the pages of the Koran gambling and excessive drinking, and the prevailing Arabic barbarism of killing female children. But most of the good that was in Mahometanism has long been merged in the evils of a debased domestic creed, and wrapped in the garments of a decaying state and an ignorant despotism. All that remains is the picturesque faith of millions in the sanctity of the Koran; their devoutness in formal prayer; their intense belief in certain ceremonials; and their fanatical hatred of infidels— with all the disastrous possibilities which still environ so powerful a sentiment.

CHAPTER III.

MODERN TURKEY.

While the shores of history are strewn with the wreck of empires which in their fall have brought much of sorrow and suffering, and sometimes disgrace, to whole masses of humanity, it remained for the Ottoman power, as it entered upon the nineteenth century of the Christian era, and commenced the seventh century of its own history, to show the world a decadent empire, storm-tossed upon waves of Russian hatred and internal disorder, and existing for a hundred years after the vital spark of nationality had gone out and been replaced by disease and corruption. In this position, and despite innumerable efforts at reform—mainly under British pressure—it has remained an incongruous burden upon the hands of Europe, a source of misery to millions of subject races, an isolated mass of barbarism resting upon the feet of Christendom.

The reign of Selim III. closed in 1807, amid scenes characteristic of Ottoman and Oriental despotism. During his eighteen years of power, this Sultan had nearly all the ills of fallen states to contend with. Internal disaffection and external attack were perhaps the least of them, and could have been dealt with had the usual instruments of Turkish authority—the Ulema, or Sacred Council, and the Janizaries—remained faithful. Apparently they were so, and Selim commenced the difficult and dangerous task of reform. He endeavoured to

Benjamin Disraeli, Earl of Beaconsfield.

The Late Earl of Derby
British Foreign Secretary during the Russia-Turkish War, 1876-1877

control the misapplication of public revenues, to curtail the powers of the Pashas, to abolish the farming of the taxes, to revive printing, to promote education, to reform the Divan or Council of Ministers, and to establish permanent missions at the chief European Courts. But his efforts were of little avail. The Greeks naturally used the press privileges to encourage revolution; the ministers were bribed by first one power and then another in the great European struggle which was going on with Napoleon; the French had to be encountered in Egypt, and traitors and Janizaries at home in Constantinople. And the Sultan had neither the ability required for a great crisis, nor the unprincipled cruelty of character which had carried many of his predecessors through difficulties as great, though of dissimilar origin.

Moussa Pasha was, in this connection, one of those seraglio fiends who have done so much to prostrate Turkey, disgrace Islam, and oppress Christians. For twenty years he had been a meek instrument in the hands of the Sultans, and, when Selim, in 1807, promoted him to high office, it was in the expectation that the more or less sacred functions of the Kaimakan would continue to lie dormant under his submissive administration. But Moussa at once began plotting with the ever-discontented Janizaries, and, in May, revolt broke out as the result, apparently, of some order given by Selim. Under the treacherous advice of the Kaimakan, the Sultan tried to appease the storm by concession, instead of sending for other troops who were near the capital, and meanwhile defending the seraglio with his body-guard. The consequence was that the Janizaries, headed by Moussa—who now threw off his mask—forced their way into the palace, deposed Selim, and placed Mustapha IV. on the throne.

For a few months matters remained thus, until Bairactar Pasha returned from the Russian campaign with some 40,000 troops, and, from the heights above the capital, issued his orders to the empire. During six months following he governed Turkey in this manner, and then decided to reinstate his former patron Selim. He entered the city and stormed the gates of the palace, demanding that the Sultan Selim be liberated from confinement. On hearing this demand, Mustapha ordered that Selim and his own brother Mahmoud should be at once seized and strangled. By their death he would have become the sole representative of the House of Othman, whom no true Turk would dare to destroy or depose. For this cherished position many of the Sultans had slaughtered all their relations. He came very near attaining it. His eunuchs found Selim, and, after a desperate resistance, murdered him, just as Bairactar's soldiers gained the gates. The unfortunate man had expired under the bowstring as the doors of the chamber were burst open; and almost into the arms of his friend the body was cast, with the words, "Behold the Sultan whom ye seek."

Meanwhile young Mahmoud was being sought for eagerly by the ministers of death. But he had been secreted by a faithful slave in the furnace of a bath, and before he was found Bairactar had dragged Mustapha from his throne, while the cannon of the seraglio announced that Mustapha IV. was dead and that Mahmoud II. had become Padishah of the Ottoman world. From his place of concealment the young prince walked up the steps of his perilous and blood-bespattered throne. For the moment Bairactar had triumphed. He became Grand Vizier, and set himself to the work of superseding the Janizaries by a new armed force. But with marvellous and fatal confidence in the apparent submission of his foes,he let the majority of his own troops return home. The result was an immediate and sudden revolt of the formidable mercenaries, the siege of his palace, the death of the Grand Vizier through an explosion, the submission of Mahmoud to temporary and overpowering forces, the return of the Janizaries to power, the curse and renunciation of all proposed reforms and European customs. And then followed a more or less disastrous war with Russia.

Mahmoud, however, was one of those characters who, in many portions of their career, throw a pleasant personal light upon the dark annals of Turkish rule and barbarism. With even a fair chance, and without favour, he might have saved Turkey. But the now developed character of the nation, the natural defects of Islamism, the external and antagonistic pressure of Russia—which preferred Turkish weakness and oppression to Turkish power and genuine reform—were too much for him. Of this Sultan—who reigned from 1808 to 1839—Sir Edward Creary says, with some degree of force and truth:

"He was neither coward nor fool; nor was he a selfish voluptuary like Louis XV., who could understand the growing miseries of a state, and the approaching overthrow of a monarchy, but rest content with the calculation that the means and appliances of pomp and indulgence were safe, for his life at least, and that after him might come the deluge. The evils that Mahmoud saw around him were gigantic, and he gave up the repose of his seraglio to grapple with them in the true heroic spirit. It would be absurd to assert that he fell into no errors; it would be rash to maintain that he was sullied by no crimes; but, take him on the whole, he was a great man, who, amid difficulty, disappointment, and disaster, did his duty nobly."

The shadow of Islam, however, was over everything which he attempted or carried out, and, eventually, it marred his career by converting the just execution of traitors into the wholesale and sanguinary slaughter of enemies; by changing a character of energy and wise ambition into one affected, in its closing years, by the debauchery incidental to his position and nation; by bringing earnest and able efforts at systematic and saving reform into disappointment and failure. Mehemet Ali, for instance, suppressed the troubles in Egypt for him; but it was by a wholesale massacre of the Mamelukes—a sort of local band of Janizaries—which stands on the pages of history as a picture of the vilest treachery and the most ruthless cruelty. The Greek war of independence was a prolonged and bitter conflict in which every species of oppressive cruelty was practised by the Turks, and, at times, retaliated by the Greeks themselves. Mahmoud's otherwise beneficial policy in making war upon Ali Pasha, of Janina, a Moslem chieftain who ruled in Epirus, and whose career had been stained by the foulest treachery and crime, turned the latter into an ally of the Greeks—whom he had heretofore treated with a ruthlessness of which few but a powerful Turkish Pasha could be capable. Thus, circumstances made the Sultan's action in attacking an oppressor of the Christians a step which gave added force to a Christian rebellion. And, by the strange turn of fortune, the subsequent downfall and death of the cruel Turk became a temporary injury to the cause of Greek freedom.

His suppression of the Janizaries is one of the most remarkable incidents in Turkish history. It illustrates the general character of the Turk, as well as the energetic and merciless will which lay at the root of Mahomet's personal policy, and enabled him, during so many years, to rule as a despot whilst inaugurating changes which promised to revolutionize the condition of Turkey. His reign had commenced with a signal manifestation of the power held by this corrupt and corrupting body of pampered troops. And for eighteen years he had to bide his time and see the Janizaries prove their military uselessness in the war with Russia and against the Greek insurgents, whilst Mehemet Ali, in Egypt, was doing what the Sultan longed to do at home—reviving Mahometan power by the adoption of European discipline, muskets, and bayonets. Every year he had also to submit to unreasonable demands from his turbulent auxiliaries, or to condone frequent instances of outrage and disorder.

But quietly, silently, and steadily he made arrangements for their subjugation. His artillery force in and around Constantinople was patiently improved and strengthened until he had, in 1826, more than 14,000 men under a faithful but cruel leader, named Ibrahim. Gradually, too, he had gathered a large body of Asiatic troops at Scutari, and in the year mentioned found himself with a Grand Vizier upon whom he could depend, and a Chief Mufti who would support him in making everything formal and according to the laws of Islam. Hence the thunderbolt issuing early in June from a great council of Ministers and Ulemas, which declared that only a regularly disciplined army was capable of contending with the infidels, and enacted immediate changes in the composition and drill of the Janizaries. The expected revolt at once commenced, and the hitherto irrepressible and all-powerful mutineers marched to the palace, with loud cries for the heads of the Sultan's chief Ministers.

Mahmoud, however, was ready for them. Unfurling in person the Sacred Standard of the Prophet, he called upon all true believers to rally round their Caliph, and then, amid the intense enthusiasm of the people, ordered his well-trained artillerymen to open fire. As the rebels pressed through the narrow streets toward the palace, his gunners poured grape shot into their struggling columns, while his troops followed them up in their quick retreat to the barracks, and there showered a continuous stream of shot and shell upon the dying remnant. Those who endeavoured to escape were cut down with the sabre, and, finally, the last of the ruthless rebels met a deserved though terrible death in the blazing ruins of the barracks, from which they had so often issued orders to their masters, and demanded the slaughter of their enemies. In Constantinople over 4,000 Janizaries were killed on this memorable day. The British ambassador of the time tells us what ensued :

"A special commission sat for the trial, or rather condemnation, of crowds. Every victim passed at once from the tribunal into the hands of the executioner. The bowstring and the scimitar were constantly in play. People could not stir from their houses without the risk of falling in with some terrible sight. The entrance to the seraglio, the shore under the Sultan's windows, and the sea itself, are crowded with dead bodies, many of them torn and, in part, devoured by the dogs."

The Sultan followed up his victory in every part of the empire with equally merciless severity, and thousands more were put to death, while the very name of the famous bodyguard was proscribed and its standards destroyed.

It was a great though bloody victory, and a splendid opportunity. The military tyranny of centuries had been swept away, and the Sultan was free at last to inaugurate reform and make an attempt at grafting new fruit upon a decaying trunk. That his efforts were doomed to failure he could not foresee, but, looking back now, we can note and admire the struggle which then commenced. An army of 40,000 men was formed, and drilled and armed after European models, and he announced that it would be increased to 250,000 in time. For the moment everything seemed to work into his hands. The insurgent Wahabites in Syria were crushed; the head of Ali Pasha had been exhibited in his divan as a warning to other rebels; the Mamelukes of Egypt, like the Janizaries of Stamboul, had been exterminated; the rebellion in Moldavia and Wallachia was subdued; the Greeks were apparently about to be subjugated by Ibrahim Pasha. And had Mahmoud been given a few years of grace and immunity from aggression or rebellion, great good might have been done, despite the fact that he embodied so much of barbarism in his own character and methods. It was the struggle of a strong ignorant man of great ability, with old traditions, customs, and corruptions. It was a blind, brave, though isolated, effort toward something better, and, as such, should have been supported by the Christian powers.

But it was against Russian policy to allow of any real attempt at improving the position of Turkey; war was declared, nominally on behalf of the people of Moldavia and Wallachia; and the humiliating treaty of Adrianople exacted, in 1829, from the unfortunate Sultan. Then in the midst of his still determined efforts, and at a time when he required every possible prestige to aid him in the gigantic task, France seized one of his African provinces; Russia forced him to sign the offensive and defensive treaty of Unkiar Skelessi, which for seven years made the Porte a sort of Russian football; Mehemet Ali, ambitious and daring, over-ran Syria and a large part of Asia Minor, and threatened Constantinople itself; Greece obtained its independence, and the whole empire became a scene of tumult, disruption, and war.

A weaker man would have succumbed to such a malignant combination. But Mahmoud held his determined way, promulgated various reforms, trained his successor in European principles, and finally received the support of England against Mehemet Ali. Death came, however, in 1839, in the midst of all his struggles, his good but futile intentions, his great but unsuccessful career. And whatever may have been his personal vices, his characteristic Turkish cruelty, his inherited environment of degradation, the reforms which he attempted were great even in their failure, and afford ample evidence of a naturally noble mind.

Abdul-Medjid was hardly a worthy or fitting successor to a militant reformer. Lord Stratford de Redcliffe, who may be almost said to have ruled Turkey from 1842 to 1856, describes him in not unflattering terms as a generous-hearted and intelligent youth, with a pervading melancholy of expression. But, in truth, "the great Eltchi" found the young Sultan an apparently facile instrument in his hands, and at first liked him because he promised to be easily moulded in harmony with his own determined views and disposition. Unfortunately, the flexible will of the new ruler was as easily swayed by strong minds against reform as he was by that of Lord Stratford in its favour. And the lack of vigour which had come to him from his cradle—he was the son of Mahmoud and one of his Circassian slaves—combined with sensual indulgence in all his later life, soon undermined the effects of his father's teachings, and the hoped for results of his own enactments.

Yet he began well. Mahmoud had taken away the power of life or death from the Pashas, and given a right of appeal against the death sentences of the courts. He had set the example, for the first time, of constantly attending the Divan in person; he had suppressed many hereditary local chiefs, or Pashas, who were so many local tyrants; he had partially reformed the system of levying taxes, and had abolished many sinecure offices. Upon his ascension, and under the advice of Reschid Pasha, Abdul-Medjid issued what has been often called the Magna Charta of Turkey. This famous Tanzimat, or Hatti-Scheriff of Gulhané, well deserved the name, so far as its principles and enunciation were concerned. Had it been carried out, an Oriental religious despotism would have been transformed into a limited monarchy, and the ruin of the Turk indefinitely postponed. The marvel is that such a change was not seen to be impossible, and that so shrewd an observer as Lord Stratford should have been deceived into hopefulness.

Writing to Lord Palmerston, on March 7th, 1832, he had stated that, in his belief, "the time is near at hand, or perhaps already come, when it is necessary that a decided line of policy should be adopted and steadily pursued with respect to this country. The Turkish Empire is evidently hastening to its dissolution, and an approach to the civilization of Christendom affords the only chance of keeping it together for any length of time." This was not very hopeful in tone, but upon his return to Stamboul, ten years later, he loyally set to work to realize the ambition of Mahmoud, and the enlightened but singularly ineffectual mandate of his successor. The Hatti-Scheriff had commenced in characteristic form. "Full of confidence in the help of the Most High," declared the Sultan, "and supported by the intercession of our Prophet, we consider it advisable to attempt, by new institutions, to obtain for the provinces comprising the Ottoman Empire the benefits of a good administration."

It then went on to provide for the security of all subjects, without distinction of creed, in life, honour, and property; to announce the equitable distribution and collection of taxes; to propose the systematic recruiting of the army. It confirmed Mahmoud's ordinance as to public trials and appeals; it asserted the right of all persons to hold property, and appointed a council to elaborate administrative reform. But the enactment was an absolute farce from the beginning. Reschid was overthrown, and a reaction ensued, in which for a time the weak Sultan fell entirely into the hands of enemies to reform, or progress, or even justice. The local Pashas again did as they liked; though, instead of acting as independent tyrants, with an occasional relapse into rough kindliness, or honesty, they were now the obsequious but powerful tools of the corrupt governing clique at Constantinople. For instance, in 1842, three Christian peasants were executed at Scutari without trial; the Pasha at Trebizond cut the throats of two alleged criminals in the public street; the governor of Mosul, maddened with drink, rushed out of his house one night, and murdered at pleasure without interference or punishment; two towns were utterly destroyed by the troops in Albania; Pera was placarded with threats against the Christians.

The general condition of the country was as bad as these local details would indicate. "Every man," wrote Lord Stratford, "gets what he can, commands when he dares, and submits when he must." Financial e͏͏rassment existed everywhere, and the most was in lucrative posts, under a governmen not afford to pay salaries, and therefore peri ted ry species of corruption and dishonesty. Brutal vi ence prevailed in the courts of law; Christian evidence was of no avail against Moslems; Christians could hardly enter the Turkish quarters of the capital itself; fraud and outrage were everywhere prevalent, while Bulgaria, Albania, Servia, and Wallachia were in a condition of chronic revolt.

Lord Stratford protested daily, and brow-beat the Sultan in his own inimitable and effective way, whilst urging the British Government constantly to " an active but friendly interference." He protected the citizens of the United States in the absence of their consul, righted the wrongs of the Dutch Jews in Syria, protected the Greek artisans in Constantinople, terminated a relentless persecution of the Armenians which had been going on for a decade, and everywhere stood by the oppressed Christians. After a determined and prolonged effort, resulting from the execution of a Christian who had been converted to Islam and afterwards recanted, he obtained the practical reversal of a law which placed every Christian, or Rayah, in Turkey, at the mercy of Moslem proselytism, which constituted part of the inexorable mandates of the Koran, and which had been responsible for many judicial murders. He was greatly helped by Reschid and Midhat Pashas—men who, under better conditions, would have been great reformers and public benefactors. As it was, they were, like Mahmoud, and Lord Stratford himself, mere temporary dykes, placed in power at intervals, and then swept away upon a vast flood of corruption, prejudice, and fanaticism. And within a couple of years of the Crimean war there came to Lord Palmerston the despairing admission of the great ambassador, that " the game of improvement is altogether up for the present, and it is impossible for me to conceal that the main object of my stay here is all but gone."

With the varied events of the Crimean war the reign of Abdul-Medjid drew to an end. He died, in 1861, at the early age of thirty-eight, and received from Lord Palmerston a deserved summary of his career : "Abdul-Medjid was a good-hearted and weak-headed man who was riding two horses to the goal of perdition—his own life and that of his empire. Luckily for the empire, his own life won the race." His brother, Abdul-Aziz, succeeded to the dignities of Moslem power amid the usual trumpets of praise and promises of reform. At first the prospect really seemed bright, but after a few fitful efforts, some attempted economies, and certain commercial concessions, the new Sultan developed into a pronounced reactionist. What Abdul-Medjid had permitted through his weakness, Abdul-Aziz now carried out by his own will. It was a curious reign in the constant alternations of Western custom and Eastern intrigue and disorder. The vast series of loans begun in 1856 were carried on to their natural termination of practical bankruptcy, while the first links were laid of a railway which was never completed or properly worked. The Sultan visited England and Europe for the first time in Turkish history, created the wildest expectations of reform, and returned with the remark that he had only seen one object of interest in his travels—a beautiful woman. An Exhibition was held in Stamboul, and succeeded by the massacres of Christians in Jedda, Lebanon, and Damascus. Hordes of Circassians immigrated from Russian oppression, and became an additional curse to their adopted country. Wallachia and Moldavia obtained their practical independence under the name of Roumania, while the persecution of Christians was maintained in the midst of rebellion in Montenegro and Herzegovina, in Crete and the mountains of Lebanon. The personal character of the Sultan was of the worst, and, in the midst of Russian invasion, in 1876, following upon a refusal to give up some of his private treasure to the ministers in order to save the nation from threatened collapse and conquest, he was forcibly deposed, and soon after died in prison. Amurath V. followed in a reign of three stormy months, and was then deposed by Midhat Pasha on the ground of :" health and insanity. With the accession of Abdul-Hamid II., on the 23rd of September, 1876, began the reign which will be chiefly remembered in history for the Berlin Congress, the Armenian massacres, and the imminence of national downfall.

" O Time ! sole empress of the mighty past,
The pillars of thy throne are on the grave
Of empires ; thy dominion is a waste,
Once animate with nations great and brave."

During this century the corpse of the Ottoman power had been more than once galvanized into temporary action and apparently revived vigour. But with the events of the present administration, it has reached a position in which it appears to merely await the axe of European partition. Lord Palmerston warned Reschid Pasha, as far back as November 24th, 1850, that "the empire was doomed to fall by the timidity, and weakness, and irresolution of its sovereign and of its ministers, and it is evident that we shall ere long have to consider what other arrangement can be set up in its place." But threatened people live long, and the Sublime Porte has been through two great wars since then. Events, however, are moving faster and faster as the end of the nineteenth century draws near, and the troubles in Armenia have shown the world that a mass of mingled intolerance, corruption, and despotic weakness cannot much longer be allowed to suppress the welfare and liberties of the countries which still suffer under the shadow of Islam, and the authority of the Sultan.

CHAPTER IV.

CONSTANTINOPLE—THE CENTRE OF ISLAM.

The beautiful capital of the Turkish power, the sacred centre of Moslem regard, is worthy of a better destiny and a nobler mission than that of guarding the last days of a decaying state, or watching over the worship of many millions of deluded Asiatic races. Below the minarets of Moslem temples and the towers of Turkish palaces are to be seen the blue waters of the rapid Bosphorus as it flows between the shores of Asia and Europe. In the far distance appear the rolling hills of Asia, while all around are sights of such singular beauty, such architectural magnificence, such grovelling and individual wretchedness, such picturesque costume and character, such natural loveliness of scenery, as only this historic Eastern city can present to the eye:

> "The glowing scene of water, leaves, and light,
>   And white-veiled dames and turban'd men are here,
> And all around the earth and sea are bright
>   And beautiful in the shining air."

Upon this historic ground flourished Byzantium in centuries before Christ, and over it swept the hosts of the Medes and Athenians, the Spartans and Romans. Upon the ruins of the ancient city Constantine, in 324, founded a new Rome, and the seat of another Christian empire. Here was established the Eastern Church, and in the famous building of St. Sophia was centred the power and prestige of Eastern Christianity.

Abdul-Aziz
Sultan and Emperor of the Ottomans, 1861-1876.

Abdul-Hamid II.
Sultan and Emperor of the Ottomans, 1876-1896.

Upon Constantinople the wave of Saracen success broke and fell, and the tide of Muscovite war was checked on four occasions within a couple of centuries. Here came the conquering Crusaders in the vain endeavour to found an empire of Latin or Roman Christianity in the high places of its Eastern brother. Over the whole scene of religious controversy and discussion there finally swept the banner of the Crescent, and the Sacred Standard of Islam was installed in the Christian Church of St. Sophia. Through all the struggles and successes of six succeeding centuries it has remained there, and in 1895 has overlooked the slaughter of Armenian Christians in the streets of what the Turks call Stamboul, as it did so many hundred years before when it was first carried by Mahomet II. over the bodies of the Christian Greeks.

For two hundred years past it has been the cherished objective point of Russian intrigue and war, the storm-centre of European diplomacy. "Constantinople," muttered Napoleon, "is the empire of the world." "Constantinople," said Peter the Great, "is the key of my back door, and I must have it." "If Constantinople be taken," said the Duke of Wellington, "the world must be reconstructed." "The Eastern Question," declared the greatest Earl of Derby, "is the question of who shall have Constantinople." And during the entire six centuries of Turkish rule it has been the home of mysterious murder, the centre of Moslem immorality, the abode of secret crime, of despotic violence, of mob revolution, of cruel slavery, of multiform intrigue. At the same time it has been the occasional scene of romance such as only Eastern lands can produce, the centre of magnificence and splendid state, the subject of Eastern song, and of prayer from millions of faithful and, no doubt, sincere Moslem hearts.

But the visitor in Stamboul does not at first think of all these memories of the past, or muse upon the vast miseries of the present. He is bewildered by the weird and wonderful beauty of skies, and seas, and soil. Its situation in these respects is as absolutely unique as is its position of control over the commerce and naval power of Russia in the Black Sea, or its advantage to that power as holding the keys of the Mediterranean and the gates of the Dardanelles. Within its walls are to be found many of the most precious products of ancient art and philosophy. Side by side with these, amidst the sombre seclusion of the Moslem harems, and resting under the shadow of absolute authority, are to be found the lighter pursuits or pleasures of Paris, and the theatres and operas of European civilization. Many of those who went to see the Columbian Exhibition, at Chicago, thought that the famous Midway Plaisance presented a fair picture of an Eastern city, or at all events of an Eastern population. But, of Constantinople, it was only a faint imitation.

There is in Stamboul an infinite, ever-changing variety of costume and language. Soldiers are there in every conceivable uniform, and hailing from distant Eastern countries, or attendant upon the numerous embassies which sit at Therapia and watch each other and the Sublime Porte with such lynx-eyed keenness; picturesque Persians from the land of the Shah-in-Shah; Frankish diplomats and European adventurers; beauties of the harem with henna-stained fingers and painted eye-lashes; Jews in black clothes and the Turkish turban; Armenian priests with dark robes and square caps, using their rosaries as they walk; lank and naked dervishes; gesturing Italians; strange peoples from the Isles of Greece; grim and towering Arabs; black and glistening Nubians; slaves and eunuchs in every variety; Turkish Pashas in fez and frock coat; warlike Albanians; terrible-looking Circassians; Syrians in their long robes; Bulgarians in coarse serge and fur-embroidered caps; Greeks covered with embroidery, tassels, and buttons; representatives of races from every country and clime.

Amidst this wild medley of national types are shouted the newspapers of the day in Greek, Turkish, French, English, Armenian, and other tongues, and to the traveller who stands upon the bridge which crosses the Golden Horn between Galata and Stamboul is presented such a scene as he can witness nowhere else. Who loves variety and change, the horrible and the beautiful, the study of human nature in its every phase and form, may here have absolute satiety. Perhaps no better description of such a scene can be given than that of the Hon. S. S. Cox, for many years American Minister in this mighty network of labour and laziness, intrigue and mystery:

"An experienced eye discerns, among the waves of that great sea, the faces and costumes of Caramania and Anatolia, of Cyprus and Candia, of Damascus and Jerusalem, the Druse, the Kurd, the Maronite, the Croat, and others—innumerable varieties of all the anarchical confederations which extend from the Nile to the Danube, and from the Euphrates to the Adriatic. . . . No two figures are dressed alike. Here are shawls twisted around the heads, savage fillets, coronets of rags, skirts and undervests in stripes and squares like harlequins, girdles stuck full of knives that reach to the armpits, mameluke trousers, short drawers, skirts, togas, trailing sheets, coats trimmed with ermine, vests like golden cuirasses, sleeves puffed and slashed, habits monkish, and habits covered with gold lace, men dressed like women and women that look like men, beggars with the port of princes and ragged eloquence, a profusion of colours, of fringes, tags, and fluttering ends of childish and theatrical decorations that remind one of a masquerade in a mad-house, for which all the old-clothes dealers in the universe have emptied their stores. . . . It seems that Constantinople is the same as it always was—the capital of three continents and the queen of twenty vice-realms. But even this is insufficient to account for the spectacle, and one fancies a tide of emigration produced by some enormous cataclysm that has overturned the antique continent."

Away from all this noise and stir and wilderness of movement—amid nature at its best and quietest—lies the suburb of Therapia and the houses of many of the foreign ambassadors. Here we find another side of Stamboul, and one which is exquisitely beautiful. Bordering the blue waters of the Bosphorus, the houses, though not amounting to much from an architectural point of view, are surrounded by sloping gardens, and breezy woods, and abundant flowers. The British Embassy of many pregnant years was thus secluded in bowery groves, filled with great English elms, and pinks, and daisies, and buttercups. Here Lord Stratford de Redcliffe laid down those masterful ideas and regulations which might have saved the Turk, the Christian, and the world from much of suffering and disgrace had the rulers of that unhappy nation not shuffled out of every obligation and promise. Here took place many conferences fraught with peace and war, reform and relapse. Here lived Sir Austin Layard, and Sir Henry Elliot, and the Earl of Dufferin. Here were held the ends of many an intricate chain of intrigue and diplomacy, the keys to many an occurrence of great international importance.

But in every direction are scenes of beauty and historic renown—a rich luxuriousness of natural charm, coupled with an entire absence of effort to do justice to the fertile soil, or to take advantage of the exquisite scenery. Nature seems to have done its best to here place Europe and Asia in a rivalry of lovely, living wildness. Up from the banks of the Bosphorus, as the traveller glides gently along in some picturesque caique, are scenes which made one of them feel that "whatever changes may darken and disfigure the globe, work the ruin of cities, and the destruction of nations, you have here beneath your entranced vision what no warring vicissitude can reach—an embodied power of purity and loveliness which time cannot impair, or man deface." And as the brilliant cupolas, gilded crescents, lofty monuments, and marble porticoes of the palatial capital of Islam come into view, swelling almost from the bosom of the beautiful waters, it is hard indeed to realize the sombre records of its memorable past.

Yet over this historic stream, and within sight of Stamboul, if not actually through its weltering streets, have passed the mighty hosts of Persia, to leave their bones whitening upon the soil of Greece; the devastating hordes of Vandal and of Goth; the leagued followers of the once mighty Crescent. The city itself is more than worthy of the surrounding beauty, and of its position as the centre of such vital conflicts. Its great buildings are many, varied, and famous. Seated upon either side of the " Golden Horn," which runs up from the Bosphorus into the very heart of its teeming population, Constantinople has its two European portions—Stamboul proper and Galata—and the Asiatic suburb of Scutari, which is a part and parcel of the city, and the centre of an ever-moving mass of boats from one shore of the Bosphorus to the other.

In Stamboul are innumerable buildings of intense interest and memorable import. Overlooking the shores of the Strait, where it swells inward from the Sea of Marmora, stood for several centuries the famous Seraglio, with its historic gate, or massive arched Porte, from which the "Sublime" Ottoman Empire obtains its diplomatic designation. Through this and other gates were the courts and marble pillars; the galleries, balconies, and clustering domes; the gorgeous decorations and architectural splendours of that home of Eastern pomp and power—the Sultan's chief palace and harem. There, during a part of the year, and through many and varied periods, had dwelt the Padischah of the Moslem world, until, in the reign of Abdul-Medjid, the beautiful and stately pile of buildings was burned to the ground.

Elsewhere are more than twenty imperial palaces, some inland and some upon the banks of the Bosphorus, but all magnificent creations of Oriental imagination and extravagance. Amongst them, Dolma Bagche, built by Mahmoud II., and Begler Bey, a later creation, and Yildiz Kiosk, the last of all, are, perhaps, the most remarkable. Around these costly dwellings are spread the most exquisite gardens, laid out with terraces, and lakes, and fountains, and cascades, and aviaries, and pavilions. Within them is all that money can purchase. During the reign of Abdul-Aziz, his harem included 5,500 servants of both sexes, while his personal expenditure is said to have exceeded $10,000,000 a year. Yildiz, a beautiful place about three miles out of the city, and on the banks of the Bosphorus, is at present the chief and official residence of him who was termed not long since in a Turkish paper:

"The finest Pearl of the Age, and the esteemed Centre of the Universe; at whose grand portals stand the camels of justice and mercy, and to whom the eyes of the kings and peoples in the West have been drawn— the rulers there finding an example of political prowess, and the classes a model of mercy and kindness; Our Lord and Master, the Sultan of the two Shores and the

High King of the two Seas; the Crown of Ages and the Pride of all Countries; the Greatest of all Caliphs; the Shadow of God on Earth; the successor of the Apostle of the Lord of the Universe; the Victorious Conqueror, Sultan Abdul-Hamid Khan."

In these palaces and over the spot where the Eski-Serai once stood are all the memories of fleeting pleasure, and dreary pain, and tortured death, which surround the myriad lives of the women who, during six hundred years, have given each successive Sultan a bodyguard of beauty and of grace. Here has been the embodied pathos of the harem life, the continuous struggle of rival ambitions, the fitful success of some one out of many hundreds, the prolonged power of some unusually able or unscrupulous woman. Here also is the luxurious and lavish wealth of centuries, accumulated as a sort of secret gilding to the life of the Sultan and the four or five hundred partners of his heart.

At some distance from the ruins of the Seraglio is the renowned Mosque of St. Sophia, with its noble dome, its varied and stately columns, its mosaic pavements, and sweep of sombre splendour. An air of intense solemnity seems to permeate the exterior and interior of this historic building, which the Sultan so greatly cherishes, which the Greek is determined to possess, and which more than one Czar has sworn to conquer. Elsewhere the Solymania mosque, with its granite from Thebes, its columns of white and green marble, its stained windows, lofty cupolas, and beautiful fountains, produces a scene of genuine Oriental magnificence. And so with many other religious edifices. Scattered throughout the city may also be seen the famous Obelisk, the marble pyramid of Constantine, the Delphic column, the pillar of granite erected to the Emperor Marcian in days of Christian power, and other memorials of the past.

Marble and richly gilt fountains are numerous and beautiful, but the characteristic centre of popular attraction in Stamboul, outside of religious hours, is the bazaar—in all its innumerable and brilliant forms. These splendid exhibitions of varied goods are perfect labyrinths of colour and beauty. Simple articles are not common, but jewelled turbans, ermined robes with flowing folds and costly material, Indian shawls of a richness which would have made a whole community of Western women—when shawls were fashionable—almost crazy with delight; muslins from Bengal, silks from China, gold and gems and ivory from Africa, are there in ever-changing variety. Intimately associated with the bazaars are the Khans, or public storehouses and places of free residence for the multitude of visiting merchants who combine to make Constantinople a great Eastern emporium.

Here also are innumerable camels, still bearing the burden of a commerce which Western enterprise has not yet transferred from the patient ships of the desert to the steaming railway horse. Here also are the Turkish baths, of which Western cities have some faint knowledge. But this is their home and centre, and here they are maintained in truly Oriental luxury and elegance. The Rev. Walter Colton said of his experience in one of them a number of years since, that he " felt for several days like a new being; it seemed as if the clinging weariness of years had been cast off, and that I had got back again amongst the sallies and impulses of childhood."

But Stamboul presents to the visitor much more than a mere kaleidoscope of beautiful scenery, historic churches, Eastern variety and merriment. It is an Asiatic centre of intrigue and story planted upon European soil, and, like Bagdad, with its Arabian Nights, often receives more attention from the standpoint of tragic memories than from that of learned detail. We have, for instance, the story of Sultan Mahomet IV., who delighted to honour a certain historian named Abdi, and kept him near his person with the special duty of writing the royal annals. One evening Mahomet asked him, "What hast thou written to-day?" Abdi answered hastily that nothing had happened to record that day. The Sultan replied by throwing a spear at the historian, wounding him severely, and observing, "*Now* thou hast something to write about."

Near St. Sophia is a large group of carved figures, which are said to represent the one hundred and twenty children and numerous wives of one of the Sultans, who had all been strangled by order of his successor. But this happened so often in Turkish annals that its commemoration seems to have been rather superfluous. Elsewhere is the grave of Ali Pasha of Janina, who, after the capture of his stronghold by Mahmoud's general, Churchid Pasha, retired to a small property near by, under promise of an act of oblivion. To him, amongst other visitors, came Mahomet Pasha, governor of the Morea, with various presents and pleasant speeches. As he rose to depart amid pledges of eternal frendship, the sabre flashed in his hand and was plunged into the heart of his host. The ingenuity and patriotism of this act is said to have been much applauded at Stamboul. It was, however, one that Ali himself had always more or less affected, and for that and other reasons he no doubt deserved his fate.

All through the traditions and stories of Stamboul runs the pathetic chord of harem loves and hatreds; of discovery and death in the dark waters of the Golden

Horn, or Bosphorus; of the merciless bowstring in the hands of the still more merciless eunuch; of multitudes sewed up in sacks, and drowned without pity or regret. Amid such memories, coupled with the enervating effects of self-indulgence and luxury, each successive Sultan grew up to man's estate, the inheritance of unlimited facilities for debauchery, and every conceivable temptation to live a wasted life. Little wonder if the majority of them succumbed to their surroundings and contributed their part to the decadence of Turkish power. Even Mahmoud II., with great inherent force of character, found it impossible to resist his environment, and in his later days fell into habits of excessive self-indulgence. Abdul-Medjid plunged into this life from the beginning of his reign, and literally killed himself at an early age.

Abdul-Aziz was a Sultan of the olden time placed amidst modern surroundings. Prodigal—with borrowed money; capricious, violent, and voluptuous; he is described as having been a powerful but commonplace-looking Turk, with full face and large fixed eyes. He was filled with fanciful and costly whims. Turkish loans were largely in the building of new palaces. Lions and tigers were brought from Africa and India; innumerable carriages and pianos were imported from Europe; cockfights were a constant source of amusement to him; and no expense was spared in keeping the harem supplied with beauties from all parts of Asia. After his return in 1867 from the European trip, about which so much was said and hoped, Miss Frances Elliot, in her delightful "Diary in Constantinople," records a conversation which was repeated to her as having taken place. "Your Majesty," said the Grand Vizier, "is, I hope, satisfied with all you have seen?" "Very much so," replied the Sultan. "At least I thank Allah that I am not blinded like those European sovereigns who put faith in so cursed a faith as the Christian."

He went on to speak of the "shameful" appearance of women at balls and receptions, hanging on the arms of strange men, the fulness of the prisons, and the starvation existing in the great centres of Europe. Miss Elliot describes Fuad Pasha as saying afterwards, " He believes that he knows as much as all. Europe put together. 'I have nothing to learn from those states,' he declares. One thing pleased him in France—a woman. (The Empress Eugenie.) In England he admired the fleet. Austria and Prussia did not interest him at all." Such a ruler could, and did, do much to hasten the downfall of his country. One of his best known ministers, for instance, was Nevrez Pasha—half knave, half fool. Like so many others, in Turkish history, he had risen to eminence from the lowest stage of Seraglio duties, and for a long time retained office through willingness to be the victim of the Sultan's undignified fondness for wrestling. Such was the monarch who met an unproven but undoubtedly violent death after his deposition in 1876.

To this royal position, without any previous training, without friends whom he could trust, without educated and intelligent advisers, without principles of high morality or any lofty conception of national duties with which to guide himself, Abdul Hamid came. Surrounded by corrupt pashas, unscrupulous eunuchs, lying mollahs and astrologers, obsequious courtiers of the worst Eastern type, Kadines and odalisques and slaves without number, he has remained ever since, through a reign of twenty troublous and tortured years. During that period he appears to have been Sultan in deed and in truth. The constitutional farce was early got rid of, and Midhat

Pasha soon dismissed to die in dignified but useless state.

Since then, so far as can be seen through a veil of intrigue and corruption, the Sultan has ruled without confidants and without other than nominal or secretarial assistance from his Ministers. His industry has been phenomenal. His courage, in the teeth of almost overpowering difficulties, has been great. His vices and his cruelty are the ordinary qualities of the Turkish governing character. During the war with Russia, at a critical moment—when the armies of the Czar faced Stamboul from the heights of San Stefano, and the fleet of England was anchored within a short distance of the capital—his Grand Vizier and Council became panic-stricken at what seemed to them a double menace. They urged instant flight into Asia, and upon the result turned questions of more than national import. But Abdul Hamid refused, and declared his intention never to abandon the capital which for four hundred years had held the throne of his dynasty. And by this decision he unfortunately saved his empire for another term of oppression and riot and massacre.

His industry takes the form of an attempt to supervise and control everything within the wide and troubled current of Ottoman affairs, and, while this exceptional quality may be deserving of praise, it undoubtedly increases confusion and encourages disorder. Mr. Shaw-Lefevre, the English politician, stated, after a visit to Stamboul, that "there is no detail of administration in his government so small or trivial that it does not come before him for his approval or his signature." This fact —coupled with the further one of every pasha or governor being appointed under his personal orders, maintained in their places by his personal will, and dependent upon what they know of his personal inclinations and policy for their promotion—indicates strongly the Sultan's responsibility for the Moslem murder and outrage of many past years.

Abdul Hamid has been described as "a most unhappy-looking man of dark complexion, with a look of absolute terror in his large eastern eyes." With the shadows of Ottoman history behind him, and the evils and dangers of his own life immediately around him, this can hardly be wondered at. The same observer refers to him as emaciated and unnatural in appearance, and declares that "his eyes haunted me for days, as one gazing at some unknown horror." But in the shades of Yildiz he none the less perseveres, courageously and doggedly, in the administration of Turkish affairs. There he lives amidst the seclusion of his enormous harem, and surrounded by the most charming of Oriental natural scenery. What may be the tortured doubts and fears of this Commander of the Faithful few or none will ever know. All that the civilized world can really be certain of is the result of the labours and secret commands by which he strives to hold together the threads of a barbaric past and a civilized present; the keys of the East and the West; and all the myriad complications and contradictions represented by the position, history, and population of Constantinople the beautiful.

CHAPTER V.

Russia and Turkey.

If Constantinople is the centre of the world of Islam, it is equally certain that St. Petersburg is now the central city, and its government the predominating power, in the Greek Church. But this fact is of more international than religious interest. Outside of Russia, the Greek and Christian faith of the East is divided into independent Churches which only look toward the Czar when persecutions or national complications make it advisable to have political pressure brought upon the Sublime Porte, or make military intervention desirable, for reasons often entirely apart from the religious issue. By Russia itself, this representative position as the great recognized power of the Greek Church has been used aggressively and continuously as a means for territorial expansion, and for the weakening of its hereditary enemy, the Turk.

It was in A.D. 988 that Vladimir, the first powerful ruler in what is now the Russian Empire, married a daughter of the Greek Emperor, at Constantinople, and was baptized in the Christian faith. From this time, during nearly five hundred stormy years, his territories and people have passed through every form of national experience and war. They succumbed to various Tartar invasions and dynasties, but in 1462 were finally established in a strong position by Ivan III., the Great, who introduced firearms and cannon into the country, almost annihilated the Tartars, took possession of Siberia, fought

Peter the Great
Czar of Muscovy and First Emperor of Russia, 1689-1725.

Poland, and asked Queen Elizabeth of England to marry him. It was in his reign that the first collision with the Turks took place. A large Moslem army had laid siege to Astrakhan, in the interest of a scheme of Sultan Selim's Grand Vizier, looking to the construction of a canal connecting the Don and the Volga. The ensuing defeat by the Russians prevented the ambitious scheme from being carried out, and placed in the Czar's hands the first trophies ever captured by Russian soldiers from the hitherto victorious Ottoman. The Khan of the Crimea— a Turkish vassal—retaliated afterwards by marching upon Moscow and sacking the Muscovite capital.

With the reign of Peter the Great, however, in the years between 1689 and 1725, began the great empire of modern Russia, as well as the persistent and historic policy of war and aggression upon the Turks. It is the custom to praise this ruler, and his ability certainly deserves all that can be said of it. But he was as cruel and merciless in his government as he was keen and unscrupulous in carrying out his ambitious designs. Barbarism was as engrained in his character as it was in that of his nation, and no visit to the dockyards of Holland or England could eliminate the quality. His revenge upon the royal body-guard, which had shared in some conspiracy at home, illustrates this fact. Over 2,000 of them were tortured and slain, many being beheaded by his own hand. So with the 14,000 Swedish prisoners whom he sent to die in the wastes of Siberia after the victory of Pultowa.

The first encounter between Peter and the Turks was in 1672, when certain Cossacks of the Ukraine appealed to the Porte for protection against both Poland and Russia. The Khan of the Crimea was at once sent to their assistance, and 6,000 Turkish troops were added to his own forces. To the ensuing threat of war from the Czar the Grand Vizier sent a most remarkable letter. "God be praised," said he, "such is the strength of Islamism that the union of Russians and Poles matters not to us. Our empire has increased in might since its origin; nor have all the Christian kings that have leagued against us been able to pluck a hair from our beard. With God's grace, it shall ever be so, and our empire shall endure to the day of judgment." For the time war was averted, but in the closing days of the century Peter joined Austria and Venice and Poland, in their almost continuous state of conflict with the Turks, and prosecuted his campaign with a vigour which the latter found not only unusual, but unpleasant. After two sieges the strongly fortified city of Azof—a menace to Russian territory for a long period—was at last conquered.

Turkey had, meanwhile, lost in many other directions, and in 1698, through the mediation of England and Holland, the important Treaty of Carlowitz was signed. For the first time, Russia and the Porte now took part in a European Congress, and, by admitting the representatives of the two non-combatant states, accepted that principle of intervention which has since constituted such a vital portion of the so-called Eastern Question. But the Czar, who had lately proclaimed himself Emperor of Russia, and whose territory was now growing with gigantic strides, would only accept a two years' truce. Austria, however, under the terms of a twenty-five years' peace, took most of Hungary and Transylvania from the Porte, Poland recovered Podolia and Kamienic, and Venice retained parts of Dalmatia and the Morea.

This was the commencement of Russian dominance, and the first great step in the external downfall of the Turks. From this period the latter were no longer feared

by Christendom as an aggressive force, but rather as
containing within their empire resources and a national
position which, in the hands of such a power as Russia,
might prove a menace to the liberties of the world, as
pronounced as they had been in the days of Solyman the
Great. In 1711, Peter again declared war against the
Turks, and this time he gave it a distinctively religious
character. Nominally, the first declaration eman-
ated from Constantinople, but it came as the natural
result of Russian intrigues amongst the Christian Greeks
in the empire, and the known fact that the Czar was
only waiting his completion of the conquest of Livonia
to march upon the coveted Crimea. And now, instead
of the usual standards, the Russian troops bore red
ensigns inscribed on one side with the words, " In the
name of God and for the cause of Christianity," and
having on the other side a large cross.

The result was a triumph for Turkey, only limited by
the short-sighted folly of its rulers. By some military
mischance, into which it is not necessary to enter, the
Russian army became hemmed in upon the banks of the
Pruth by unbreakable Turkish lines and a wall of Turkish cannon. Peter might have been destroyed, his army
annihilated, Russia put back for hundreds of years, and
the Turk reinstated in much of his old-time power. But
the conquering spirit had gone out of the Moslem commanders, and the result was the celebrated Treaty of the
Pruth, commencing with the preamble that, " By the
grace of God, the victorious Moslem army had closely
hemmed in the Czar of Muscovy, with all his troops, in
the neighbourhood of the river Pruth, and that the Czar
had asked for peace," which had been granted with the
following conditions:

I. The surrender of Azof and all its dependencies.

II. The destruction of certain offensive Russian fortifications.

III. No further interference with the affairs of the Poles or the Cossacks.

IV. The direction that no Russian ambassador should, in future, reside at Constantinople, because of intrigues with the Greeks, etc.

V. The release by Russia of the captured King of Sweden.

And for these petty and comparatively unimportant concessions, Peter the Great and his captive army were allowed to depart, with the farewell intimation in the Treaty from the Grand Vizier, that "the royal and infinite goodness of his thrice powerful and gracious Lord and Padischah was entreated to ratify these articles, and to overlook the previous evil conduct of the Czar." The fact is that, at this critical moment in the history of the Turk and the Russian, the venality of the Grand Vizier had been played upon successfully by a Russian envoy, and the spirit of corruption had won another victory over the ancient conquering spirit of the Moslem.

A dozen years later occurred the first alliance of the two great rivals. That it should have been a solemn treaty of eternal peace seems a rather amusing fact, but the objects of the arrangement were quite sufficiently serious. It was, in brief, a partition of Persia. The Czar was to take the provinces near the Caspian Sea and extending into the heart of Persia, while the Sultan was to reach northwards and assume an extensive territory hitherto forming debatable ground. The latter obtained a fetva, or mandate, from the religious authorities of Islam, sanctioning hostilities against the hated and heretical Persians, and expressly requiring all orthodox Mahometans to put the men of that nation to the edge of the sword and reduce their wives and children to slavery. After a prolonged war, however, in which the celebrated Nadir Shah gained victories over both the Turks and the Russians, peace was finally made between the three powers upon a basis of the boundaries previously existing.

The Porte would now have been very glad of a period of rest, but the Empress Anne, fresh from her iniquitous attacks upon Poland, and having made all possible use of Turkey as against Persia, decided that it was a good time for another war with her recent ally. Marshal Munnich's campaign in the Crimea which followed was marked by atrocious cruelty, the destruction of many defenceless towns, the burning of monuments and libraries and schools, the capture of Oczakof and the slaughter of 17,000 Turks. Meanwhile, Austria joined in the war against Islam, and in 1738 the victorious Munnich told the Czarina that "now is the time to march upon Constantinople." During the following year this was attempted, but checked by the defeat of the Austrians at Krotzka, and ended for the time by the Peace of Belgrade.

In the succeeding reign of Catharine II., Russia was joined by Prussia in the shameful occupation of Poland, and, of course, paid no attention to the strong remonstrances of the Porte. Curiously enough, the Poles, fighting for freedom, and the Turks, fighting for the preservation of their dominions—the one Christian and the other Mahometan—more than once sympathized with each other in this century of their declining power. But the barbaric sweep of the Muscovite, together with the clever and unscrupulous diplomacy which has won more for Russia than ever its armies have done, was too much for either Pole or Turk. In 1768, for instance, Obresskoff, the Russian Minister, was summoned before the Grand Vizier to explain the presence of 30,000 troops in Poland

**IMAGE EVALUATION
TEST TARGET (MT-3)**

when he had pledged himself in writing, and on behalf of the Czarina, that they should be reduced to 7,000 men. "Traitor, perjurer!" cried the Vizier, "hast thou not owned thy faithlessness? Dost thou not blush before God and man for the atrocities which thy countrymen are committing in a land which is not theirs?" And the public opinion of to-day cannot but feel that when a Christian power merited such reproaches at the hands of a Turk, the disgrace was indeed signal. Obresskoff, in accordance with the still haughty temper of the Ottoman, was sent to the famous prison of the Seven Towers, and war was again commenced.

The result might have been anticipated with such an ambitious and brilliant leader as Catharine on the one side, and the enervated, corrupt, and ignorant Turkish commander on the other. To complicate matters for the Porte, an insurrection of the Mamelukes broke out in Egypt, and Georgia rebelled against his authority. Following this a Russian flotilla intercepted in the Black Sea the supplies of the Turkish capital; a Russian fleet landed troops upon the soil of Greece and endeavoured unsuccessfully to advance upon Stamboul; Azof was captured, and Russian authority established in Moldavia, Wallachia, and Bessarabia. In 1774 the humiliating Treaty of Kainardji was signed, by which the Porte declared the Crimea independent, as well as Bessarabia, and undertook to give "free exercise for the Christian religion" in Moldavia and Wallachia, together with "humane and generous government." It also promised "to protect constantly the Christian religion and its churches, and it also allows the ministers of the Imperial Court of Russia to make, upon all occasions, representations as well in favour of the new Church at Constantinople as on behalf of its officiating ministers."

Poland was not referred to, and Catharine now proceeded to carry out her policy unhampered by Turkish protests. A smaller matter, but one very painful to the Turk, was the recognition of the Czarina's right to the title of Padischah, or Empress, which had been hitherto refused. This treaty strengthened Russia enormously, and gave an added impetus to Catharine's schemes for the completion of the great Peter's policy of expansion to the shores of the Bosphorus. A Russian Prince was named Constantine, after the last of the Greek emperors, and openly procla.ned as destined for the throne of Constantinople. In 1779 the Empress and Prince Potemkin actually proposed to offer aid to England against the American colonists in return for support against the Turks. French diplomacy, however, prevented the matter from going beyond the region of schemes. A little later Catharine boldly annexed the Crimea and adjacent territories, without cause or reasonable pretext, and, on resistance being made, sent an army of invasion which, upon one occasion, massacred 30,000 Tartars of every age and sex, and compelled myriads to flee the country—amongst the rest some 75,000 Armenian Christians.

During 1787 the Empress marched through a part of the Crimea in great state, and at the head of 200,000 men. Upon one occasion a triumphal arch was inscribed with the words, " Route to Constantinople." And throughout this period, as well as in much of the succeeding hundred years, Greece, Roumelia, Macedonia, Montenegro, the Danubian provinces, and parts of Asia Minor, swarmed with Russian emissaries preaching Muscovite friendship and promising Muscovite support. A secret treaty was also made with Austria, during a visit paid by the Emperor Joseph to Catharine's camp upon the shores of the Black Sea, and the Empress tried to persuade him into an immediate partition of Turkey. War not unnaturally broke out a little later, and lasted, between the Turks on the one side and Austria and Russia on the other, with varying success, until 1791. The most memorable incident during its progress was Suwarrow's storming of Ismail—a great Turkish fortress on the Danube. For months it had resisted Potemkin, but six days after his instructions to Suwarrow, " You will take Ismail, whatever the cost," it fell, amid scenes of carnage and crime rarely equalled in history, and during which the defenders were massacred without stint or mercy. To quote Byron's powerful lines in this connection:

> " Let me put an end unto my theme!
> There was an end of Ismail—hapless town !
> Far flashed her burning towers o'er Danube's stream,
> And redly ran his blushing waters down.
> The horrid war-whoops and the shriller screams
> Rose still; but fainter were the thunder's grown ;
> Of forty thousand who had manned the wall,
> Some hundreds breathed—the rest were silent all ! "

The temporary Peace of Jassy followed, and the Russian frontier was extended to the Dneister. Russian emissaries were immediately afterwards sent into Georgia, and other Persian or Turkish territories in Asia Minor, to stir up the inhabitants, and in 1796, when Catharine suddenly died, she was preparing an army of 450,000 men and a great fleet with a view to a determined advance upon Constantinople. For the time, however, these great designs were abandoned by her successor, who now became more or less mixed up in the Napoleonic wars. In 1798 a treaty of alliance was, in fact, concluded between Turkey, Russia, and Great Britain against France. But in 1801 this was abandoned by the Sultan for friendly relations with the French, and in 1806 war again broke out with Turkey. It grew from Russian demands for an offensive and defensive alliance, and for the recognized right to " protect " all the subjects of the Sultan who professed the faith of the Greek Church. This little extension of the Treaty of Kainardji—however agreeable it might have been to some of the Christians of Turkey—was naturally an impossible one to its rulers, and war was declared, despite the threats of the British ambassador, who wished to again combine the Turk and the Russian against Napoleon.

The war continued until 1812, when the Treaty of Bucharest was concluded, and the Russian frontier advanced to the Pruth. An interesting feature of this struggle was a prolonged negotiation between Alexander and Napoleon concerning the proposed final partition of Turkey. There were two schemes discussed. Under the one, Russia was to have the Danubian principalities and Bulgaria, and Austria was to be given Bosnia and Servia, while France was to take Greece, Albania, and Candia. Under the second one, Austria was to be given the additional bribe of Macedonia and the important harbour of Salonika, France was to take Cyprus, Syria, and Egypt, besides the countries above mentioned, while Russia was to have the Danubian principalities of Moldavia and Wallachia, Bulgaria, Thrace, and the Asiatic provinces touching upon, or near, the Bosphorus. Constantinople proved the vital point in the arrangement and the ensuing dispute. The Turk might be driven to the banks of the Euphrates in theory, but the disposal of his capital was too much for the would-be conquerors, who, in a few years, were destined to meet in a death-grapple at Moscow. Both wanted Stamboul, and, of course, neither obtained it.

During the fourteen years which followed the Treaty of Bucharest nominal peace prevailed between the Turk and the Russian. In 1826, however, Nicholas I., who had just come to the throne of the Czars, made certain demands, which it seemed very difficult to comply with. But Mahmoud II. was in the midst of his struggle with Greece and other rebellious subjects, and was, therefore, forced into signing the Treaty of Akerman, and the acceptance of some very humiliating conditions regarding Servia and other matters. Then followed combined action by England, France, and Russia for the freeing of Greece, and the battle of Navarino in 1827, by which the Turkish navy was practically annihilated. Though this happened in a time of nominal peace, it was soon succeeded by another war with Russia, in which the Turks displayed splendid but useless bravery. And, despite the loss of the fleet, the first year's campaign proved almost a drawn game. But in the succeeding year the Russian armies reached Adrianople, and there the treaty of that name was negotiated and signed on September 14th, 1829. By its terms Russia obtained the mouths of the Danube and sundry important places in Armenia and Turkish Asia.

But the chief result of this last humiliation was the secret treaty of Unkiar Skelessi in 1833. By this arrangement, made at a moment when Turkey was almost on its knees before its great Egyptian vassal—Mehemet Ali—Russia promised her aid, and in return received the privilege of passage for her vessels through the Bosphorus and the Dardanelles, and the guaranteed exclusion of armed ships belonging to any power with which she might be at war. The absence during this period of Sir Stratford Canning (Lord Stratford de Redcliffe) from Stamboul facilitated the *coup* on the part of Russia, and it was not until 1841 that the Convention of London between the great Powers and the Porte changed the situation, and made these important waters once more Turkish. The Porte, however, was not really liberated from the iron bands of this treaty until the Crimean war had sent the Russian bear shivering back into his fastnesses.

In the famous preliminaries to that war occurred another Russian effort to partition Turkey. Peter the Great had tried to do it alone; Catharine II. had endeavoured to bribe Austria; Alexander I. had negotiated with Napoleon; Nicholas I. tried to tempt England. To the British ambassador, Sir Hamilton Seymour, he, in 1853, offered Egypt and Crete as Britain's share of the spoil; the Principalities, Bulgaria and Servia, he thoug.t, should be independent states under Russian protection. Constantinople might be temporarily occupied by his troops. "The sick man," he observed, "is dying. We have on our hands a sick man—a very sick man." By the prolonged struggle in the Crimea which followed, Russia received a decisive set-back; the Danubian principalities were relieved from her "protection"; the Danube and its mouths were made absolutely free; the Black Sea—for some time a Russian lake--was neutralized; the Christian subjects of the Porte were placed under European, instead of Russian, protection. But the respite thus received by the Turk, though long in comparison with previous ones, was short in reality.

In 1870 the Black Sea clause of this Treaty of Paris was torn up by Russia, and in 1877 Alexander II. declared war against Turkey, after various preliminary aggressions, and by the Treaty of San Stefano succeeded in almost destroying its national identity. To some extent, England and Lord Beaconsfield changed this by the Congress at Berlin, but none the less had the "sick man" now to be recognized as a permanent and very troublesome dependent state—living upon the jealousies of Europe and constituting an ever-changing Eastern Question. Of this latter problem and its kaleidoscopic details, there are now three distinct divisions. One is caused by Russia's ambition and aggression, the second by Turkish despotism, the third by Anglo-European anxiety and jealousies. Russian ambition can be easily understood by a glance over past pages. A hundred and fifty years ago, the Muscovite had only one maritime outlet; now the Caspian and Black Seas are Russian lakes. From Turkey has been taken, within a century or so, more than half its European territory, and immense slices in Asia. Persia is more or less a Russian dependency, and that power seeks, and will no doubt obtain, an outlet into the Persian Gulf and the Indian Ocean. It has long sought and lately received a similar outlet by way of Corea. Towards India it has moved through all the vast recesses of Central Asia; over the lands of the ancient Tartar and Turk and the modern Khanates of Khokand, Bokhara, and Khiva; through Merv and Sarakhs to the very gates of Herat, as that lofty fortress frowns from the borders of Afghanistan and guards the interests of British territory.

Through all this great extent of country Russia has advanced with brilliant but barbarous generals, such as Skobeloff and Alikhanoff, until she holds the eastern keys of India almost within her grasp. But there is virtue in that word "almost," and Lord Beaconsfield spoke sound statesmanship when he once said that "the keys of India were in London, not Herat." Of the character of this nation, which claims, on the ground of civilization and Christianity, to have a right to rule in Constantinople, its own record speaks abundantly, and adds greatly to the complications of the Eastern Question. As late as 1881, Geok Tepe was besieged by the Russians in the course of

their determined onslaught upon Turkestan. They finally, by force of numbers, captured the place, and Charles Marvin tells the result :
"Even when the Turcomans, no longer offering resistance, streamed out in a disorderly mob across the desert, men, women, and children mingled together, no mercy was shown to them. Artillery followed in their rear, and mowed them down, until darkness put an end to the pursuit. During that few hours' chase the thousand pursuing Russians slaughtered 8,000 of the fugitives. Hundreds of women were slain. Six thousand five hundred bodies were also found afterward under the fortress. . . . The whole country was covered with corpses."

Of the second division in the Eastern Question, it need only be said here that Turkish despotism and cruelty to the Christians speaks for itself. Of the third, England has good reason to feel aware. Skobeloff used to declare that the aim of Russia was not India, but Constantinople. The menace to India was to be employed as a means of obtaining the longed-for entrance into the Mediterranean. By this achievement Russia would have in the Black Sea a vast naval reservoir and an inaccessible place from which to build, recruit, and send forth her ships. In Constantinople and the Sea of Marmora, with the protecting Bosphorus and Dardanelles, she would possess an unapproachable fortified exit from the Black Sea, and an unequalled centre from which to dominate the Mediterranean, sweep the shores of Africa and Egypt, control the Suez Canal, and menace British commerce with India and the distant East. Hence the Eastern Question in all its varied phases, from the ambitious designs of Peter the Great to the desperate barbarism of Abdul-Hamid II.; from the victory of Clive, at Plassey, to that of Wolseley at Tel-el-Kebir ; from the Asiatic struggles of Napoleon to the massacres in Bulgaria, or Greece, or Armenia.

CHAPTER VI.

The Greek Church and Eastern Christianity.

The early history of Christianity is a proud portion of the annals of the Greek faith, as it is of the rise of Roman Catholicism. In the East the Church of Christ was founded; in the West it has received its greatest and most beneficent expansion. Persia, Armenia, and Arabia were the first countries into which it spread; Rome was the first Western city in which it took root. For three hundred years there was no distinct division in its ranks. The Christian, whether in Asia or Europe, had to endure too strenuous a persecution, and too violent sufferings, to permit of any extensive controversy with others of the same faith. In A.D. 303, the Emperor Diocletian actually decreed the destruction of the Holy Scriptures and the death of all Christians. Under this edict 15,000 adherents of Christianity were massacred in Asia Minor during a single month; 140,000 were put to death in Egypt; and a total of 700,000 are said to have died in prison.

With the accession of Constantine the Great, his conversion to Christianity, and his removal of the capital of the Roman Empire to the shores of the Bosphorus, all was changed. Prosperity brought dissension, and dissension soon created disunion. Gradually, as the Church grew in power and numbers, the great metropolitan sees of Rome and Constantinople developed differences in administration and belief which created a distinct line of

Catherine II.
Empress of Russia, 1762-1796.

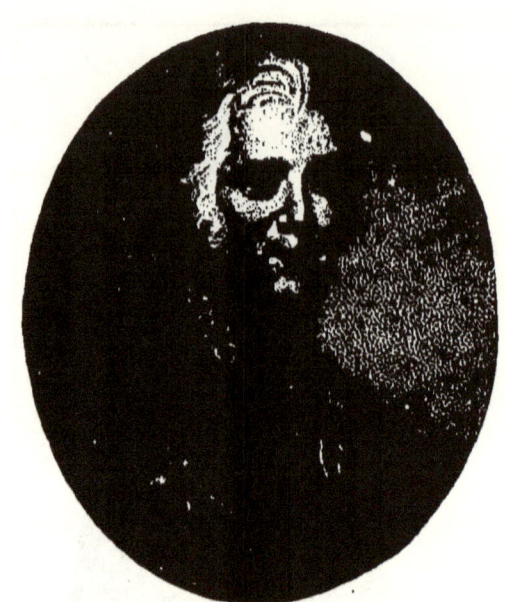

Alexander I.
Emperor of Russia, 1801-1825

cleavage between the Pope and his Western branch of the Church, and the Patriarch and his followers in the East. The controversies turned, in the main, upon the use in the Western Church of unleavened instead of leavened bread in celebrating the Holy Communion, the belief in the existence of purgatory, and faith in the infallibility of the Pope. Upon these and minor points a partial separation came about in the eighth century, and a final severance in the eleventh. The Nicæan and the Athanasian Creeds formed then, as they do now, the principal articles of faith in the Greek and Eastern Churches.

The Bulgarians accepted Christianity in this latter form during the ninth century, the Russians a hundred years later. For a long time the Metropolitan of Moscow was subordinate to the Patriarch of Constantinople. Peter the Great, however, proclaimed the independence of the Russian Church, although up to the present there remains a shadowy spiritual supremacy in the most ancient Patriarchate. So with those of Jerusalem, Antioch, and Alexandria. The Russian people, as a whole, accept the Greek, or, as they term it, the Orthodox Catholic faith. The points in which it most vitally differs from that of Rome are the denial of the supremacy of the Pope, the prohibition of ecclesiastical celibacy, and the encouragement of Bible study in the mother tongue. Divine service is performed in the national language, and singing is unaccompanied by music. Splendid churches are very numerous, and form many a strange contrast to the poverty-stricken villages and the huts of the peasantry.

Peter the Great closed up the monasteries and robbed the Church of much of its wealth. Catharine II. followed him with great success in this direction; and appropriated its entire immovable property to the use of the State. The result of this and sundry curious internal regulations was that for centuries the mass of the Russian clergy were deplorably poor, working their own little bits of soil; living like the meanest of their parishioners; and ignorant to an inconceivable degree. Matters have greatly improved during the last fifty years, and now the better class of clergymen form a distinct and superior type; and the Holy Synod possesses a capital of some £5,000,-000.

In Greece, the vast majority of the people belong to the Greek faith. In hating the Turks they are inclined to like the Russians. As being of the same great Church, though entirely independent in religious as in national jurisdiction, more than one Grecian government, and notably that of King Otho I., has been very subservient to Russian influence and intrigue. And the Greek faith, being bound up with their secular history and a part of their prolonged struggle for independence, has become woven into the very warp and woof of the national life. For a long time the Church in Greece was dependent upon the Patriarch of Constantinople, and through him, as a violent and impassioned champion of the Czar, upon the ruler of Russia. Naturally, the latter wished to retain this recognized unity, however slight it might be in practice, and despite the fact that Russia itself was independent of the Stamboul Patriarch. But the Greeks finally established their own Patriarch and Holy Synod. In conquering their national freedom, they claimed to have succeeded to the rights of the Eastern Emperors. Surely, therefore, they could decree the independence of their national Church.

Like most Eastern Churches, it is connected with the State in a more or less intimate relationship. The Holy Synod, which has jurisdiction over all ecclesiastical matters within the kingdom, is composed of five prelates, of whom the Metropolitan of Athens is chairman. Before the annual session commences, each member takes the following somewhat remarkable oath:

" Majesty, upon the sacred character with which we are invested, we certify that, ever faithful to your Majesty, our king and our master, submissive to the constitution and laws of the country, we will not cease to apply all our efforts to accomplish, with the aid of God, our duty in the administration of the Church, preserving intact, like all the other orthodox Churches of Christ, the holy apostolical and synodical canons, as well as the holy traditions. As witness of this oath, we invoke the All-Powerful. May He grant to your Majesty long days, and perfect health, maintain your kingdom unshaken, render it prosperous, *aggrandize* it, and fortify it for all ages."

A royal commissioner, appointed by the king, then attends, without voting, the sittings of the Synod and countersigns every document or decision. The Church is a very paternal organization in Greece. If any one seeks to disturb its orthodox or national position by means of preaching, teaching, or writings, the Holy Synod demands the suppression of the evil at the hands of the civil authority. It inspects all publications intended for the use of the clergy, or the youth of the community, and pamphlets, pictures, or books bearing on religious subjects. Should they oppose or be detrimental to any branch of religious dogma, or Church ceremony, it claims the assistance of the government. The mass of the clergy hold the same indifferent and undignified position which their colleagues in Russia have. They live more comfortably, because the climate is not so rigorous, and the Greek is naturally lazy in disposition. But they are ignorant, and do not hesitate, in times when fees and alms are not very lucrative, to till a field, or open a shop, or keep a public house. Edmond About, the great French author, after travelling through the Morea, declared that "the country clergy of Greece will be capable of instructing the people after they have themselves been to school."

He adds a very depressing summary of the condition of the Church, and one which is of value as showing the blackest side of a branch of Christianity which has also its bright and noble aspect. Unfortunately, however, a Church is judged by the masses of external humanity rather from its faults than its virtues, and, no doubt, the cause of Christianity in the East has been often disastrously affected by the qualities of its professors in the Greek branch of the Church, and the shortcomings of the Church itself. After terming it "a petrified religion," M. About goes on to say that "the only duties which it prescribes to men are the signs of the cross made in a particular manner, genuflections at such a place, the recitation of certain interminable formulas which have become a dead letter, the observation of certain fasts, the remaining idle during a multitude of festivals, and, finally, the obligation of feeding the priests, and enriching the churches by perpetual alms."

This is the comment and description of a caustic observer, who prefers finding faults to discovering the more beneficent influences of the Church. It is not unlikely that an Eastern critic, travelling through England, or America, or Germany, would also discover ample evidence of formalism and indifference to the real teachings of Christianity; much hypocrisy and irreligion; the greatest contradiction between precept and practice; the innumerable failures in finite efforts to reach an infinite ideal. But absolute condemnation of Western Christianity based upon such facts would have no weight amongst those who understood the situation, or the characteristics and peculiar difficulties which each nation, as well every individual, has to separately encounter.

So, in forming any fair judgment of the Greek Church, whether in Russia or in Greece, in Bulgaria or in Asiatic Turkey, wide allowances must be given for the influences of history and environment, the temperament of the people, and the drawbacks incidental to all Eastern countries. Take, for instance, the annals of the Church in its various Eastern divisions outside of Russia. It faced, and fought, and to a great extent stamped out, the heresy of Arianism, which sought to deny the divinity of Christ. It had to contend with that of Nestorius and Eutychius, which, then, and since, has had greater success because of being more insidious and indirect—although tending to the same end. It had to encounter the constant interference of the Greek Emperors and the machinations of wire-pullers at court, who were as potent ten centuries ago as they are to-day in Congress or Parliament. After the Moslem conquest, it had to face all the terrible evils of a cruel and merciless religious despotism. From the extremes of temptation afforded by national connection with the corrupt and falling Empire of Byzantium, it had to meet the depths of persecution and national effacement offered by Turkish rule. It was compelled to deal with the continuous hostility of Latin or Roman Christendom and the ancient antagonism of the Crusaders, as well as the modern efforts of the Roman Catholic missionary.

During the greater part of seven hundred years, it was isolated from the Western Church and Western Christians, and plunged in the midst of almost continuous war and invasion, or intrigue and rebellion. It has had to contend with the peculiar characteristics of Eastern love of detail and minute disquisition, Eastern fondness for display and ceremony, Eastern tendency to looseness of morals and life. And while these difficulties might be easily matched in Western Europe by a general survey of the situation there, it must be remembered that over and above these specific evils there has now existed for five hundred years the towering shadow of Mahomet, bearing all the influence of teachings which combined immutability with immorality, and thus appealed to what was for long the dormant keynote of Asiatic character and of many of the races which over-ran and intermingled with those of the European countries stretching away from the shores of the Bosphorus.

Yet amid all its wrangles and internal conflicts, all its troubles and external oppression, all its temptations and difficult environment, the Greek Church has maintained the distinctly vital principles of Christianity intact. Where the Gospel was first preached and Christian churches first organized, there the lamp of Christian faith may still be found. And its history has not been inglorious. When, in A.D. 538, the magnificent Church of St. Sophia, at Constantinople, was completed, after an expenditure of $70,000,000, the Emperor Justinian was so impressed with its exquisite beauty and stateliness that he exclaimed, "I have surpassed thee, O Solomon!" The Greek Church extended Christianity over the Slav and the Bulgarian, and really laid the foundation of the Russian nation which was to afterwards so greatly menace the Moslem oppressor of Christians. It greatly contributed to keep alive the light of Eastern literature, and sought, in the main, despite many superstitions, much vanity, and useless pomp, prevailing ignorance and vice, to advance morality and right living. It to-day boasts a membership, through various independent branches, of 2,000,000 in ˉreec ˀ, 2,000,000 in Servia, 5,000,000 in Roumania,

2,400,000 in Bulgaria, and a scattering of several millions in Asiatic and European Turkey, to say nothing of the 70,000,000 in Russia.

The Greek Church also claims to have preserved intact the original and orthodox Christian ritual. Its service comprises a number of hymns and psalms appropriate to numerous festivals, or to the liturgy. Of course, under the dominance of the Turk, the ritual has been shorn of much old-time splendour, and, in fact, has gone frequently to the other extreme in both church building and religious ceremonial. Prominent amongst the doctrines taught is that of Transubstantiation, or belief in the transformation of bread and wine at the sacrament into the body and blood of Christ. Baptism involves a complete immersion, and the anointing with holy oil. Women are not allowed to riot in excessive freedom, but are taught the maxim of St. Paul, "I suffer not a woman to teach, nor to usurp authority over the man." Confession must always precede the taking of the Communion. But it is in a very attenuated form, and is described as merely a conference between the individual and his priest. A forty days' fast is enjoined, but not imperatively, before Christmas, and during Lent. There are very few monks, or orders of that nature, within the Church. Monasteries flourished for a time during the rich and Christian days of Byzantium—as they also did in Russia—but the Turks confiscated their property in much the same impartial way as did Peter the Great and Henry VIII. in their respective spheres, and the orders rapidly declined thereafter, until now they have almost disappeared.

Whatever the faults of the Greek, or other adherent of the Greek Church, and they are many, he is never ashamed of his religion. In this respect, Eastern Christians generally, as well as the Turks themselves, should put to shame a multitude of the careless professors of Christianity in the West. Even M. About, with all his caustic bitterness, has to admit that, in Greece, "each one observes his religion because he believes in it, and no one fears to appear ridiculous in fulfilling its duties." And, however this devotion to the Church may fall short in its application to the characters and daily life of the people, it has an all-important effect upon the national development of the past and present. The twelve millions or more of orthodox Greek Christians in Bulgaria, Roumania, Greece, Servia, and other portions of what is, or has been, the Ottoman Empire, look consistently and continuously to Russia for assistance and support. That the Czars have taken advantage of this feeling to promote useless rebellions; to further their own selfishly aggressive and autocratic aims; to limit the liberties of aspiring states such as modern Bulgaria; is not the fault of the Greek Church in itself.

The history of the Christian faith in Russia is a noble one. Some years ago—in 1888—the nine hundredth anniversary of its introduction into ancient Muscovy was celebrated at Kiev, amidst great ceremony and rejoicing. Messages of congratulation and Christian greeting were received from all over the world, and notably from the Archbishop of Canterbury, who sent a sympathetic letter, drawing attention to the common principles and interests of the Church of England and the orthodox Church of Russia. The hymn composed for the occasion, and sung with the utmost enthusiasm, was a characteristic and picturesque production :

"By Russia's faith is our state free and stable. Glory to Vladimir, the Prince of Kiev—the anciently throned! Nine centuries are past; on the foam of the ninth wave, the shield of our faith is secure, the bequest of bygone times is strong, the banner of orthodoxy is waving, shining forth afar. Rejoice, O Prince Vladimir —isapostolic Prince! Endeared to the heart of the people, the elect of the holy faith, to-day, O Prince, we sing thy day together with the whole Russian land. If the land is not to be measured, if the inhabited places on it cannot be counted—to God of strength be prayer, to Prince Vladimir be the praise! Glory!"

This curious commingling of national and religious congratulation is borne out and approved by history. Not only did Vladimir merit admiration by his complete change of character and life and rule after his conversion, but Yaroslav, his son, in a long and prosperous reign (1019-54), extended Christianity, good government, and the boundaries of the state at one and the same time. During two hundred years thereafter the dominions of Kiev produced a degree of enlightenment and scholarship such as could be found nowhere else in Europe, except in some isolated cities, or in the Greek Empire. But in 1236 the Tartar hordes, numbering half a million of men, sprang from out the gloomy depths of Central Asia, and swept over the country in a flood of devastation and death. And for more than two succeeding centuries the Church kept itself alive amongst the people; did much to mitigate the miseries of Tartar rule; acted as peacemaker between rival princes and hostile races; won the respect of even the monarchs of the Golden Horde; and finally trained the Russian spirit up to the conquest of its national independence. But after the Tartars came the Catholic Poles with those numerous invasions which have since been so terribly avenged. And in the midst of struggles, internal and external, with Tartar, or Pole, or Turk, was the ever incessant effort of Rome to obtain a reunion of the churches. For good or evil, however, it has been vigorously and successfully resisted, and to-day Russia may boast of being almost a religious unit and the head of a Church which materially aids in her national and territorial expansion.

There is, of course, a darker side to the picture. The Church has been, to a great extent, the obedient servant of the Czars, and, while working earnestly for national independence, has acted with equal effectiveness in the suppression of peasant liberties. How far it might have developed a capacity for the proper exercise of freedom amongst people who are certainly not yet even approximately fitted for it, is an open question. But it might, at least, have ameliorated to a far greater extent the practice of slavery, and the position of the emancipated peasant of to-day—whose place is so well indicated in a certain poetic appeal from a Russian to his master or lord :

> "My soul is God's,
> My land is mine,
> My head's the Czar's,
> My back is thine!"

And surely a strong and patriotic clergy might have done much to modify the historic horrors of Siberia.

Leaving, however, its local environment in Russia, it will be seen that, in any general survey, the historic position of the Greek Church is complicated by many important considerations, and its future controlled by movements far beneath the ordinary surface of affairs. Its religious influence is widespread, and must be judged by popular surroundings and racial qualities. Its history reflects, in the general balance of unprejudiced judgment, great impulses for good upon the countries and peoples of the East. Its place in controlling the past relations of the Russian and the Turk is far more important than the shadow of a connection between its really independent branches would indicate. Its influence in evolving liberty amongst the Balkan States and preserving nationality amongst the peoples of Russia has been greater than its power of soothing Russian savagery or modifying the weaknesses of the Greek character. Its weight in the settlement of the Eastern Question, so far as Turkey is concerned, has been important and far-reaching, and may be still more so in the future. Finally, a favourable and eulogistic summary of its past and present might well be quoted from Dr. Neale, the latest English historian of the Orthodox Church :

"Extending herself from the Sea of Okhotsk to the palaces of Venice, from the ice-fields that grind against the Solovetsky monastery to the burning jungles of Malabar—embracing a thousand languages, and nations, and tongues, but binding them together in the golden link of the same faith—offering the tremendous sacrifice in a hundred liturgies, but offering it to the same God, and with the same rites—oppressed by the devotees of the false Prophet, as once by the worshippers of false gods—she is now, as she was from the beginning, multiplex in her arrangements, simple in her faith, difficult of comprehension to strangers, easily intelligible to her sons, widely scattered in her branches, hardly beset by her enemies—as were her divine founders—yet still, and evermore, what she delights to call herself—One only, Holy, Catholic, and Apostolic."

CHAPTER VII.

A SURVEY OF EUROPEAN TURKEY.

There is no country, or collection of countries, in the world with so varied and conflicting a history, such antagonistic and diverse populations, such a record of continuous external war and internal disorder, as the Turkish Empire in Europe presents; and, in order to understand the condition of the Christians, the character of the Turk, the policy of Russia, or the future of Islam, it is absolutely necessary to know something of the separate identity, though combined annals, of these unfortunate countries.

Yet, despite the most vital interests to the contrary, the Christian races and independent states are all alike keen rivals, and sometimes bitter enemies. They are a unit only in hatred of the Turk, and in the determination to use Russia or Austria, or some other external influence, in helping forward the humiliation and destruction of Islam. In no one country—excepting Greece, and Servia, and Roumania—is there any real unity of religion, and only in gallant little Montenegro is there substantial unity of race. They seem unable to combine among themselves, even against the Turk; and the Serbs and Bulgars, the Roumans and Albanians, are constantly fighting each other, instead of directing all their energies to driving out of Europe the power which has so long oppressed and maltreated their peoples. Now that the chief of these countries have been practically inde-

Nazim Pasha
Turkish Minister of Police during the Armenian Massacre in Constantinople.

Kiamil Pasha
Grand Vizier, 1896.

pendent for years, they ought surely to have been able by this time to combine and concentrate their strength in support of the mixed races which are still scattered over European Turkey, and amongst whom their own nationalities are largely represented. Certainly they have had ample reason to hate the Turk. Writing in 1637, concerning the Ottoman dominions in Europe, Sandys, the historian, thus describes what he had himself seen:

"These countries, once so glorious and famous for their happy estate, but now, through vice and ingratitude, become the most deplored spectacles of extreme misery; the wild beasts of mankind having broken in upon them, and rooted out all civilite, and the pride of a sterne and barbarous tryant possessing the thrones of ancient and just dominion; who, arguing only at the height of greatnesse and sensualitie, hath, in tract of time, reduced so great and goodly a part of the world to lamentable distresse and servitude under which it now faints and groaneth. . . . Large territories are dispeopled or thinly inhabited; goodly cities made desolate; sumptuous buildings become ruins; glorious temples either subverted or prostituted to impietie; true religion discountenanced and oppressed; no light of learning permitted, nor virtue cherished; violence and rapine insulting over all, and leaving no security, save to an abject mind and unlookt on povertie."

In the main, this picture illustrates the condition of affairs during the succeeding two hundred years in all these historic lands, and indicates the position to-day of those which are still under the government of the Turk. Throughout the territories in question, and in the rest of the Empire, the mixture of races and religions is so great as to almost defy analysis, and yet so important in connection with the general question as to absolutely require it. Ubicini, Bianconi, Farley, Denton, MacColl, Girardin, Kunitz, and Sir George Campbell all differ in their totals.

The following figures, however, compiled from various authorities, may be considered as approximately accurate:

	Moslems.	Christians.
Turkey in Europe	2,000,000	2,800,000
Bulgaria	700,000	2,400,000
Bosnia and Herzegovina	500,000	900,000
Servia	15,000	2,000,000
Roumania	2,000	5,000,000
Montenegro	10,000	220,000
Greece	25,000	2,200,000
Asiatic Turkey	12,000,000	2,000,000
Egypt	6,800,000	300,000
	22,052,000	17,820,000

These last totals represent the Turkish Empire of the past; those of the present include about 14,000,000 Mahometans and 5,000,000 Christians. Egypt is hardly an Ottoman dependency now, and the other countries mentioned are practically independen But these figures by no means dispose of the problem. More than one-half of the Moslems in Europe are not Turks by nationality; whilst millions of the Christians in the above totals are Greeks by nature and loyalty, as well as by Church. Mixed up with the Greeks in all these countries are numbers of Roman Catholics, Protestants, Armenians, and adherents of many other divisions of Christianity. To add to the complexity, there are as many Roumans outside of Roumania as there are in it; many Serbs are to be found in Bosnia and Herzegovina as well as in Servia; Bulgarians in large numbers are located throughout Turkish Macedonia, Thrace, and Albania, as well as in Greece and their own country; Greeks are more numerous outside of Greece than within its borders.

But amidst all this seething mass of conflicting races the central fact looms clearly into light, that about a million Ottomans planted in Europe are now holding in abject bondage nearly four millions of other races; that, supported by their vast reserve in Asia, they have for centuries held many other millions in subjection; that they have done this through stern and deliberate oppression, applied by means of a theocratic government, in which religion is made the great motive power and force. In this government the Sultan is the nominal head and representative of the Prophet, and he, therefore, rules the empire with absolute power. But it must be done in accordance with the sacred laws of the Koran, which is thus made the keystone of the whole constitutional arch. The Koran, however, has to be interpreted and explained, and the official who performs this duty is the Sheik-ul-Islam—the Grand Mufti of Constantinople, the spiritual head of the Moslem world, the greatest man in the empire after the Caliph himself.

He is, consequently, the veritable incarnation of Islamism in its most intolerant and bigoted form, and as no laws are valid without his sanction, he is the real ruler of Turkey. This fact explains much that is otherwise vague in the modern annals of the Turk. The Sultan, however, is none the less a despot, and so long as his commands, or the laws of the State, are not contrary to the Koran the Grand Mufti must accept them. But the instant they conflict with his interpretation, no Mahometan owes them obedience. Hence the collapse of the efforts at reform made by one or two of the Sultans, and the utter indifference paid to the Tanzimat, or the Hatt-i-Humayoun, by which legal equality and the protection of the State were accorded to the Christian "infidel." The promises and guarantees in this respect were made by the secular power against the dictates of the spiritual, and therefore have been, and must continue to be, absolute dead letters.

With the Sheik-ul-Islam is associated the Ulema, a sort of order or governing class, which includes the Imams, or ministers of religion; the Muftis, or doctors of law; and the Cadis, or Mollahs, who preside over the Courts. All these officials are controlled by the Grand Mufti, and guided in their ministrations by his interpretation of the Koran as it affects the secular matters coming under their guidance. In his management of financial, commercial, or diplomatic affairs, the Sultan is, however, supreme, and acts merely through his Grand Vizier or Prime Minister—a personage not nearly as important as the Grand Mufti, and hardly equal in rank or influence to the Chief Eunuch of the Imperial harem. There have been notable exceptions, but not as many as might be imagined from the perusal of histories which have to deal with the visible actions of the Vizier, and cannot adequately trace the invisible power of the others.

The natural result of such a system of government is the exclusion of Christians from all equal treatment or the slightest consideration at the hands of a true believer. What says the Koran?:

"O, prophet, attack the infidel with arms, and the hypocrites with arguments; and treat them with severity; their abode shall be hell, and an ill journey shall it be thither. . . .
Adversity shall not cease to afflict the unbelievers for that which they have committed, or to sit down near their habitations until God's promise comes."

And as the same sacred book gave Mahometans the right to do what they would with the conquered or captured infidel who refused to profess Islam, it follows that atrocities such as those of Bulgaria or Armenia may be expected in the future, as they might well have been prepared for in the past. A certain form of servitude is, however, granted the Jew or Christian who cannot be conveniently destroyed, and of this the countries of European Turkey have had ample knowledge and experience. It may be summed up in practical application as follows :

I. A capitation tax—called "the humiliation tax" —for the right to live from year to year.

II. A tax in lieu of military service—from which all Christians are excluded—assessed upon all males from three months old.

III. Extraordinary taxes; such as that for the Sultan's visit to England in 1867—which are never afterwards removed.

IV. Advance taxes; such as that of 1877, when the Christians had to pay two years in advance, and then pay the sums over again at the usual time.

V. The hospitality tax; by which, since A.D. 637, every Christian householder who is a subject of the Sultan is bound by law to provide three days' gratuitous hospitality to every Mahometan traveller or official who may choose to ask it. This practically means the placing of his movable property, his provisions, his house, and, more than all, his family, at the mercy of the savage brutality of any armed Turk who happens to come along.

The reports of English consuls upon this point are too horrible for quotation.

In addition to the torture of these conditions, the Christian who is unable to pay the above taxes is by law a rebel; while, despite all international arrangements and Imperial pledges, his oath is not now, and never has been, accepted in the so-called courts of law and justice. And, up to 1843, any Christian who was forced into an acceptance of Islam and afterwards recanted was subject to death, and duly executed. In that year Sir Stratford Canning addressed one of his strong remonstrances to the Porte upon the occasion of the judicial murder of a young Armenian for this cause, and received the following reply from the Grand Vizier:

"The laws of the Koran compel no man to become a Mahometan; but they are inexorable both as respects a Mahometan who embraces another religion, and as respects a person not a Mahometan, who, having of his own accord publicly embraced Islamism, is convicted of having renounced that faith. No consideration can produce a commutation of the capital punishment to which the law condemns him without mercy. The only mode of escaping death is for the accused to declare that he has again become a Mahometan."

France joined England in the ensuing protest—which resulted in submission after a preliminary act of defiance by the public hanging of another apostate at Broussa. The *right* was, of course, not surrendered, but the *practice* was changed from public execution to more private assassination or persecution. Of the various races which have had to endure this system of government, or to fight for their lives against it, the most striking is the two hundred thousand people who dwell in mountainous Montenegro. The struggles of Greece, the sufferings of Bulgaria, and even the bravery of the Herzegovinians, pale in comparison with the heroism of their history. It was over five hundred years ago that some 35,000 Christians in the principality of Zeta, bordering on the Adriatic Sea and surrounded by the mountains of Herzegovina and the plains of Servia, retired step by step before the hosts of the Turk, until they finally took refuge in the small, rocky, and mountainous district of Tsernagora, or Montenegro.

There they swore to endure every hardship and the misery of continual struggle with overwhelming forces rather than submit to the alternatives held out by Islam—

death, slavery, or the Koran. The man who wavered in
his determination, or ran away from the enemy, no matter
what the reason, was to be hunted out of the country by
women at the point of the distaff. In this spirit they
gave up the richness of their fertile soil, and the beauty of
their happy homes, to commence a wild and prolonged
contest for faith and freedom. And now, during four centuries, writes Mr. Gladstone, in an enthusiastic eulogy,
"they have maintained in full force the covenant of that
awful day, through an unbroken series of trials, of dangers,
and of exploits, to which it is hard to find a parallel in
the annals of Europe, perhaps even of mankind."

All around them the conquering Moslem held sway.
Country after country fell; the empire of the Serbs, the
kingdom of the Bulgars, and the kingdom of Hungary
were shattered, as had been the great Byzantine power.
Yet at times, when all Europe was threatened, Vienna
besieged, Poland stripped of its territory, or the Muscovite rolled back into his eastern recesses, army after army
of Turks was dashed in vain upon the rocks of Tsernagora.
In 1712, from 50,000 to 100,000 Moslems assailed the
little country, but were beaten back by an army of 12,000
men under the Prince-Bishop Danilo, and with a loss of
20,000. It was upon this occasion that one of three spies
returned to his chieftain with the picturesque statement;
"So many are the Turks that, had we three all been
pounded into salt, we should not have been enough to
salt a supper for them." In the succeeding year 120,000
of the best troops which could be collected assailed the
mountaineers, but only succeeded in burning the chief
monastery, and carrying off a number of women and children into slavery.

Again, in 1722, Has an Pasha renewed the attack
with 20,000 troops, but was beaten by a thousand Mon-

tenegrins, and he himself captured. Three years later another invasion was similarly defeated, and, in 1732, Topal Osman, at the head of 30,000 Turks, had to fly with the loss of his camp and baggage. These, however, are but instances in a continuous struggle, which, in 1768, the Porte decided to finally put an end to. The invading force under the command of the Turkish Pashas of Roumelia and Bosnia was, at the lowest estimate, 70,000 men—the highest is 180,000—and, to add to the peril of the Montenegrins, ammunition ran short in their little army of 10,000, while the Venetians refused the entry of supplies through their territory on the sea coast. It seems almost incredible, but the beleaguered and hunted heroes first captured a lot of powder with 500 men from a large division of the invading force, and then routed the Turks with a slaughter of 20,000 men, the capture of 3,000 horses, and an enormous quantity of colours, arms, munitions, and baggage. Such was the flood of war and baptism of blood which Tsernagora has had to encounter.

But this was not nearly all. During the passing centuries their increase of population had naturally been small; in 1800 it only totalled 55,000, but by 1876, when their last great struggle took place, it was about 200,000. The achievements upon this occasion were worthy of their history. On July 28th, they defeated Muktar Pasha, lost seventy men, and killed 4,000 Turks. At Medun, 20,000 of the enemy were defeated by 5,000 Montenegrins, and each mountaineer seems to have slain a man. On September 6th, Dervisch Pasha was beaten with a loss of 3,000 men. On October 7th, 6,000 men again drove back Muktar Pasha, and a force three times as great. Finally, an armistice closed the war, so far as the heroes of the Tsernagora were concerned, after a total Turkish loss, which the historian

Goptchevitch places at 26,000. And the force directed against them is stated at the enormous figure of 130,000. It is safe to say that in all the annals of mountain warfare—gallant little Switzerland included—there is nothing to equal this record. Well does it deserve that eloquent tribute by Tennyson :

> "They rose to where their sovran eagle sails,
> They kept their faith, their freedom, on the height,
> Chaste, frugal, savage, arm'd by day and night
> Against the Turk ; whose inroad nowhere scales
> Their headlong passes but his footstep fails.
>
> O smallest among peoples ! rough rock-throne
> Of freedom ! Warriors beating back the swarm
> Of Turkish Islam for five hundred years,
> Great Tsernagora ! Never since thine own
> Black ridges drew the cloud and brake the storm
> Has breathed a race of mightier mountaineers."

Their freedom is now recognized by the world, and a small yearly sum is paid by Austria and Russia to the hereditary Prince—Nicholas I.—as aid in the development of his little territory. And, by the Treaty of Berlin and subsequent international arrangement, it has been very wisely extended to the seaboard through the cession of Dulcigno. The Church of the people is orthodox Greek, and the few thousand Mahometans now in the country are the result of the recent approach to the sea.

Akin to the Montenegrins in bravery, and in the possession of mountain fastnesses, are the Albanians. But there all resemblance ends. Despite the heroic struggles of Scanderbeg in an earlier century, the independent and somewhat ruthless character of the average mountaineer, the troublesome achievements of numerous bodies of brigands, and a general hatred and contempt for the modern Turk, the Albanians have for hundreds of years lost all claim to national independence. Both in Upper and Lower Albania, as they stretch south from Bosnia over the countries known to ancient history as Illyria and Epirus, there are varied elements of religion and nationality. The large landowners are, in the main, Mahometans, perverted from their original Christianity, and oppressing the peasantry with a spirit of typical intolerance and Moslem cruelty. Scattered throughout the mountainous regions are numerous chiefs, exercising control over villages built like eagle's nests in almost impenetrable fastnesses, and at times acting as leaders in brigandage and lawlessness. Elsewhere, and especially in the beautiful table-land of Janina, Greek enterprise has promoted commerce, and established excellent schools and prosperous towns.

Before the Turkish conquest the Albanians, as a whole, professed Christianity, but it seems to have taken little real root amongst the people. Nominally, masses of them are still Christians; but the wild, turbulent spirit of the race appears at first to have inclined very many to the aggressive faith of Islam. In Epirus, or Lower Albania, two other substantial reasons contributed to the conversion of sections of the country. After the defeat of Scanderbeg in 1478, the Sultan was so angry at his prolonged resistance that he ordered the destruction of the Christian churches, or their transformation into mosques, and commanded that all Epirots should be circumcised on pain of death. In 1812, when Ali Pasha obtained—and for three years held—a sort of independent sway over the country, he forced whole villages to confess Islam. But as the character of the Turk and the aggressive force of Mahometanism have declined, its influence has also weakened, and the progress of the Greek Church has been correspondingly increased.

At the present time it is said that a Moslem Albanian will swear with equal vigour by the Blessed Virgin or the Prophet, while he affects considerable indifference as to the relative merits of the Koran and the Bible. The Christian part of the population is, upon the whole, superior to the Mahometan in character and conduct, but all alike seem to be influenced by a native and natural savagery which combines in itself the virtues and vices of pre-civilization days. They will plunder with pleasure, and fight with cruelty from the pure love of fighting. They are vindictive, but honourable, never breaking a pledge, though ruthless in revenging a wrong. But, above all, they respect women, and the curious custom prevails of ensuring the safety of travellers by sending them through mountain fastnesses infested with brigands, accompanied only by a female guide and guardian.

Taken as a whole, the million and a quarter Albanians living in these districts are a most unsatisfactory race. The majority are of the Greek faith and claim national Greek affiliations, but a strong minority are Mahometans. There are also 150,000 devoted Roman Catholics or Mirdites. Politically, they look in the main to Greece, and in 1878 formed a league to resist partial annexation to Austria and Bosnia. From this date there was continuous fighting with the Turks until 1883, when they finally submitted, after an unsuccessful appeal to Europe for union with Greece. Since then there has been a condition of more or less chronic brigandage and disorder. The Albanian, however, is not limited to his own regions, and may be found all over European Turkey and in Greece, contributing a picturesque but unruly element to the universal Turkish chaos.

Another interesting country in this Moslem medley is Macedonia. Touching Servia and Bulgaria on the north, Turkish Adrianople on the east, and Greece on the south, it is a living bone of contention between the three countries which hope to some day dominate the Ægean Sea and the Dardanelles. Historically, it is the home of Philip and Alexander the Great, the seat of a one-time mighty empire, the centre of a kingdom which was conquered in turn by the Ostrogoths, the Romans, the Bulgarians, and the Turks. Of all the mixed racial elements which Turkish Europe boasts, this particular section is the most intricate and perplexing. At the same time it is extremely important as indicating which of the three dominant States in this part of the world has the best ethnographic claim to succeed the dying power of Islam. All three are struggling for superiority in Macedonia. It is absolutely essential to the formation of a new Greek empire, and equally so to the extension of Bulgaria or Servia. But the diplomatists at Berlin were unable to agree as to the distribution of the races, and none of the Governments concerned can be expected to give reliable figures—least of all the Turk.

The balance of expert opinion, however, is in favour of the Bulgars, and M. de Laveleye, after minute research, describes the western part as being inhabited by Albanians, the eastern part by Bulgarians, the northern by Serbs, the centre by Bulgarians, and the coasts and many of the towns by Greeks. Interspersed are Wallachs or Roumans and many Jews. Upon the whole, three-quarters of the population appears to be of Bulgarian extraction, and to this estimate Prince Bismarck has given his authoritative approval. The people generally, being the nearest of all the Christian populations to the centre of Turkish power, have suffered greatly from its permanent brutality. And, in addition to this, the Greek element has persistently persecuted the already cowed Bulgarian peasantry, whilst the oppression of Albanian brigands has been added to the terrors of Islam and the bigotry of the Greek. The Bulgars in Macedonia have thus been ground between an upper and a nether millstone. When they refuse to accept Christianity according to the Greek Church, they are often unscrupulously misrepresented and betrayed into the power of Turkish Beys to be dealt with in some underhand and cruel fashion.

This struggle for national extension is, in fact, revealing a very unpleasant and black page in the history of the Greek Church. It certainly introduces another element of warring discord into the tangled troubles of the Turkish population, and the difficult problems of the present and the future. But, to clearly grasp the threads of destiny in this curious patchwork of conflicting nationalities and religions, some separate consideration of the important history and characteristics of the more independent States of Bulgaria, Servia, Roumania, Bosnia, and Greece is absolutely essential. Without it the reader would be unable to either see the difficulties of the present, or to accurately estimate the chances of the future.

CHAPTER VIII.

THE STRUGGLES OF MODERN GREECE.

The Greeks of to-day are the product of combined suppression and oppression; the more immediate result of centuries of Turkish government. As a nation, they have been born again out of two thousand years of war and invasion and intermixture with other races. Millions of them are scattered throughout European and Asiatic Turkey, and everywhere they exercise a marked influence through qualities which, like their religion, present a curious picture of complex Oriental and Western influences. Whether in Greece or out of it, they are actuated by two strong principles—hatred of the Turks, and pride in the past glories of their historic country.

How far this latter feeling is justified in their racial connection with the heroes of antiquity is a matter of serious doubt. The ancient Hellas, from its subjugation by Rome in B.C. 146, has gone through every variety of settlement and conquest. It was over-run by the Goths and Vandals after the fall of Macedon, and was conquered about 580 A.D. by the Avars, a race of Tartar extraction. "These Avars," writes the Patriarch Nicholaos to the Emperor Alexis in 807, "have held possession of the Peloponnesus for 218 years, and have so completely separated it from the Byzantine empire that no Byzantine official dare to put his foot in the country." This race appears to have been a completely dominating power in the Peninsula, and to have made more than one successful war upon the so-called Greek Empire at Constanti-

Henry John Temple, Viscount Palmerston.

Sir William Fenwick Williams, Bart., of Kars

nople. In the ninth century the Scythian Slavs occupied the country, and were shortly succeeded as conquerors by the Bulgarians, who were themselves pretty well Slavonized by this time. Hence the modern sympathies of Greece with the Slavs of Russia. But, however successful or otherwise the ethnologist may be in grappling with the intermixture of these varied races, there seems little reason to doubt that the qualities and greatness of ancient Hellas have not fallen upon those who now occupy its mighty soil.

The old-time race has disappeared, and though many customs and traditions have been preserved the process of racial assimilation which has been going on for so many centuries has replaced it by another and different people. Yet the modern Greek is as proud of the soil upon which he treads as were the heroes of Athens, or Sparta, or Macedon. He believes himself to be their lineal descendant—the just heir of their history and fame. He cherishes their achievements, and to him memories of Thermopylæ, and Marathon, and Salamis are as dear as are those of Blenheim and Waterloo to the British citizen of to-day. During all the wars and struggles which followed the conquest by the Turks in 1456, and amid the succeeding suppression of everything that was worthy of their intellect and brilliant past, the Greeks preserved their national pride, and cultivated the memories of which Byron sang in the dawning of the new and second national life :

> "They fell devoted, but undying ;
> The very gale their names seemed sighing ;
> The waters murmured of their name ;
> The woods were peopled with their fame ;
> The silent pillar lone and gray
> Claimed kindred with their sacred clay ;
> Their spirits wrapped the dusky mountain ;

> Their memory sparkled o'er the fountain ;
> The meanest rill, the mightiest river,
> Roll'd mingling with their fame forever.
> Despite of every yoke she bears
> That land is glory's still, and theirs."

With such a feeling of national pride, the people of Greece had to endure for nearly four hundred years the burden of Turkish misgovernment, alternating with an occasional triumph of the Venetian over the Turk. Had they, however, preserved their old-time character as well as memories much of the history of this part of the world might have been vastly different, and a beneficial civilization long since established upon the banks of the Bosphorus in place of the creed and sword of Islam. The Hellenes, mixed in race as they were even then, had a large individual place in the history of the Eastern or Greek Empire, and from the time of Alexander of Macedon their language and literature permeated the annals of many countries in the distant East.

With them and amongst them early Christianity took singularly strong root, and gave the name of Greek to the extension of that religion in much of Asia Minor, in all Russia, and throughout various parts of European Turkey. While the mass of the people were undergoing an almost complete transformation of national character, its name was being writ large upon history in the decaying empire of the Byzantines and the rising Christianity of Russia.

Between the Turk and the Greek no possible sympathy could exist, nor assimilation take place. The differences in religion, apart entirely from those of race, were sufficient to keep them in constant antagonism. Races have intermixed a myriad times in the history of the world, and the blood of more than one could be found in that of the Greek himself. But the follower of

Islam possessed a religion which set him absolutely apart in marriage, family, and social relations, from the Christian, while his religious fanaticism and pride of supremacy were as great as he conceived his laws and enactments to be immutable. Moreover, the Mahometan law in regard to land was the antipodes of the Greek or Christian conception of such ownership, and was grounded on the religious belief that, in the first instance and the last resort, "all the land belongs to the Caliph, the shadow and vicegerent of God upon earth."

And as time passed, the ordinary feelings of the conquered towards the conqueror became a thousand degrees enhanced by the barbarities of Turkish government. For a long period the Greeks were subject to the child-tribute by which the flower of their children were borne away every few years to be trained up as Janizaries at Constantinople. There was no justice to be had by the Christian as against a Turk; there was no security for life; nor was there any safety in property. Needless to say, no measures were taken to promote education, or to regulate agriculture, industry, or commerce. Every male from seven years up was subject to oppressive taxes, and in this respect the Turks watched over their subjects with a vengeance. The Koran says of the "infidels" in such a connection: "Oppress them until they pay poll-tax and are humbled." And this religious duty was certainly a pleasant one to the average Mahometan.

The result of the system was a natural one. For three hundred years the Greeks were deprived of every chance of education or opportunity of intellectual activity. The few learned or able men rising out of such conditions emigrated to Italy, or to the Hellenic Islands held by Venice, and there lifted the lamp of Grecian literature to Western nations. But more than this. The historian Timayenis tells us that "neither the complete submission of the vanquished, nor the payment of the taxes, nor the tribute of blood, satiated the savage cruelty of the Turk. The archbishops and bishops of the Church were hanged like the worst of malefactors in Constantinople; hundreds of Christians were butchered in the churches of Smyrna; hundreds of patriots were roasted to death in Attica, Euboea, and elsewhere. No family was safe; no woman dared to appear in the streets; nobody's life was secure—because a Turk was promoted in proportion to the Christians he could claim for his victims."

Hence the unsuccessful rising of 1770 in the Morea, where a number of Greeks joined the invading Russian army, shared in its temporary successes, and took chief part in many vengeful cruelties upon captured Turks. But Orloff and his allied Greeks were defeated near Tripolitza, and the latter were massacred without mercy by their victors. The reign of Selim III. which followed, by its unusual encouragement of literature, gave an opportunity for the revival of Greek patriotism, and the cultivation of the dormant love of letters. The national poet, Rhiga, rose to the level of the occasion, and helped to light the flame of freedom which blazed into the succeeding War of Independence.

A society was formed called the Hetæria, which, after some reverses, obtained a strong though secret footing amongst Greeks everywhere, and also enrolled in its ranks a great many Russian officers. All over European Turkey, Asia Minor, and in parts of Russia, its branches were organized, under the terms of an injunction which indicates the intense bitterness felt towards their Turkish rulers: "Fight for thy faith and thy fatherland. Thou shalt hate, thou shalt persecute, thou shalt utterly destroy the enemies of thy religion, of thy race, and of thy country." Early in 1820 preparations were in readiness for the revolution to begin, when the chiefs of the movement were given the singular good fortune of seeing the Sultan Mahmoud engaged in war against a most formidable subject, Ali Pasha of Janina. Nothing could have been more propitious for their cause than this struggle between the powerful oppressor upon their own borders and a Sultan whose ability and determination were sufficiently great to promise them a prolonged, if not doubtful, contest.

For two years the old "Lion of Janina" kept the best troops of the Sultan at bay, and gave the Greek insurrection an opportunity to obtain a strong footing in the Peninsula. By the time he had been captured and put to death, nearly all Greece had risen and driven back the Turks. The war thus begun was carried on with a degree of ferocity which might almost have been expected under the circumstances.

During a brief period fortune seemed to smile upon the revolutionists, and in December, 1824, the French ambassador at Constantinople wrote to his government that "the brilliant feats which they have accomplished during this year have strengthened the work of their regeneration." But in the next two years a storm of war broke over them very different in force from the scattered efforts of Albanian hordes and Turkish irregulars. Mahmoud had transferred the task of conquest to his great dependent, Mehemet Ali, of Egypt, and that ambitious leader was only too delighted to grasp the opportunity. He at once despatched a large army under Ibrahim Pasha, composed of seasoned troops, and supported by ample pecuniary resources and a constant naval communication between Alexandria and the Peloponnesus.

The famous siege of Mesolonghi followed, and for a whole year the Greeks maintained a really heroic defence against great odds. Under their leaders, Mavrokordatos and Kitsos Tsavelles, the 12,000 inhabitants—of whom about 5,000 could bear arms—fought and starved and fought again, until their last desperate sally in April, 1826, resulted in the downfall of the town, and the wholesale massacre of men, women, and children. Many of the women, however, died by their own hands, or in explosions purposely arranged in order to prevent their falling into the power of the victors. Here also died Lord Byron, whose patriot verse had done so much to raise a friendly feeling in Europe for the struggling and oppressed nationality, and for those great memories of the past upon which he knew so well how to touch. Meanwhile, the Greek fleet, under command of the gallant Kanaris, had greatly distinguished itself against the infinitely superior naval resources of the Turk. To this superiority, however, the battle of Navarino put an end in 1827.

In this year also Russia declared war against Turkey, and thus further aided the Greeks, whilst Ibrahim found that he had failed to obtain the success which he once anticipated. And, in 1828, a French army of 20,000 men, under command of Marshal Maison, with the consent and approval of England, occupied the Morea, and soon drove the Egyptian and Turkish troops out of the country. Meantime the powers of government—such as they were—had been in the hands of a president, Court Capodistrias, whose ambitious aims created many difficulties during the years immediately preceding the recognition of independence. He was a Corfiote by birth, a Russian by adoption, republican in tendency, arbitrary in disposition, and naturally jealous of the great Powers and their monarchical policy. Sir Stratford Canning (Lord Stratford), to whose unceasing, strenuous, diplomacy Greece owed so much during this period, and who really controlled the creation of its constitution and the marking of its boundaries, summarized the situation at the time very clearly. After a reference to the difficulties caused by the poverty of the country and people, he says:

"Yet they had need of an imposing authority, of a government adapted to their wants, their weaknesses, their passions, and their obligations, capable at once of fostering their good and restraining their evil tendencies, of forming them into a community progressive by means of industry and inoffensive on principle. In their existing condition, democratic or popular forms were little calculated to secure their external peace, to conciliate the good will of their neighbours, or to win for them the confidence of Europe. I did not therefore hesitate to recommend a kingly form of government, subject, of course, to constitutional limitations—foreseeing that the Crown would have to descend on the brows of a foreign prince to the extinction of all envenomed rivalries at home."

In 1830 the independence of Greece was recognized, and Russia, England, and France undertook the responsibility of arranging its constitution and boundaries. The latter, as finally fixed, excluded Thessaly, Albania, and Macedonia, and by doing so, left for the succeeding sixty years a vexed Greek question to be added to the other Turkish complications. The fact is that Great Britain feared the influence of Russia in the new kingdom, and naturally opposed its too great extension. And the indirect aid afterwards rendered by Greece to Russia during the Crimean war proved sufficiently the truth of the feeling—one which all Sir Stratford Canning's representations could not moderate. The constitution was arranged, however, in accordance with the latter's views, and the Crown was offered to Prince Leopold—known in history as the husband of the lamented Princess Charlotte of England, and as the sagacious King of the Belgians. He at first accepted, but then declined it.

The truth is that the condition of the country was so deplorable, the rivalries amongst the people so keen, and their reputation in Europe for dishonesty so great, as to have fairly staggered him. Despite their heroic resistance to the Turks, and prolonged sufferings under Turkish rule, the sympathies of Europe had been as yet insufficient to overpower the antipathies of the past. Writing in 1831, Sir Stratford Canning himself observed that: " It grieves me to the heart to say that I hear nothing good of the Greeks as I approach their shores. No fresh crimes, and that is all. But disunion and party hatred and political intrigue carried to the worst extremes." To this kingdom of confusion came Prince Otho of Bavaria in 1832, and in it he remained until the revolution of 1862 expelled him from the country and resulted in the accession of George I., son of the King of Denmark.

It was prior to the latter choice—more by the three protecting Powers than by the people of Greece—that a curious movement arose in favour of presenting the Crown to Mr. Gladstone. The English leader was not only popular by virtue of his having practically transferred the Ionian Islands to the Hellenic Kingdom, but also by his life-long devotion to Grecian literature and Homeric study. The proposal did not become an international one, but the correspondence of Mr. Freeman, the English historian, and Mr. Finlay, the Grecian historian, reveals some interesting particulars. Both strongly favoured the idea. Of a more important nature was the Greek agitation in favour of Prince Alfred—afterwards Duke of Edinburgh and of Saxe-Cobourg-Gotha. In a pamphlet published at the time in Athens, a Greek named Koulouriotes declared that "if the European Powers endeavour to force on us any other king than Prince Alfred, we will choose a republican form of government." But international jealousies intervened, and the present ruler was duly crowned.

During this half-century the condition of the people has, upon the whole, steadily improved. Liberty at first brought disorder and brigandage and crime in its train, but gradually the population has risen in some degree to its opportunities, and the Greek of to-day, though far, indeed, from the ideal presented by his great ancestors or predecessors, is the citizen of a Kingdom where education, religion, and constitutional freedom are bearing their natural and beneficial fruit. The finances of the country are still deplorable, and the indebtedness of 30,000,000 francs to England, Russia, and France incurred in 1832 has never been liquidated, and perhaps never will be. The politics of the community are very stormy and the rivalry of Tricoupis and Delyannis has produced results beside which the contests of Gladstone and Disraeli look pale and weak. But none the less has the population doubled in number, the revenues immensely increased, telegraphs been widely established, the fleet of mercantile vessels increased to over 5,000 in number, ruined towns changed into prosperous centres, new ports opened, and Athens raised from an historic ruin and a collection of hovels to a royal city of 50,000 people. Many newspapers have been established, as well as a university and observatory, a palace and a legislative chamber. In 1880, as a result of the Treaty of Berlin, the boundaries were further extended and Thessaly acquired, while some twenty years before the Ionian Islands, largely peopled with Greeks, had been voluntarily handed over by England with a view to strengthening the nation as a whole, and pleasing the Hellenic susceptibilities of the Islanders.

Meantime, in many of the other islands connected with Greece by history, and language, and race, liberty has been excluded and Turkish tyranny perpetuated. A melancholy case in point may be seen in Chios. In 1822, the Greek inhabitants were persuaded to join their copatriots in the mainland revolution. Ali Pasha was at once sent by the Porte to suppress the rebellion, and found the population totally unprepared and a consequently easy prey. Out of its hundred thousand inhabitants, this Turkish barbarian is reported to have slaughtered within seven days over 70,000 people, and to have sent 10,000 to Asia Minor for sale as slaves. In this latter action he was anticipating Ibrahim Pasha, who failed a little later in his effort to conquer Greece, but succeeded in sending some 30,000 of its people to Egypt for a similar purpose.

A still more terrible illustration of Islamic barbarity is that exquisite Isle of Crete, or Candia, which Homer described as being "in the midst of the Black Sea, beautiful and fertile, wave-washed roundabout, with a population infinite in number, and ninety cities." But centuries of historic oppression—under the Saracens from 820 to 961, under the Venetians from 1204 to 1669, and under the Turks from the latter date to the present time —have left but a conparative remnant of population, and villages in the place of cities. In the fifty years following 1770, the condition of Crete has been described as that of a man on a rack. The persecutions of the Christians during that prolonged period were almost intolerable, and the cruelties of the Janizaries, who governed the island, brutal to the uttermost degree. But in 1821 a massacre of several thousand Christians was followed by a demand that the mountaineers, who had retained some faint spark of influence and liberty, should give up their arms. The result of these incidents and the concurrent rebellion in Greece was a rising of the Cretans.

For a time they were successful, and, under the gallant leadership of Antoni Melidoni, swept the island from end to end. All too soon, however, troops began to pour in from Turkey and Egypt. In one march, or raid, of these invaders, 20,000 men, women, and children were put to the sword. Eventually, combined bribery and military strength suppressed the rebellion, and it was not until 1866 that the Cretans again rose in a body. The barbarities of this latter war are indescribable. Under Mustapha Pasha, and his successor, Omar Pasha, many villages were burned after surrender, entire populations murdered or worse, thousands destroyed by massacre, and other thousands killed by brutal ill-treatment or starvation. Petition after petition had come to the great Powers asking for annexation to Greece, and describing the lamentable condition of the country before this last uprising, but without effect. One of these pathetic documents, dated as late as May 15th, 1866, and addressed to the Queen of Great Britain, says:

"We pay enormous taxes, which are increased year by year. . . . Justice is a thing unheard of. We have no tribunals worthy of that name; nor have we any laws. Our children, from want of public instruction, wallow in ignorance. We are not admitted into the public service. We have no roads or bridges. Our evidence is of no avail against that of a Mahometan. The excesses committed by the Turks are rarely punished. We have never enjoyed any of the advantages enjoyed by the poorest subjects of civilized nations. We are the slaves of another race."

Such has been the state of affairs in the "Isles of Greece," as well as upon the mainland, wherever Islam reigned, or reigns supreme. As Greece suffered, so did these and many other islands. But the day of signal retribution may yet come, if only the Greek character can develop to the high level of its possibilities. Its defects are still many. Vanity is carried to a laughable degree, and one visitor to Greece says, in a rather hostile description, that to the minds of its people the events of Europe have their centre and end in Greece. If England has a universal exhibition, it is to put on view the products of Greece; if France has a revolution, it is in order to afford interesting matter to the Athenian papers; if the Emperor of Russia covets Constantinople, it is for the purpose of laying it at King George's feet. This is, of course, caricature, but it portrays a national quality as marked as the gasconade of France, the spread-eagleism of America, or the insular pride of England.

Vanity and bravado, subtlety in argument and thought to the point of chicanery, fondness of gain to an extreme degree, and a frequent tendency amongst all classes to deal in falsehood rather than in truth, are the chief national defects. To counterbalance these are the fine physical characteristics of the race, the love of freedom, and the national instinct of equality, often concealed under fluent but unmeaning phrases and designations. In appearance very many of the Greeks resemble statues by Praxiteles, or Phidias, but their muscular strength hardly equals the appearance. The women are beautiful and graceful, and the domestic virtues are, perhaps, better cultivated in Greece than in any other country which has endured the yoke of Islam. But the union of endurance, swiftness, strength, agility, and manly beauty which made the ancient Greek so great is not common and time alone can tell how far these qualities may be developed.

One factor in the extension of their power the modern Greek has to the very fullest degree. He is to be found everywhere throughout the Turkish Empire. In Constantinople there are from two to three hundred thousand —chiefly Fanariots, or descendants of the Greeks resident in the capital when it was at the head of the Eastern Empire. They are noted for sharp business dealings, and in the provinces outside of Stamboul are everywhere found as tax-gatherers and somewhat merciless officials of the Moslem government. Aside from this special and very unpopular class, the Greeks are to be met with wherever fortunes may be made, commerce pushed, or maritime adventure found. A fringe of Greek population runs around the Ottoman Empire wherever it touches the sea, and the activity of the people makes them the centre of work and business wherever cities are to be found. In this latter connection they are no mean rival of the keen Armenian. Smyrna boasts 120,000 Greeks, and, in short, Greek boatmen and Greek merchants, the Greek language and the Greek costume, are omnipresent in Turkey.

This growing influence—greater than the mere national power of Greece—will be a vital factor in achieving, or struggling to achieve, the national ambition. To destroy Turkish power and re-enter Constantinople is the Greek dream, and to attain this end its people will do much and suffer much. In the inevitable break-up of the Ottoman Empire, this would most certainly result if the Powers of Europe could be induced to trust the Greek character and feel confidence in Greek pledges. As a nation they are superior in many ways—in activity, intellectuality, and historical claim—to the Bulgarian, who also aspires to the possession of Constantinople.

But they have no sense of gratitude and little sense of honour, and in many ways, small and great, have won contempt and angry denunciation from both England and France. The two Powers which will—with Russia—have the most to say regarding the future of Turkey are thus antagonized in advance, and this fact alone gives the rival claims of Bulgaria to the stewardship of the Bosphorus an important advantage, which almost counteracts the widespread force of Greek settlement and financial influence. What the final result will be no man can prophesy; but the Eastern Question, with all its varied phases, has yet to hear in strong and confident tones from the modern Greek and his throned representative at historic Athens.

View of Suj Bulak, Kurdistan.

Nicholas I,
Emperor of Russia, 1825-1855.

CHAPTER IX.

BULGARIA AND THE TURKS.

Of all the subject races which have endured the dominance of the Turk, none have suffered more bitterly and continuously than the Bulgarian. With the exception of the Armenian, none have been the victims of so much oppression, degradation, and outrage. Yet they have managed to stand together in a more or less compact nationality, and to-day hold a position of prosperity and increasing power only marred by characteristics developed under centuries of cruel misgovernment, and accentuated by the present evils of Russian intrigue.

In all the historic storms of war and struggle and barbarian strife which have swept over the Balkan Peninsula, they have had a share. Originally, the Bulgars were only a wandering portion of some race of uncertain extraction located on the lower banks of the Volga. They came across the Danube in the fifth century, and settled amongst the Slavs, by whom the eastern part of the Peninsula was populated. Through intermixture with this race, and the adoption of their manners and customs, while maintaining some strong characteristics of their own, they have practically become one of the branches of that great Slavonic family which includes Russia, Servia, and parts of other countries in European Turkey. For centuries they were a warlike, aggressive people. The history of the Bulgarian Kingdom, from its foundation in 674 to its conquest by the Turks in 1396, is indeed a wearisome story of almost continuous conflict between its rulers and the Greek Emperors at Constantinople—or Byzantium, as it was then called. Even before the kingdom was really established the antagonism of races showed itself in a Bulgarian siege of the Christian capital, which was only saved from capture by the skill of Belisarius. Afterwards, under the leadership of Czar Kroum, Adrianople was occupied, Byzantium forced to pay tribute, and a treaty of alliance entered into with Charlemagne. One of Kroum's successors—Michael Boris—was converted to Christianity in 864, and constituted a church which, with some exceptions, maintained its autonomy separate during several centuries from that of either Rome, or Constantinople, or Russia. During the tenth century, after successful wars with the Magyars of Hungary and the Greeks, or rival Christian power to the south, Bulgaria reached the summit of its national strength.

Its ruler, Simeon, assumed the title of " Emperor of the Bulgarians and of the Wellachians, Despot of the Greeks"; took possession of the very suburbs of Byzantium; and reigned over the whole Peninsula. The ruins of his capital, Preslau, illustrate the passing power of kingdoms, and prove the Asiatic splendour of his palaces, the beauty of his churches, and the magnificence of his court. Another, and previous, King of Bulgaria—Johannes—actuated, no doubt, by national hostility to the head of Eastern Christendom at Byzantium, had acknowledged absolutely the spiritual supremacy of the Pope, and upon one occasion defended himself in a most remarkable letter, from the Pontiff's reproaches concerning a defeat he had inflicted upon the Byzantines. " I have received my crown," he wrote, " from the Supreme Pontiff; they have violently seized and invested themselves with that of the Eastern Empire; the Empire which belongs to me rather than to them. I am fighting under the banner consecrated by St. Peter; they with the Cross on their shoulders which they have falsely assumed. I have been defied; have fought in self-defence; have won a glorious victory; which I ascribe to the intercession of the Prince of the Apostles."

But this connection with the Church of Rome was only a transitory one, and, upon the whole, the Bulgarian Church up to the Turkish conquest was an independent unit. Some centuries later began those peculiar expressions of Russian religious sympathy and practices of Russian intrigue and intervention which lie at the base of so much of the Eastern Question. Meanwhile, the country had fallen completely into the hands of the Mahometan power, and its Church under the jurisdiction of the Greek Patriarch at Constantinople, who had been allowed by the Turks to retain his spiritual position, and such authority as he might still be able to wield. The conquest was a thorough one, and the Bulgarian Empire now absolutely disappeared from view. Nothing but some ruined fortresses and a few popular songs were left to mark the power won and retained, amid torrents of blood, in days when fighting seems to have been a normal condition, and peace something strange, if not absolutely remarkable.

To make matters worse, their neighbours hardly looked upon the Bulgarians as Slavs, or felt that racial sympathy which, later on, brought them the help of Russia in fighting the Turks, and the hindrance of Russia in the building up of their own national position. Isolated, ignored, and debarred from all communicatior with the civilized and Christianized world, they lapsed into a position only slightly affected by their nominal

Christian profession, but very strongly controlled by a character of inherent morality and kindliness. No doubt, amid the toil and hardship of a life in which there was little of brightness or hope, the faith of their fathers found much individual expression, despite the ceremonial abuses and corruption of their Church and the oppressive cruelty of the Moslem. And, as time passed, the people became divided into two distinct classes. The poor, who had remained, at least nominally, true to their Church and national feeling, gradually deepened in their faith and patriotism as the Ottoman yoke became more and more unbearable. The richer classes, on the other hand, adopted Islam in order to save their property and obtain immunity from persecution.

But as the faith of many became more real, the expression of it became less and less possible, and the sufferings of the people greater. Their moral and intellectual qualities could not avoid being affected in some degree. Their dress was even made a mark of servility to the governing Turk. Their means of livelihood became the subject of every species of exaction and illegal tax. Their families were made liable, every five years, to the terrible blood tax, by which the ranks of the Janizaries were forcibly recruited from the finest children of the province. No Bulgarian woman was safe from seizure or outrage at the hands of Turkish pashas, officials, or so-called police. Even the most ordinary, wretched, insignificant Turk was infinitely superior to any Christian in the eye of the Moslem law, and his will and word were sufficient against a multitude of miserable Bulgarians.

Such a condition of affairs could not but produce some disastrous effect upon the character of a race which is still a splendid one physically. It gradually but surely undermined, in many places, the national spirit; cowed the bravery which had once made them conquerors; weakened imperceptibly, but none the less surely, the popular ideas of right and wrong; taught them to cringe before the overmastering and vindictive Turk. What else could be expected from an unarmed people—utterly defenceless in law and fact—in the face of Turkish troops and irregulars, Turkish police and private individuals, all armed to the teeth? Prior to the last Russo-Turkish war and its preliminary—the ghastly Bulgarian massacres—the appearance of a solitary Turk coming towards a village would be the sign for all women to either hide themselves or else flee into the country, while the men concealed any little valuables they might have, and prepared to give the terrible visitor the best the place could offer in the way of food and provisions. Against the unarmed and helpless villagers any crime was possible, and terrible were those sometimes committed. The slightest opposition to the Turk's will, or the least sign of violence or reprisal, meant a probable massacre in the ensuing week, or possible torture and death in the case of individual revenge.

Naturally, such conditions developed an intense and suppressed hatred of the Turk which overcame even the peace-loving disposition of a people who were only too anxious for the right of indulgence in quiet farm work and the enjoyment of their domestic life. And before the dawning of 1876, with all its inconceivable horrors of torture, outrage, impalement, and massacre, other troubles had come upon them. In 1864 the conquest of Circassia by the Russians had caused a migration of some 20,000 Circassians from their mountainous districts into Turkey. The Sultan, with great liberality and hospitality, welcomed this influx of foreigners, and calmly " placed " them in armed thousands throughout Bulgaria. This meant that a wild, semi-barbarous body of men, strong in physique, but unaccustomed to labour, and quite accustomed to take what they required or desired by force, was planted amongst the unarmed and helpless Christian peasantry, with power to add a fresh terror to the exactions and oppression of the Turk.

Meanwhile a determined effort was being made by the Greeks who held official positions under the Porte, and who ruled the people in a religious and educational sense through their fealty to the Greek Church, to Hellenize the race. The Greek language was taught everywhere to the exclusion of Bulgarian, and all that could be done to suppress national feeling and memory was done. Oppressed by the Turks, harried by the Circassians, educated by the Greeks, and deceived by the Russians, it is indeed a marvel that this people has been able to rise out of their troubles and assume even the halting national position which they occupy to-day. But before the attainment of that independence there came a baptism of blood such as few other people have had to face, and such as the nineteenth century has seen under no other government than that of the Turk.

The Bulgarian horrors are pretty well known by name; their details can be guessed at, but hardly described; their result very nearly wrecked the Turkish Empire, and certainly helped at the polls to defeat a great British leader. At the beginning of 1876 the Porte was in a very difficult position. The Herzegovinians were in revolt. Bosnia and Montenegro were known to be in readiness to join them. Moldavia and Wallachia were just about declaring their independence under the name of Roumania, and knowledge of the condition of things in Bulgaria naturally made the Turkish authorities anticipate a rebellion there. Russia was also known to have numerous emissaries all through these countries, stirring up the people to aid in the war which seemed imminent. These circumstances afford some explanation—they can offer no excuse—for what followed in Bulgaria. Undoubtedly the Sultan gave strong orders concerning the instant and stern suppression of any attempted revolt, and in the existing state of affairs this was sufficient ground for pillage and massacre, without any further direct orders from Constantinople. But it is also certain that the commanders of the Bashi-Bazouks, or irregular Turkish cavalry, the chiefs of the armed Circassian bands, and the officers of the regular troops sent in to " preserve order," were all aware that the murder of Christians was an aid to promotion, as their plunder was a sure path to wealth. And, as it turned out, the greater the massacres, the higher were the honours bestowed.

Exactly how the troubles commenced can only be guessed at. Early in May, 1876, it seems probable that there were two or three small bands of insurgents in the country, mostly recruited from men whose homes had been harried by Turk or Circassian, and in whose breasts the ruin and loss of everything they cherished had produced an active hatred, instead of the too common condition of dumb despair. But, small and unimportant as these bands were, they furnished ample excuse to the Turkish forces—regular and irregular. The massacres promptly commenced, and were at first as carefully concealed as those in Armenia have since been.

Gradually, however, news filtered through the Ottoman lines, and, despite the utmost precautions of the authorities and threats against all who spread rumours of the kind, horrifying details reached the ears of ambassadors, and finally filled the columns of English papers. Investigation ultimately brought to light the whole dreadful record. It appeared that regular troops under direct orders from the Sultan were on the scene of operations during the entire series of massacres; that they watched, and, in many cases, assisted in the wholesale murder of a helpless population by Bashi-Bazouks and Circassians; that Chefket Pasha, the centre of the terrible scenes at Boyadjik, was immediately afterwards decorated and given a high place in the Sultan's palace; and that Achmet Agha, the hero of similar events at Ba'ak, had been rewarded with the order of the Medjidie. So much for the question of responsibility.

The massacre at Batak was a peculiarly awful one. A large number of helpless Bulgarians, men, women, and children—about 1,200 in all—took refuge in the local church, which happened to be a very solid building and capable of resisting the efforts of the soldiery to burn it from the outside. They therefore fired in through the windows, and ultimately got upon the roof, tore off the tiles, and poured blazing oil and burning cloths upon the wretched victims within. Finally the door was forced in, and the massacre completed amid scenes which absolutely beggar description. But Batak was only part of the district or sandjak of Philippopolis, in which the total number of persons massacred is estimated by Mr. Schuyler, the American Consul-General at Constantinople, at 15,000, and by Mr. Baring, of the British Embassy, at 12,000.

But perhaps the worst of all, in a series where degrees of horror are almost imperceptible, was that at Boyadjik. It was committed by regular troops, assisted by the Bashi-Bazouks. The villagers in this case came out in a body to the commander, Chefket Pasha, stated that they had gathered together for protection against the Bashi-Bazouks and Circassians, urged their claims to protection and offered to surrender their arms. He promised mercy to the suppliants at his feet, and then, as soon as they had returned to the village, the order was given to storm it and massacre the inhabitants with the usual accompaniments of outrage and torture. Of this scene Mr. Baring writes, under all the limitations of a knowledge that his ambassadorial chief, Sir Henry Elliot, as well as the British Government itself, were desirous of avoiding grounds of rupture with the Porte, that :

"What makes the act of Chefket so abominable is that there was not a semblance of revolt. The inhabitants were perfectly peaceful, and the attack on them was as cruel and wanton a deed as could well have been committed. . . . Nana Sahib alone, I should say, has rivalled their (Achmet Agha's and Chefket Pasha's) deeds."

Sir Henry Elliot, of course, protested and urged punishment, while the Sultan denied or minimized the massacres, and conferred honours upon the perpetrators. Outside the district already referred to, the proceedings were as atrocious as those faintly indicated, and fully as many more helpless Christians were murdered, the children being slaughtered or sold as slaves, and the women who were not killed reserved for Turkish harems. Altogether some 20,000 Bulgarians were massacred, while the generals—Achmet Agha, Raschid Pasha and Chefket—defiantly and publicly declared that they had in their pockets the definite official order to slay, burn, and terrorize. Needless to say the "insurrection" was suppressed, and the leaders returned to received rewards and divide their booty in Constantinople. What plunder the troops obtained is incalculable, but it was as easy to take under the circumstances as was the slaughtering process described to Consul Reade by one of the Turks with true Moslem callousness : "When I tell you that even our schoolboys killed their five or six Bulgarians, what can you imagine that I did ?"

The reception of the news in England was varied. At first there were grave doubts, and Lord Beaconsfield, in view of the crisis created by Russia's avowed determination to this time break up the Turkish Empire, endeavoured to sooth the public alarm and prevent a wild and panicky policy of surrender to that ⁿower. To prevent Russia obtaining Constantinople was, he pointed out, the true British policy—in the interest of England, not in defence of Turkey. But Lord Derby, the Foreign Secretary, was finally authorized to write Sir Henry Elliot, that "any sympathy which was previously felt here toward that country has been completely destroyed by the recent lamentable events in Bulgaria. The accounts of outrages and excesses committed by the Turkish troops upon an unhappy, and for the most part unresisting, population has raised a universal feeling of indignation in all classes of English society." He further spoke of the almost insuperable obstacle thus placed in the way of England defending Turkish territory against possible Russian aggression. About the same time Lord Salisbury—then Secretary of State for India—wrote to a stormy meeting at the Mansion House that: "Every one must concur in reprobating the abominable crimes which have been committed in Bulgaria; and a desire to relieve the Christian populations of those regions from a renewal of the atrocious oppression under which they have suffered is felt as strongly by members of the Government as by any other Englishman."

But this was not enough for Mr. Gladstoⁿ came out of his retirement and demanded instar No matter if the Bosphorus became a Russian ⟨ ⟩nnel, the Turkish peninsula a Russian stamping ground, or th Mediterranean a Russian sea, justice must be done, the Turks cleared out of Bulgaria, and, if possible, out of

Europe. This "loathsome tyranny" must be checked at any cost. "Never again," declared the eloquent leader, "while the years roll on in their course, so far as it is in our power to determine, never again shall the hand of violence be raised by you; never again shall the dire refinements of cruelty be devised by you for the sake of making mankind miserable in Bulgaria." His burning pamphlet entitled "Bulgarian Horrors" created a sensation in Europe, and, although not at the moment leader of his party, the tremendous campaign of the next six months against Turkey, against Lord Beaconsfield, and against the whole foreign policy of the Government, practically placed him at its head, and certainly contributed to his electoral triumph in 1880.

Meanwhile Russia had declared war and settled the question for the time being by over-running the Principalities and Bulgaria, and accepting the alliance of Servia and the aid of the rebellion in Bosnia. Eventually her armies came within sight of Constantinople, and forced from the Porte the Treaty of San Stefano. With the signing of this compact, by which Turkey became practically a shorn and helpless vassal of the Czar, there developed one of the most acute stages of the historic Eastern Question. Lord Beaconsfield had to face the problem of either sacrificing British pledges and traditional policy and Imperial interests, by letting Constantinople fall into the hands of the great rival of England, or else interfere in the teeth of the popular passion aroused by Mr. Gladstone against the Turk and all his concerns. He chose the former, and the Treaty of Berlin was the result.

By this arrangement Bulgaria was created an autonomous province, tributary to the Sultan, but independent so f as concerned its internal government and affairs. o elia, however, which naturally pertained to it by the nationality, language, and customs of the majority of its people, was still left under Turkish rule. And henceforth its acquisition or annexation became the chief immediate object of Bulgarian policy. At first the country fell completely under Russian influence, and its infant Parliament was opened at Tirnova by a Russian—Prince Dondoukoff Korsakoff—in the presence of Russian soldiers and amid the booming of Russian guns. Shortly afterwards the new constitution was promulgated and found to be fairly liberal in its terms, while Prince Alexander of Hesse was elected Prince of Bulgaria on April 29th, 1879, under the title of Alexander I., and with the approval of the Czar. Before settling down to the duties and difficulties of his position, the Prince made a tour of the European Courts and paid a visit to Queen Victoria. Upon his return the Russian troops evacuated the Principality, and nominally, at least, the country was left to experiment in self-government.

During the next five years all was confusion and disorder. Lifted out of centuries of despotic oppression by an alien power into the light of constitutional liberty, the Bulgarians naturally did not know how to use their privileges, while to add to these complications came the continuous intrigues of Russian emissaries and officers and the pressure of a Russian Government bent upon making Bulgaria a dependent State, and its people a part of the great Pan-Slavic movement. Hence the distinct formation of a Russian and an anti-Russian party. In numbers the latter was, of course, the chief, and indeed the national party, but the former was backed by Russian prestige and Russian gold. Prince Alexander, assisted by Karaveloff, placed himself at the head of the national aspirations, struggled against foreign interference, and by the necessary exercise of almost autocratic power tried to temper the system of government to the requirements and capabilities of his people.

In 1885, he boldly proclaimed the reunion of Roumelia--or South Bulgaria, as it is now termed—with the Principality, and amid great national enthusiasm the people armed for a struggle which seemed imminent. But Turkey only protested, and the expected war broke out in another quarter. For some years the Servians— who also obtained their freedom in 1878—had been upon bad terms with the Bulgarians. Despite the folly of quarrelling in the face of their mutual foe, the Turk, and in spite of some measure of blood relationship between the races, their rivalries and jealousies had been growing in strength until the annexation of Roumelia aroused still further the passions of the Serbs, and induced King Milan to declare war upon the 13th of November. A few weeks of active and varied fighting followed. Bulgaria was invaded by 40,000 Servians, and its troops defeated at Tru, and Kula, and Widdin. Then Prince Alexander routed the invaders at Slivnitza, and at the Dragoman Pass—where the Servian loss was estimated at 6,000—and turned the tide of war by entering Servia and winning several other victories. Finally, an armistice was concluded through Austrian intervention, and in January, 1885, mainly by the influence of Sir William White, the British Ambassador at Stamboul, the practical union of Bulgaria and Roumelia was admitted by the Porte through the courteous fiction of Prince Alexander being appointed to represent the Sultan in the latter part of the new Bulgaria. And in March, peace was signed with Servia.

Then came the tragic result of Russian intrigue. Alexander had shown himself altogether too virile and able a ruler, too representative of the national aims of the people, too desirous of strengthening the national independence, too anxious to extend the national territory. So, one day in the August following his return from the war, a conspiracy was organized by Russian sympathizers and purchased officers, and the Prince surprised, kidnapped, and carried off a prisoner; while Zankoff, a former pro-Russian premier, formed a provisional government at Sofia. This, however, was promptly repudiated by the army and the people, and a loyalist government was temporarily established at Tirnova, under the strong and determined leadership of Stambuloff. Within a few months the rebel government were prisoners, and Prince Alexander, who had in the meantime escaped, or been allowed to escape, returned to his capital in triumph.

Realizing, however, the almost impossible difficulties of governing the country against the will of the Czar, he soon afterwards abdicated and left the State for which he had done so much, and in which he had won such deserved popularity. For a time after this the situation in Bulgaria was a grave one, and the Eastern Question seemed to have assumed a new phase. General Kaulbars was sent to Sofia with the generally accepted aim of making the country a Russian dependency, while Russian warships were despatched to Varna. He found, however, that the mass of the population was opposed to his policy, and that whatever was done must be done under cover. Austria and Great Britain also protested vigorously against these evident designs, and Lord Salisbury denounced the aggression of Russia during a speech on November 9th in no halting or uncertain terms. He referred to the gallant Prince who had been overthrown by officers "debauched with foreign gold." He spoke of the "encroachment after encroachment upon the rights of a free and independent people, witnessed with the deepest regret and most earnest reprobation," and then eulogized the struggling State in most generous language :

" The people of Bulgaria have had no long apprenticeship in freedom. They are but recently released from the enervating influence of the subjection under which they had been placed, and yet the courage, the resolution, the tenacity, the determination to secure their national and individual freedom, would have done credit to races which have enjoyed freedom for centuries, and will lend a happy augury to the beginning of that which I believe will be a brilliant history."

Eventually, Russia was side-tracked, in a diplomatic sense, and Prince Ferdinand of Saxe-Coburg was chosen ruler by the Sobranje, or Parliament, over the head of the Russian mominee—Prince Nicholas of Mingrelia. Prince Waldemar of Denmark, and Alexander himself, had previously refused the perilous honour. The years which followed have been, upon the whole, a period of substantial progress amongst the people; hampered by inevitable Russian intrigues and occasional small revolts. But the strong hand of Stambuloff, rather than any qualities in Prince Ferdinand, have held the country together and guided it along the path of development and independence. The brutal murder of this great Bulgarian, in 1895, is only another of the sins which must be laid at the door of Russian schemers playing upon the still brutalized instincts of a portion of the population, and making the weak character of the reigning prince a cover for frightful crime.

Time, and education, and progress will remedy this, and gradually suppress outbreaks of the barbarism which which has here and there been developed. And the recent baptism of little Prince Boris into the Greek Church, while it may or may not mean a fraternization with Russia, will give to the people—if he lives—a native ruler with a national name, and inspired in all probability with the national ambition of "on to Constantinople." To succeed in this great policy, however, the Bulgarians have to grow greatly in strength and wisdom, to keep free of Russian complications, to retain the good will of England, and defeat the rivalry of Greece and Servia.

The Late Prince Gortschakoff,
Chancellor of the Russian Empire.

Alexander II.
Emperor of Russia, 1855-1881

CHAPTER X.

SERVIA AND ROUMANIA.

As with Bulgaria, the history of Servia is a deeply shadowed record of oppression and struggle. The dismal features of Turkish misrule and cruelty, so familiar in the history of all these Balkan States, may be seen here to the fullest extent. So also with the machinations of Russia, complicated in this particular case by the rival influence of Austria. Lying south of Hungary, and peopled by a race of Slavonic extraction, who accepted Christianity and the tenets of the Greek Church about 640, Servia has been alternately during many centuries a free State and a conquered football of the Byzantine or the Turk.

In A.D. 1150, the country was subjugated by the Emperor Manuel, of Constantinople, but thirty years later recovered its independence, and in 1356, under the great Emperor Dushan, became a really powerful State. Joining with Bulgaria, which at that time possessed much of influence and prestige, this ruler over-ran a wide territory, and even seriously menaced Constantinople. In 1389, however, the Turkish Sultan, Amurath I., undertook the conquest of the countries around the Christian capital, and on the plains of Kassova succeeded in defeating the combined forces of Servia, Hungary, Bulgaria, Bosnia, and Albania. The Sultan was himself killed, but the victory proved a decisive stepping-stone to the accomplishment of his policy. And, some years after the taking of

Constantinople in 1456, Mahomet II. over-ran Servia and entirely subjugated its people. During the succeeding three hundred years, with the exception of a rebellion in 1737, and aid given to the Austrians against Turkey in 1788-90, the country remained fairly quiet under the iron heel of its Moslem rulers.

But, in 1801, events reached a crisis through certain chiefs of the Janizaries taking the government into their own hands and massacring the heads of the communes and the leading inhabitants of the country. A general insurrection, which practically continued until 1820, broke out under the leadership of the famous Kara-George, who succeeded in winning a signal victory over the Turkish army in September, 1804. The country was then organized politically, placed under the protection of Russia, and the first Senate called together. Between this period and 1813, when the Ottomans in overwhelming numbers invaded and reconquered the country, Russia had played her usual game of deception and intrigue. If Servia proved itself willing to become a submissive dependency of the Czar, it would receive due protection; but if its leaders and people showed a desire for real independence, they were to be left to the mercy of the Turks. And as Kara-George had not the slightest intention of freeing his country from one yoke to place it under another, Russia alternately helped and deserted its unfortunate allies.

In 1815, Milosch Obrenovitch headed the insurrectionary movement, and succeeded in again driving back the Turks. He obtained in 1820, after a prolonged struggle, the Sultan's recognition of the right of Servia to govern itself, and choose its own Sovereign, upon the payment of an annual tribute to the Sublime Porte. Then followed the usual efforts of Russia to obtain control of the new government and to oppose the extension of liberal principles. Finally, Milosch—like Alexander of Bulgaria in after years—was found to be altogether objectionable to his would-be masters, and in 1839 was forced to abdicate. His son Milan was elected Prince, and on his death in 1840 was succeeded by his brother of the same name. Two years later he also was compelled to abdicate, and for the next sixteen years the country was ruled by Alexander, son of Kara-George. In 1858, he was forced by a successful insurrection to flee the country, and Milosch was recalled, reigning vigorously and well until his death in 1860. He was succeeded by his son, Milan III., whose reign is noted for the organization of a national army, the evacuation by Turkey of the fortresses still held by its troops, the partial formation of constitutional government, and the rise of the Servian statesmen, Kristich, Ristitch, and Garashanine. In 1868 this Prince was assassinated, and his place taken by Milan IV., who was crowned King in 1876, and reigned until 1889, when he abdicated, and was succeeded by his son, the youthful Alexander II.

During all this period of struggling progress, the difficulties connected with their rulers were the least of Servia's troubles. Something has been said about Russian intrigue. Emil de Laveleye—a not unfriendly critic —declares that, " wishing still to keep it (Servia) dependent, Russia was opposed to the growth of its liberty and power, and encouraged internal discord. It, therefore, follows that the Servians have not retained any feelings of gratitude towards the Russians. The same policy has been pursued in Bulgaria." The plan of the Czars has always been to use these countries against the Turk, and then, if they were not amenable to ideas of dependence upon Russia, to promptly desert them until an opportunity for new plots might again arise. Writing in 1863, Lord Palmerston told Baron Brunnow that: "As regards the Russian Government, I look upon the insurrection (in Poland) as a just penalty awarded by Heaven for the intrigues fomented by that Government in instigating rebellion against the Sultan in Moldavia, Wallachia, Servia, and Bosnia. For the present, Russia herself suffers the evil she wishes to inflict upon a neighbour. In this I refer to the 100,000 rifles the Russian Government has clandestinely sent to Servia and Bosnia, and to the host of *agents provocateurs* likewise despatched by Russia to stir up rebellion in Turkey."

To *use* the Christians of the Ottoman Empire, whether in Europe or Asia, not to help or really free them, has ever been the policy of the Czars. When they refused to be facile instruments, their freedom became a matter of indifference, and time after time, treaties made with the Turk contained little or no reference to the interests of the States which had fought so well under the eagles of the Russian leaders. In 1878, however, came the critical moment in the history of these Balkan countries. Servia, Bulgaria, and Roumania all declared war against Turkey, and assisted Russia with their fullest strength. And in the ensuing Treaty of San Stefano they were duly declared independent of the Porte, but under conditions which practically made them dependent on Russia. Lord Beaconsfield and the Treaty of Berlin changed this, and gave Servia an absolutely national independence, with its own sovereign and constitution, and an enlarged frontier.

Thus ended the dominance of the Turk in the land of the Serbs. During four hundred years it had lasted with crushing effect upon an industrious agricultural community which, like that of Bulgaria, only desired the right to live, and work, and practise its religious principles in quietness and peace. In the beginning of the nineteenth century very few of the peasantry in Servia could read or write, and only a small proportion of what may be somewhat doubtfully termed the upper classes. Most of the latter had been compelled to profess Islamism on pain of losing their property, and perhaps their lives. Constitutional liberty was, of course, a farce, and remained so for a long time after the recognition of a line of Servian princes. When not interfered with and checked by Russia, it was crushed or made inoperative by the pressure of the Turkish troops, while during the revolts which took place from time to time, or the earlier wars in which the capital—Belgrade—was the prize fought for by Christian and Moslem, by Austria, Russia, Hungary, and Turkey, the inhabitants of the country were subject to all the miseries and cruelties of Moslem conquest or invasion.

Whether in the struggles of Kara-George, the troubles of 1862, or the war of 1876-7—in which Servia lost some 8,000 men, and had 20,000 wounded—the people were compelled to endure all the ruthless practices of Turkish warfare. One of the methods of revenge or punishment was by impalement. It is not necessary to describe this terrible, torturing, lingering death, but the fact of its frequent use is undoubted. Hundreds of Servians fell victims to it. Ranke says that "men were impaled, and children, in derision of the rite of baptism, were thrown into boiling water." Kinglake, in describing a journey through Servia in 1845, speaks of two skeletons which he himself saw by the roadway, still propped up in their place of death. He also describes a building erected by the Turks, "of a pyramidical shape, and made up of 30,000 skulls, which were contributed by rebellious Servians in the early part of this century." Ranke again speaks of a number of Servians who, upon one occasion, laid down their arms on promise of pardon. Some hundred and fifty were at once beheaded, and " the more important, to the number of thirty-seven, were impaled. These were all young, high-spirited, and brave men, of good descent." Such were the methods of warfare which patriotic Servians had to face.

Since obtaining its independence in 1878, the youthful kingdom has not been altogether fortunate. Ristitch, the Conservative leader, has been an able man, but somewhat subservient to Russia, while the beneficial influence of Kristitch and Garaschanine has been checked by the undue Conservatism of King Milan on the one side, and the undue power of the Radicals on the other. The latter, as is so often the case, desire to adopt principles and methods of administration entirely unsuited to the present development of a people who are still ignorant to a degree, accustomed to a primitive commercial system, and to living by the most imperfect methods of old-time farming. There has been practically no educated aristocratic class in the country which could moderate revolutionary ideas and help forward popular progress by degrees. Naturally, therefore, much of confusion and intrigue, looseness in government, and despotic reactions, constitute the legislative history of the country from the dawn of Parliamentary liberty in the beginning of the century to its full nominal realization at the present time. And even now, as evidenced by the differences in 1888 between the King, who favoured Austria, and Queen Nathalie, who favoured Russia, external intrigue still flourishes, and still throws a shadow over the national institutions.

Financially, too, the little kingdom has been unfortunate. King Milan did not prove an economist, and the greatest danger of small and ambitious States now menaces Servia. Its national debt amounts to between fifty and sixty millions of dollars, and has steadily increased since 1875—the interest now reaching one-half of its entire revenue. Of course, the war with Turkey in 1876, and the unfortunate contest with Bulgaria in 1885, were responsible for part of it, while $20,000,000 has been spent upon a railway connecting Belgrade with Constantinople, which may, in time, prove remunerative. But none the less is this a heavy burden for a country with two millions of a population—a people possessed of great ambition, and utterly ignorant of financial considerations.

Still, with all its misfortunes, the country is now free from the Turkish blight, and has time on its side in the work of development which lies before all the Balkan States, and which might be so greatly aided by their friendly combination, but is so greatly hampered by their mutual rivalries. For, like Bulgaria and Greece, Servia aims at some day winning Constantinople—obtaining as a preliminary the part of Macedonia from which once sprang the empire of Dushan, and which is now known to its people as Old Servia. At present, however, the race does not seem to be with the Serbs. Their debts are heavy, and their King Alexander is a young man of no promise, and poor character. When the time comes for driving the Turks out of Europe, it seems probable that the one of the three Balkan powers which can produce a great king, or virile leader, will be the country most likely to obtain the coveted prize. Meantime, the most needed policy for Servia is peace, economy, and patience.

To turn from the stormy politics and many troubles of Servia to the settled calm and general prosperity of Roumania is somewhat of a relief. This most populous, united, and contented of all the Balkan States is almost a surprise to the average student or visitor. Its five or six millions of people are so largely homogeneous in race and religion; so prosperous in trade and progressive in agriculture—the great staple of the country; so fortunate in their rulers, and so comparatively well versed in constitutional government; as to make the country a genuine example to the other States which have torn themselves out from the toils of Turkey.

Yet its history has been sufficiently tempestuous and varied from the time when it formed a part of ancient Dacia, and after a prolonged contest was subdued, in A.D. 106, by the Roman Emperor Trajan. A couple of centuries later it was abandoned to the tender mercies of the Goths, and from that period to the middle of the ninth century was successively conquered by the Huns, over-run by the Scythians, subdued by Charlemagne, and subjugated by the Magyars of Hungary. From this latter date until its conquest by the Turks in the fifteenth century, its annals are much confused and decidedly uninteresting; but after that event the Provinces of Moldavia and Wallachia, or the Danubian principalities, as they were often called, became a sort of football, tossed from Russian to Turk and back again. In the many wars between these two powers, the principalities were, as a rule, invaded and occupied by Russia, and, after the struggle was concluded by some sham peace or temporary cessation of overt hostilities, they would be evacuated and left to the cruel consideration of their former masters.

Through it all, however, the Roumans retained more of practical independence and suffered less from Turkish brutality than perhaps any other dependents of the Porte. They had the advantage of being more or less a national unit, and their country, placed as it was along the north bank of the Danube, and containing important fortified towns such Bucharest and Jassy, Galatz and Giurgevo, received more consideration than might otherwise have been the case. Controlling so much of the shores of the Danube as they did, and almost reaching in territory to its outlet into the Black Sea, the Principalities were always an object of European interest, and were thus kept freer from Ottoman tyranny than either Servia to the east, or Bulgaria to the south. In 1812, during one of its numerous invasions, Russia took part of Moldavia, presumably as a reward for its unselfish interest in the welfare of the people, and nine years later, so as to equalize matters, the Roumans were severely treated by the Turks for having risen to the assistance of Greece. In 1829, however, the two principalities were formally placed under Russian protection by the Treaty of Adrianople, and so remained for twenty years, when the Porte once more asserted its authority and appointed Prince Stirbey, Hospodar of Wallachia, and Prince Ghika, Hospodar of Moldavia. The Crimean war and another occupation by Russia followed, until the Paris Conference of 1858 decreed the practical independence of the provinces under a nominal recognition of Turkish suzerainty. The result was the election of Alexander Couza as Hospodar or Prince of the combined provinces, and their union, in 1861, under the name of Roumania.

After considerable opposition from the Sultan, and much discussion amongst the Powers which had helped Turkey in the Crimean war, the union was formally recognized. In the British Parliament it was opposed by Lord Palmerston and Mr. Disraeli, and defended by Mr. Gladstone and Lord Salisbury. The latter, then just commencing his public career, and known as Lord Robert Cecil, made his first speech on the Eastern Question in this connection, and declared that :

"If Europe supports the claims of Turkey, the Principalities will be left to the mercy of the Turkish

Government, the most oppressive and rapacious of governments. Whilst Turkey is still standing they must be under this rule, and when she falls, as fall she must, they will be a spoil which the other powers will divide amongst them. I hope that the House of Commons will, under these circumstances, show itself the friend of liberty."

During the thirty years which followed, the country steadily progressed in constitutional government, in material prosperity, and in population. Commencing the period with three millions of people, it has now nearly double that number. Of course, there have been ups and downs, and more than one revolt, before government affairs became shaken into a firm and stable system. In one of these changes Prince Couza was overthrown, and Charles of Hohenzollern-Sigmaringen elected, in 1866, by popular vote to be Prince of Roumania. Fortunately for the country, he accepted the Crown, was recognized by the Sultan, and assumed the government amidst general enthusiasm. Since then, assisted by the grace and charm of his wife—known also to the world as Carmen Sylva, the poetess—he has laboured unremittingly, and upon the whole wisely, to build up the national interests and protect the national territory.

It has not been an easy task, but external events have at times helped materially. In 1874, for instance, Austria, Germany, and Russia informed the Porte that they claimed the privilege of making separate treaties with Roumania. To this serious blow at his supremacy, nominal as it was, the Sultan naturally objected, and ...e years later Prince Charles concluded a convention with Russia by which its troops were allowed to cross Roumanian territory in their projected invasion of Turkey. A month after this arrangement the country naturally drifted into its declaration of war against the

Porte, and a formal declaration of independence. Roumanian troops distinguished themselves with the Russians at Plevna and elsewhere, and the absolute freedom of the country was recognized in the Treaty of San Stefano, approved in the Treaty of Berlin, and formally recognized by England, France, and Germany in 1880. The Prince was at once crowned King, and set himself to preserve his country from the fresh dangers arising out of Austrian intrigues along the Danube, and the usual Russian schemes to subvert institutions which now seemed to menace its influence over what had once been, in all but name, dependent provinces.

The former trouble was averted, in 1885, by the bold entry of Roumanian troops into Silistria, and a policy well in accord with that action. The latter was checked by the prolonged and popular administration of Bratiano, and the crushing of an insurrection which broke out in 1888—encouraged, as was well known, by Russian emissaries and Russian gold. Since then, the King has been persistently devoted to the creation of an army and its improvement year by year, until it is now understood that, for its population, Roumania has the best drilled and equipped troops in all Europe. And side by side with this military development is the somewhat unusual condition of increasing revenues, a frequent surplus over expenditure, and an excellent banking system. The national debt is about $137,000,000, but does not seem to be burdensome, while the trade of the country is encouraged by the presence in the community of a number of commercial foreigners, who, to some extent, offset the seventy per cent. of the population engaged in agriculture, pure and simple. Of these there are three or four hundred thousand Jews, 50,000 Germans, and 15,000 Armenians. There are also a number of Swiss and Greeks, while the railway and similar interests are mainly in the hands of English residents.

Roumania is fortunate in being not only a comparative unit in the nationality of its people, but in possessing an extraction and characteristics which separate them from the Slavs of Russia, and preserve them, to some extent, from the wide-reaching plots and plans of Slavonic enthusiasts in the Austrian Empire and elsewhere. It is also fortunate in possessing a really national Church in the sense of one which appeals to the great mass of the population. And, though a branch of the Greek Church, it is independent in name and practice, and is ruled by its own Patriarch and local synod.

As a race, the Roumans are intelligent and quick-witted —more so than either Servian or Bulgar—but rather inclined to be rash and whimsical. They have no great national ambition outside of their own country, although there are nearly as many Roumans (4,500,000) scattered throughout the other Balkan States and Turkey proper as there are in Roumania itself. For this reason they are more likely to remain at peace and continue the work of building up their own institutions and prosperity than are the intensely ambitious and restless communities of Greece, or Servia, or Bulgaria. One external trouble they have. Freed from Turkish oppression, and now safe, in the main, from Russian intrigue, Roumania is, like Belgium, subject to an international arrangement by which belligerents are allowed to pass through its territory in time of war. Practically this means Russia, as being the strongest neighbouring power, and the only one likely to desire the privilege. Until the agreement is abrogated, Roumanian independence in time of war is a farce, and it is this cause which makes King Charles devote so much energy and money to the strengthening of his army—

a force which will have to be seriously reckoned with in the next war between Russia and the Ottoman Empire.

The Roumans have been unusually fortunate, indeed, in their King. They now have a complete constitutional system, working smoothly and harmoniously, and due, in the main, to the fact that their sovereign has understood its workings from the first, and has been able and willing to help his people towards its full development. Could the rulers of Servia and Bulgaria rise to the same level of their opportunities, and then unite with him and with Greece, in a common union for offence and defence, the future of the Turk in Europe might be settled without foreign intervention, and to the lasting welfare of these Christian people, and of their unfortunate brothers scr tered through the present domain of the Sultan. This may be a dream, but it is one lifted out of the regions of impossibility through the example set by Roumania in freedom of government and wisdom of policy.

CHAPTER XI.

BOSNIA AND HERZEGOVINA.

Alike in race and historic misery, the populations of Bosnia and Herzegovina have been mixed up in almost innumerable conquests, wars, and revolutions; united to-day and separated to-morrow; the victims of Hungarian aggression; the wretched subjects of Ottoman misrule. The one State is fertile, but has been long desolated by war and taxation; the other is mountainous and poor, but none the less racked by oppressive exactions. Allied by nationality and language with the Croats to the north, the Servians to the east, the Montenegrins and the northern Albanians, the people are affiliated with the general mass of Slavonic races which are supposed to look to Russia as the centre of their hopes and aspirations. Yet, by virtue of Austrian influence, and the liberty accorded to the Croats and others by that Empire, the issue is complicated through a sympathetic desire to develop under Austrian rather than Russian protection into the great Jougo-Slav State of their patriotic national dreams.

In the dawning of their history, Bosnia and Herzegovina formed part of ancient Illyria; were conquered by the irresistible Roman, and still retain ruins of that great civilization. They were afterwards over-run by the Goths, and then for two centuries became the scene of ruthless massacre and tyranny at the hands of the Avars, who, during the same period, occupied Greece and the

Alexander III.
Emperor of Russia, 1831-1895

Nicholas II.
Emperor of Russia, 1895.

greater part of the countries which formed a background to Christian Byzantium. In the seventh century began the ethnographic situation which now prevails. The Croats then occupied Croatia and northern Bosnia, while the Serbs, of the same race and language, peopled Servia, southern Bosnia, Montenegro, Dalmatia, and the Herzegovina. Incidentally the former were converted to Christianity by missionaries from Rome, and the latter were carried into the Greek communion by the eloquence of Cyril. Hence a complication which tends to keep apart at the present time two peoples of similar origin and instincts.

For a prolonged period these various countries retained a sort of uncertain national coherence. Whenever a strong prince or leader arose, they seem to have naturally come together; otherwise they drifted apart into more or less confusion and hostility. In 874 the name Bosnia appeared for the first time, when Budimir became king of Croatia, Dalmatia, and Bosnia. Thirty years later, Brisimer, King of Servia, annexed Croatia and Bosnia, and in 1091 a new development came in the overthrow of the nominal supremacy which had been all this time retained by the Byzantine Empire, through a successful invasion by King Ladislaus of Hungary. His successor, in 1103, added to his titles those of King of Bosnia and of Herzegovina. During the next two hundred years the country was racked by religious conflicts and persecution. The Franciscan monks revived Catholicism, and the Hungarian kings endeavoured to promote their aims by the attempted extirpation of a peculiar sect of Christianity—the Bogomiles, or disciples of the Albigenses—who had obtained much popular support. Blood flowed like water in a struggle which the Bosnians fought because it seemed to be connected with a possible national independence, as much as for any special religious convictions.

Finally, the great Emperor of Servia—Stephen Dushan—freed them in 1355, and under his successor, Stephen Tvartko, the much troubled countries enjoyed a period of peace and prosperity. Serajevo, the present capital, was founded; order, justice, and toleration established; and the people given a breathing spell just as the Turk appeared on their national horizon. Thirty thousand Bosnians were engaged in the memorable battle of Kassova, which gave Servia to the Moslem, but Bosnia, under Tvartko II., was left to face a further period of independence, and, as it unfortunately turned out, of civil war and intense religious persecution, instead of unified preparation for the coming and inevitable onslaught.

When, therefore, Mahomet II. advanced upon Bosnia, in 1453, with an army of 150,000 men, there was nothing which could resist him. The whole country was laid waste, 30,000 young men were circumcised and enrolled amongst the Janizaries, 200,000 prisoners were sold as slaves, many towns were burned or destroyed, the churches were turned into mosques, and the land was confiscated by the conquerors in accordance with the laws of the Koran. For a long time, however, isolated fortresses held out, and it was not until 1527, when the battle of Mohacz had given Hungary to the Turks, that Jaitche, the last rampart of Bosnian independence, fell to the invaders. At this time a curious and important incident occurred. Exasperated by the prolonged persecutions received at the hands of Hungarian Catholic rulers, and from the last King of Bosnia himself, and no doubt influenced by the necessity of saving their wealth and lands from the Turk, the great mass of the local magnates, or, as they were afterwards termed, the Beys, adopted Islam, and from that time onward stood in the forefront of every struggle with Christian nations, or local persecution of Christian votaries. They fought in the vanguard of the wars which gave Hungary to the Moslem, as well as in the struggles for the possession of Vienna. And when their external influence and aggressive power ceased with the decadence of the Turk, they became the most fanatical and cruel of Christian oppressors.

Numbering some 400,000 out of a population of a million and a quarter, these converts to Islam naturally controlled, to a great extent, the internal government of Bosnia. They had imbibed to the full the Turkish contempt for Christians, the Moslem tendency to persecute, fleece, and ill-treat them, and the instinctive Moslem dislike to progress, novelty, or education. More than once the Bosnian Mahometans have risen against the Porte itself. The Beys defied Mahmoud II. and his reforms, drove out the Turkish governor, and headed a rebellion which succeeded in pillaging Bulgaria, while they even ventured to proclaim an intention of dethroning the Sultan as being " sold to the Giaours." Again and again, between 1820 and 1850, they revolted against the Ottoman Government, not because they wanted liberty or equality, but because they feared the Sultan was going to deprive them of that power over the Christian peasantry which they so cruelly misused. Unlike nearly all the other insurrections in the various countries of European and Asiatic Turkey, through all the pages of its bloodstained history, these risings were dictated by extreme Mahometan fanaticism, and not by Christian aspirations after liberty.

Of course, the latter class in the country—the Rayahs—had nothing to do with the rebellions, and could

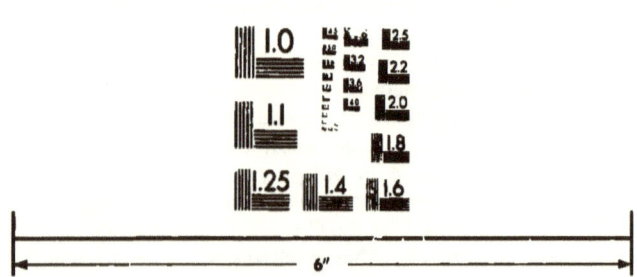

IMAGE EVALUATION
TEST TARGET (MT-3)

Photographic
Sciences
Corporation

23 WEST MAIN STREET
WEBSTER, N.Y. 14580
(716) 872-4503

only rejoice when, in 1851, Omar Pasha finally crushed the power of the Beys by taking away their chief privileges. But this did not remove them from the country, nor deprive them of the land. Between this date and 1875, the Moslem proprietors, exasperated by the nominal guarantees given the Christian peasantry by the Porte, despoiled and ill-used the miserable farmers to a greater extent than before, while the latter, of course, had no appeal except to Mahometan judges and hostile Turkish officials. The result was a wholesale exodus to Austrian territory, followed by events which finally placed them under the protection and government of the Austrian power.

To these Beys a Rayah was only a dog, an enemy whom he would be justified in killing at once, were it not that he was a useful source of revenue. And the means of wringing taxes out of the miserable peasantry were characteristic. An Austrian author, Gustave Thoemmel, tells us that the fiscal agents used to frequently hang unwilling or incapable taxpayers to trees above a large fire, or fasten them without clothes to posts in the middle of winter, or cover them in the same season of the year with cold water, which froze upon their stiffened limbs. Complaint was useless, and might result in their being thrown into prisons beside which those of Ferdinand Bomba in Naples, or those described by Prince Krapotkin as existing in Russia, are mere rose-coloured palaces.

Meanwhile the history and condition of Herzegovina was proceeding on almost parallel lines, although the natural union of the peoples, as well as the greater part of their national aspirations, had been more or less crushed into the ground. During the fifteenth century it had come under the control of Austria—or, rather, its dependency, Hungary—but in 1694 was ceded to the Ottomans at the Peace of Carlowitz. Its people have since suffered, though not quite to the same extent as Bosnia, from the exactions of local Beys and the cruelties of marauding Turks. The population is only a few hundred thousand, and, being scattered amongst mountainous districts, has always been able to hold its own to better advantage than the inhabitants of the richer but more accessible plains. In 1861 a Christian insurrection, fostered by the Prince of Montenegro, broke out against the Beys and the Turks, but was suppressed with the usual accompaniments of violence and outrage.

An illustration of the treatment accorded the peasantry is told by M. de Laveleye in connection with the death of Aga-Tchnigitch, who, in 1836 and thereabouts, was Governor of Herzegovina. He had been busy for some time collecting the *haradasch*, or capitation tax imposed upon Christians as a mark of their servitude, but had found that the miserable rayahs had been stripped of everything. Neither torture for themselves nor the most brutal ill-usage for their families could apparently wring from them the Government tax, to say nothing of the additional levy for himself. Finally, one evening, the Governor was resting and smoking his pipe near one of the villages, while a number of rayahs were suspended to a tree close by. To amuse himself, he had a large fire of straw lighted under their feet ; but their cries proved an annoyance rather than a pleasure. Finally he roared out to the soldiers : " Make an end of these Christians ! Take some well-sharpened yataghans, some sharp-pointed stakes, and some boiling oil ! Let loose the powers of hell. I am a hero." Just at this moment, however, he was surprised and instantly slain by a Montenegrin foray.

Such were the rulers of these countries, and such the conditions prevalent for many centuries. Even as late as

1876-77 atrocities were committed equal to any recorded in the past, and rivalling those in Bulgaria, or in the Armenia of to-day. In the years mentioned the Christians of Bosnia and Herzegovina and Montenegro, as well as of Servia, joined in rebellion and war against the Turk. The invasion and crossing of the Balkans by the Russian armies were to all alike a beacon of hope, and one which no amount of experience in Russian selfishness and intrigue could obliterate. The Porte at once sent a large number of irregular troops into the country, with a result not dissimilar to that in Bulgaria. They went there with the knowledge that the insurrection was to be suppressed at all hazards, and in Bosnia and Herzegovina they ultimately succeeded, although driven back by the Servians and Montenegrins.

Fire and bloodshed were promptly served out to the unfortunate rebels with true Turkish luridness. Whole villages and towns were burned and the inhabitants massacred. Entire districts were transformed into deserts. Those even suspected of hostility were systematically killed, and their heads exposed upon stakes. More than a hundred thousand of the people fled into Austrian territory, and were fed and taken care of by Austrian money. But the end came when the Treaty of Berlin, recognizing the affiliation of these peoples with Austrian Croatia, the impossibility of organizing a beneficial independent government, the difficulty of annexing to Servia countries which contained nearly half a million of militant Mahometans, and the generally friendly feeling towards Austria itself, handed Bosnia and Herzegovina over to that Empire for administration and government.

This action was strongly denounced at the time in England. Mr. Gladstone, of course, could see no good in any part of the Beaconsfield policy at Berlin, and he never had liked the internal policy of Austria itself. That country had naturally obtained a reputation in accordance with the prolonged rule of Metternich, the known views of the old-time Holy Alliance, and the suppression of Kossuth and the Hungarian rebellion of 1848. But times had now greatly changed. The Empire which recognized Parliamentary rule in Hungary, in other provinces, and at Vienna itself; the Empire of Andrassy and Haymerle, Deak and Kallay, was very different from that which Mr. Gladstone described, in 1879, as having been the intolerant foe of liberty and friend of despotism.

By those most concerned, the transfer, or annexation, as it really was, received a welcome only subdued by the presence and acute indignation of the Mahometan Beys and landowners, who now felt their power to be indeed gone. They made one last effort, and in 1878, following the Emperor's proclamation to his new subjects, rose in a rebellion which was naturally helped, so far as was possible, by the Turks themselves. In July the Austrian army advanced into the country, finding its chief difficulty in the fortresses still scattered here and there, and in the Herzegovinian recesses to which the insurgents ultimately retreated. Within four months, however, the troubles were suppressed, and on November 9th a general amnesty issued.

Since then the Austrian Government have inaugurated many small reforms, and slowly, but surely, the evils of prolonged oppression are being counteracted. Order and equity are at least the aim in taxation, although it will be years before they can be fully realized in practice. The presence for a long period of the 14,000 men who formed the Austrian army of occupation has promoted local stability and security, and is gradually developing that confidence in the permanence of strong government and the execution of law and justice, which is the first essential of development in trade or agriculture. The latter occupation is more backward in Bosnia than it has been in any of the countries which have been blighted by the Turk—and that is saying much. But under improved conditions of taxation and government, it is now slowly advancing.

Under the free religious system of the very much mixed up Austrian Empire, the 500,000 Moslems, the 600,000 Greek Christians, and the 300,000 Roman Catholics in Bosnia and Herzegovina are enabled, and obliged, to live in at least outward harmony and toleration. In connection with the Greek Church a great reform has been enacted by the abolition of a system through which the infamous Phanariote tribe at Constantinople were enabled to sell its bishoprics and benefices to the highest bidder—thus spoiling the peasants and starving the rural priests—or popes, as they are locally called. Under the rule of the Beys and their Turkish successors education did not exist in the community. As with the negro slaves in the old days prior to American emancipation, education was considered a dangerous thing for an inferior people or class. Now, under a free State system, it is being slowly developed, and, strange to say, in a land of such fanatical devotion to diverse faiths, Orthodox, and Catholic, and Moslem are, in many places, being taught together.

Roads are also being built, mainly at Austrian expense, and a successful postal system has been established, while the marriage laws of the community are being guarded so far as the varied religious beliefs will permit. Especially is this the case in connection with that universal practice of the Mahometan—the abduction of young women—which for centuries prevailed to such a merciless extent, and about which a Turkish Pasha, who was once sent to Widdin, in Bulgaria, for the purpose of examining into the violence complained of by local Christians, smilingly, and no doubt sincerely, remarked: "I do not see wh.t these rayahs have to complain about. Are not their daughters much happier in our harems than in their huts, where they die of hunger and work like horses?"

These are now conditions of the past, and great indeed is the gulf between what has been and what may be. To say that a great future lies before these populations under the pact of peace and conditions of confidence created by Austrian supremacy would be stating too hasty a conclusion. Before that happens, differences in religion as acute as ever Ireland has experienced will have to be surmounted, to say nothing of the results of centuries during which the national spirit has been suppressed and the national character degraded. But, none the less, time may bring about the development hoped for by Bishop Strossmayer, and the junction of Croatia, Servia, and Bosnia with little Herzegovina, and still smaller Montenegro, revive in far greater strength the historic empire of Dushan.

Much, indeed, must be accomplished before that dream can be practically considered, but it is by no means an impossible one, and could be quickly precipitated by the rise in Servia of an able ruler who would be willing to accept the nominal supremacy of Austria in return for a *carte-blanche* given him to bring into efficient working union these countries of similar race, but rival religions. Meanwhile Bosnia and Herzegovina are in a position to progress slowly but steadily in national education, in material welfare, and in that patriotism which can only rise out of crystallized national intelligence.

CHAPTER XII.

EGYPT AND THE OTTOMAN POWERS.

With the Egypt of the Pharaohs, the Ptolemies, the Jews, or Cleopatra, the Powers of Europe have to-day little concern. They care nothing about the history which reaches into the most distant antiquity, and includes the conquests of the beautiful land of the Nile by Nebuchadnezzar of Babylon, by Cambyses and Xerxes of Persia, by Alexander of Macedon, or even by the Romans. But with the Egypt which fell under the dominance of the conquering Saracen in A.D. 638; which became then, and has ever since remained, Mahometan in religion; which was the refuge of the last heir of the Bagdad dynasty—the effete, but still somewhat sacred holder of the rights inherent in that family or royal race; which handed those powerful privileges over to its Turkish conqueror, Selim I.; which has seen the struggle between Napoleon and his British enemies almost within the shadow cast by the Pyramids; which has felt the rise of a new power under Mehemet Ali, and its collapse under the Khedive Ismail; which sent Ibrahim Pasha to make Turkey tremble and create a situation of imminent war between England and France; which is now one of the storm-centres of the Eastern Question—with this Egypt they are very intimately connected.

Like every other country which has felt the sword of Islam, Egypt has had a more or less miserable history, and one stained by mingled cruelty and crime. The

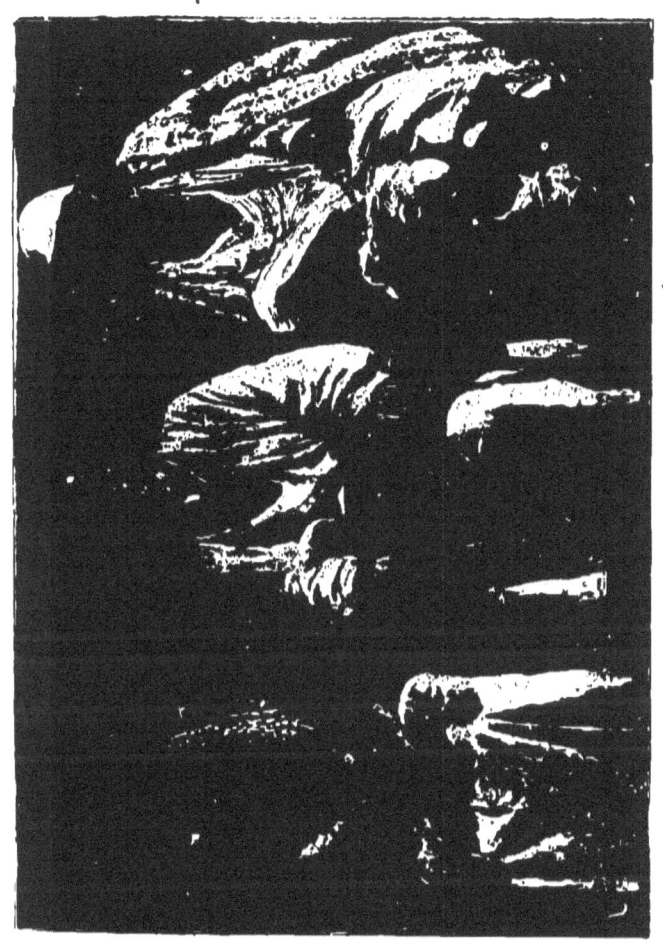

The Riots in Stamboul—Wounded Armenian Women in the Hospital.

Interior of a Kurdish Tent.

records of that singular body, the Mamelukes, illustrate this fact. Like the Janizaries, they were a body of outside slaves incorporated by Mahometan sovereigns into the service of themselves and the State. Unlike them, however, they very early in their career completely overpowered the reigning Sultan and put one of their own leaders in his place. Composed mainly of Circassians; trained to war in its every detail; forming a compact mass of splendid cavalry; and inspired by success with that conquering pride which makes heroes and creates power; the Mamelukes over-ran Syria, and ruled Egypt and part of Arabia, until conquered by the Sultan Selim in 1517—some three hundred years after their first organization.

This successful but barbaric Sultan overpowered Persia, over-ran Syria, invaded Egypt, and at the battle of Ridania defeated by means of his artillery the splendid cavalry opposed to him. Upon the plains lay the bodies of 25,000 Mamelukes, and in Cairo, which surrendered after a three days' siege, scenes ensued which appear almost incredible, and over which Satan himself might have sorrowed. Selim had proclaimed an amnesty to such Mamelukes as would surrender, and on the faith of this promise hostilities ceased, and eight hundred of their chief men voluntarily submitted—and were immediately beheaded. The Sultan then ordered a general massacre of the wretched inhabitants, and Sir Edward Creasy, the historian, estimates an ensuing butchery of some fifty thousand human beings. Under promises of safety, Kourt Bey, the bravest of all the Mamelukes, and a leader who had made even the Turks shrink before his onslaught at the battle of Ridania, was persuaded to surrender. The conqueror received him seated on his throne and surrounded with all possible grandeur.

Looking at him, he said, "Thou wast a hero on horseback—where is now thy valour?" "It is always with me," was the laconic answer. Then followed a prolonged and characteristic interview. The Sultan was aggressively insolent to a fallen foe; the Mameluke was bravely truthful and direct in his speech. At last the end came, and to some question Kourt Bey replied in words splendidly illustrative of Mahometan courage and fatalism:

"By Allah," said he, "we were not overthrown because ye were braver in battle or better horsemen than we; but because it was our destiny. For all that has a beginning must have an end, and the duration of empires is limited. Where are the Caliphs, those champions of Islamism? Where are the mightiest empires of the world? And your time also, ye Ottomans, will come; and your dominion shall in time be brought to nothing. As for myself, I am not thy prisoner, Sultan Selim, but I stand here free and secure, by reason of thy promises and pledges."

But what was honour or a promise to the Turkish Sultan! Amidst a stream of invective from Selim's lips, the head of his manly foe was stricken off by an attending executioner. After some little further struggle, Egypt came entirely into the hands of the Turks. Three thousand prisoners were impartially slaughtered, and the last Mameluke Sultan—the brave and chivalrous Touman Bey—perished under Selim's orders. The latter, by virtue of this conquest, at once became the recognized suzerain and protector of the holy cities of Arabia—Mecca and Medina—and assumed the spiritual sovereignty of Islam, with the titles of Caliph, Vicar of Mahomet, and Commander of all the Faithful. Into his possession also came, through solemn transfer from the last descendant of the Abbaside dynasty of Bagdad, now living a retired life upon the banks of the Nile, all the visible insignia and tokens of that high office. They included the sacred standard and sword and mantle of the Prophet, and gave the Sultan and his successors the power, at certain critical moments, of invoking the aid of all loyal Mahometans throughout the swarming centres of Asia and Northern Africa.

During the succeeding three hundred years, Egypt remained under the rule of various Mameluke Beys and Turkish Pashas. The authority of the Sultans, however, waned as the power of the Empire in Europe diminished, and the Mamelukes revived, from time to time, the local supremacy which they had once made so widely effective. But in 1798, when Napoleon Bonaparte, with 30,000 soldiers, landed in Egypt, and stormed the city of Alexandria, Turkey woke up to the fact that a new and greater Eastern power than any yet established was a possibility, and that even the slight hold she now had over Egypt, and its tributary or neighbouring countries, was in danger of extinction. The vivid imagination of Napoleon had been impressed with the site of Egypt as the home of ancient empires, and there is no doubt that he hoped to found one which might sweep over all Asia and excel those of Genghiz, or Alexander, or Timour, as greatly as the skill of his soldiers and the forces of his cannon excelled those of any which could be brought against him. And, as the great military sphinx of modern history stood in the shadow of the graven Sphinx of ancient annals, we can well conceive the flitting thoughts of Asiatic conquest which passed through his sombre soul.

The first power which would have had to give way was that of the Turk, and, though the struggle between the fanaticism of the soldiers of Islam and that of the more or less infidel soldiers of the great republic could only have resulted in ultimate victory for the genius and artillery of the French conqueror, it would have been a conflict worthy of the blood-stained soil of the East.

But the battle of the Nile and the skill of Nelson saved Turkey, and, indirectly, the Indian Empire, at which Napoleon really aimed. It gave time for an alliance to be formed between England, Turkey, and Russia, and produced the first of the many phases of the modern Eastern Question. Meanwhile, however, Napoleon quickly over-ran Syria, storming Jaffa, and capturing 2,000 Turks, who were promptly shot or bayoneted in great batches of silent and composed victims. His scheme had been to gather around him an immense auxiliary force—which could have easily been obtained by any conqueror in the prevailing condition of these countries—and march straight from the Euphrates to the Indus. Afterwards, Constantinople could be taken.

All these vast conceptions, however, were checked by the unsuccessful siege of St. Jean d'Acre, although his subsequent victory over the Turks at Aboukir left him in complete control of Egypt. But he was disgusted with his only partial success, and, shortly after, sailed to France to found a Western empire, instead of attempting further to realize his Eastern dreams. In 1801, three years after Napoleon's ambitious invasion, the British troops, under Abercrombie, drove the French out of Egypt, and replaced it under the nominal authority of the Turk. While these events were transpiring, Mehemet Ali, one of the most remarkable men whom the Moslem world has produced, was growing in power and position. Born in Macedonia, about 1765, he had served in the Turkish army against the French, and had soon learned the value of European arms and tactics over the antiquated mode of warfare practised by the soldiers of Islam.

Like other Mahometans of ambition, he soon rose to the rank of Pasha, and, eventually, was given the right to wield the nominal power of Turkey in Egypt. But he was not the stamp of man who endures a nominal position for any length of time, and his first determination was to get rid of the Mamelukes. They were still the dominant force in the country, and held positions everywhere, in command of its various districts and divisions. Their rule was harsh enough and cruel enough to warrant suppression, and to deserve the most thorough subjugation for themselves. But it afforded no excuse for what followed, when, in 1811, Mehemet, with a great show of cordiality and hospitality, invited the famous cavaliers in a body to his palace, and there caused them to be slaughtered without warning or mercy. An Englishman, who was in Cairo at the time, gives the following description of what occurred:

"Nothing can be imagined more dreadful than the scene of the murder. The Mamelukes had left the Divan, and were arrived at one of the narrow passages on their way to the gates of the citadel, when a fire from 2,000 Albanians was poured in on them from the tops of the walls, and in all directions. . . . A few almost harmless blows were all they attempted, and those who were not killed by the fire were dragged from their horses, stripped naked, and, with a handkerchief bound round their heads and another round their waists, were led before the Pasha and his sons, and by them ordered to immediate execution. Even then the suffering was aggravated, and, instead of being instantly beheaded, they were not at first wounded mortally. They were shot in different parts of their bodies with pistols, or stuck with daggers. . . . All these, and, in short, every one, however young and incapable of guilt, or however old and tried in his fidelity, the more elevated, and the more obscure, were hurried before the Pasha, who sternly refused them mercy, one by one, until he was assured the destruction was complete."

With the annihilation of these fierce servants and frequent rivals commenced a period of military achievement which soon made Europe ring with the name of Mehemet Ali, and recalled the days when Islam was an active and irrepressible power, flashing the scimitar of the Prophet in the open face of all Christendom.

Assisted by his brilliant son Ibrahim, the Pasha of Egypt sent his armies into Arabia; crushed the Wahabites, whose fiery sectarianism had so long defied the Sultan; conquered Nubia and Sennaar; formed and drilled and officered an efficient army upon European principles; prepared and manned a naval force; improved the harbours, constructed docks and roads, and built the great Mahmoudieh Canal between the Nile and the Mediterranean; and in 1825 responded to the call of his Suzerain by sending an army into Greece under the command of Ibrahim.

Though it was impossible for the latter to really conquer a country which was battling to a man against the invader, he did all that skill and a disciplined force could do in that direction. He recaptured the chief cities and fortresses which the Greeks had won from the Porte; besieged and stormed Mesolonghi, and entered Athens in triumph during June, 1827. But it was a brutal and fruitless war. The wholesale massacres, the great numbers of Greeks sent to Egypt as slaves, the hundreds of pairs of ears nailed over the Seraglio gate at Stamboul, as trophies of success, proved that the Moslem was still a Moslem, whether he called himself a Turk or an Egyptian. It was a misfortune consequent upon centuries of suffering that the Greeks were almost as treacherous and cruel as their invaders. But, then, they were fighting for home and country, for life and liberty.

During the three years after Ibrahim had been compelled—in 1828—to leave Greece by the intervention of the Powers, Mehemet Ali remained quiet, consolidating his authority, and preparing to establish a great Mahometan dominion upon the ruins of Turkish power. That he did not ultimately succeed in building up an empire greater than that of Saladin, and stronger than that of Mahomet II., was due to the intervention of European Powers, and not to lack of genius and conquering skill in himself. He was given the Pashalic of Crete by the anxious Sultan, but was naturally refused that of Syria, for which he then pressed. In 1831, therefore, he threw off his somewhat shadowy allegiance, and Ibrahim, who was at once sent to invade Syria, succeeded in capturing Acre, and in defeating the Turks at Ems, at Beylau, and at Konieh. This last victory placed Asia Minor at his feet, and the conqueror was proceeding to march upon Constantinople, when the Porte appealed to Europe, and received the support of Russia, France, and, eventually, of England.

Naturally, the European nations had no desire to see a new and greater Moslem power installed on the Bosphorus, and the curious picture was, therefore, seen of 12,000 Russian troops encamped near Scutari in defence of the Crescent, and a French fleet hurrying to the rescue of the Sultan. For the time Ibrahim was checked, and the succeeding negotiations ended in Mehemet being confirmed in his governments of Crete and Egypt, with the addition of the Pashalics of Jerusalem, Tripoli, Aleppo, Damascus, and Adana. This was practically the cession of an empire to Egypt, and had Mehemet kept his ambition within moderate limits he might have slowly but surely expanded, and organized his territories into a great and permanent power. But he lacked patience, and, in 1839, once more threw off the Sultan's supremacy, refused to pay further tribute, and again despatched Ibrahim into Syria at the head of a conquering army. This was the last struggle in which the Crescent—carried though it was by a rebel against the Caliph—has been the banner of a brilliant and successful leader. But how different the method of war! Byron has described the old-time victorious Moslem army:

> "The tent is pitched, the Crescent shines
> Along the Moslem's leaguering lines,
> And the dusky Spahi's bands advance,
> Beneath each bearded Pasha's glance;
> And, far and wide as eye can reach,
> The turban'd cohorts throng the beach;
> And there the Arab's camel kneels,
> And there his steed the Tartar wheels,
> The Turcoman hath left his herd,
> The sabre round his loins to gird."

But here all was different, and a Moslem army might be seen, clad to a certain extent in European garments, carrying European arms, and fighting under a leader saturated in European military ideas, though retaining much of the natural Moslem ferocity of character. And at Nezib, on June 25th, Ibrahim defeated the Turkish forces, numerous and well-appointed as they were, capturing great stores of artillery, baggage, and provisions, and inflicting a blow upon the Sultan from which his Empire could hardly have recovered if he had not once again called Christian Europe to its rescue. In July, 1840, England, Russsia, Austria, and Prussia signed an agreement to settle the disturbing questions between the Sultan and his ambitious vassal, in the general interests of European peace. For a time, however, it looked as if France was going to support Egypt, and a general war appeared imminent, in which the Eastern Question, in a most acute form, would once more have to be dealt with under the ancient shadow of the Sphinx.

But, finally, Lord Palmerston and M. Guizot came to terms, and England undertook to act for the powers in Syria. Napier, therefore, bombarded Beyrout; Acre was captured by Sir R. Stopford, assisted by Austrian troops; the Egyptians were driven out of the country; and Mehemet's position ultimately defined as that of hereditary Pasha of Egypt, under the condition of paying a large tribute to the Sultan, and of supplying him, if required, with military and naval forces. This ended the aggressive career of the Napoleon of Egypt, and he henceforth—until becoming insane in 1848, and his death in the succeeding year—devoted himself to building up the internal condition of the country. In this work his energy seems to have been marvellous, his expenditures were almost boundless, his exactions were merciless, and his ingenuity equally striking.

It was, however, entirely based upon an impossible conception. To improve and develop agriculture, to create manufactures, to beautify the country, or to open up its resources, were all alike hopeless when attempted at a fatal expense to the flesh and blood of the nation. The unfortunate peasant or fellah was treated as a slave, paid by a bare sustenance of the coarsest kind, and with hardly sufficient clothing for ordinary purposes. Upon public works he was compelled to labour without pay, and often without food; he was bastinadoed without mercy by rascally subordinate officials; he was treated like a brute, and had to live like a beast; and the lives of thousands were sacrificed to dig great canals, build palaces, or erect works of more of less national utility.

Yet with all his cruel despotism and his personal faults, Mehemet Ali did a great work for Egypt. Had his successors come up to or near his standard, the land of the Pyramids would not to-day be resting under the protection of Great Britain. Since his time, however, for good and evil, his descendants have ruled Egypt in the following order :

    Ibrahim................. June-November, 1848
    Abbas................................ 1848-1854
    Said.................................. 1854-1863
    Ismail................................ 1863-1879
    Mehemet Tewfik.................... 1879-1892
    Abbas II............................ 1892 ——

The events of the half-century which has passed away since Mehemet Ali's death have illustrated anew in Egypt the evils of Mahometan rule. The founder of this dynasty was a great man, and was therefore able to uphold the power of his country despite radical faults in religion and government. But Abbas had none of his grandfather's qualities. A solitary, worthless ruler, living in palaces built in desert places, surrounded by cringing slaves, and wild beasts kept in huge menageries, he lived uselessly, and died from strangulation at the hands of two boy slaves who had been sent him from Constantinople. Said Pasha was directly his opposite in character and person, and appears in history as a bold, frank, and reckless man, fond of society and travelling. In 1862, he visited Italy, France, and England, and in the course of his reign brought the army up to a total of 50,000 men, while forming a singular troop of gigantic Nubians, whom he clad from head to heel in black chain armour and mounted upon the blackest of horses.

The Khedive Ismail was an extraordinary character. During his reign of sixteen years he lifted Egypt into the full light of Western civilization—so far as it could be grafted upon Eastern barbarism ; suppressed for the Sultan a rebellion in Arabia ; received in reward the hereditary title of Khedive, or King ; opened a legislative chamber at Cairo ; visited Paris, and on his return attended the opening of the Suez Canal ; sent Sir Samuel White Baker to suppress slavery in the Soudan ; and increased the national debt from $25,000,000 to $445,000,000. Following the deposition of a ruler whose career had at first promised to so greatly raise his country in the eyes of the world, but whose wild extravagance had ultimately brought it to bankruptcy and ruin, came the succession of French and English controllers of Egyptian finance, out of whose efforts, and the ensuing complications, came the war of 1882, the Soudan campaign, the occupation by British troops and the administration of affairs by British officials.

In the prolonged attempt to disentangle the financial and other complications of Egypt, Mr. Stephen Cave and Mr. Goschen, Mr. Rivers Wilson and Sir E. Malet, Lord Dufferin and Lord Northbrook, Sir H. D. Wolff and Sir Edgar Vincent, succeeded one another in varied action and with varied views. But the man who has had the most to do with the country in the last ten years —the real ruler of Egypt—is Evelyn Baring, Lord Cromer. Like Lord Stratford de Redcliffe in his intercourse with successive Sultans, this British representative knew how to compel Oriental civility and surrender by the utter absence of nerve or fear. He possesses a really marvellous ability in brow-beating the Khedive or his ministers into submission at moments when failure might perhaps involve a European war, or some dreaded international complication. By his influence, and as the result of British occupation, the country is now advancing with leaps and bounds. The national system of irrigation, upon which so much depends, has been immensely improved and extended; the local army has been strengthened and bettered in every way; the iniquitous corvee—or tax upon labour—and the whips used in once frequent punishment of the helpless fellah, have been abolished; taxation of all kinds has been lightened and properly placed; the condition of all classes has been rendered such that prosperity is possible even for the fellaheen themselves; and the finances have been put into such a shape that Egypt can now pay the interest on its huge national debt, together with the tribute to Turkey, and still have a balance for internal improvement or external war.

The leading ministers of the Khedive, notably Riaz Pasha, Tigrane Pasha, and Nubar Pasha, have been compelled to help in this process—the two latter, by the way, are Armenians—and have been described by a recent traveller and author, Mr. Richard Harding Davis, as cultivated, educated gentlemen of refined tastes and wide ambition. But, like all Mahometans, they work better and more wisely under the control of a great Power than they would at the dictation of their own wills, or in subservience to an ambitious and independent Khedive. What the future of Egypt may be is no small part of the Eastern Question, but it is one which England seems to now have pretty well in hand. At present, it suits the British Government not to antagonize European Powers by open annexation, and Lord Rosebery, when Foreign Secretary in 1893, and representing the only party which could ever even consider such a possibility as evacuation, told Lord Cromer, in the course of an elaborate despatch, that:

"All these considerations point to the conclusion that for the present there is but one course to pursue—that we must maintain the fabric of administration which has been constructed under our guidance, and must continue the process of construction, without impatience, but without interruption, of an administrative and judicial system which shall afford a reliable guarantee for the future welfare of Egypt."

Of course, this means that no party in England can ever propose seriously to evacuate the country. There are no Christian interests or population to protect—except some 300,000 Copts scattered amongst the five or six millions of Moslems—but there are the vital factors of a huge financial system, in which British investors are mainly interested; a growing trade, chiefly in British hands; a large yearly expenditure upon objects connected with the British protection of the country; and a real progress which would surely collapse under native government. More important still is the fact that evacuation would, in all probability, be followed by French occupation and a joint Russo-French control of the Suez Canal—one of England's main routes to India. Equally influential is the feeling which has taken time to grow in the British mind, but which must surely have come sooner or later—that Egypt is practically a dependency of England, and that its surrender, for whatever reason, would involve a great loss to the Empire.

These combined reasons make Egypt British to all intents and purposes, and will probably keep her so in spite of Turkish, French, and Russian hostility, or the puny efforts at home of scattered and really uninfluential Radicals, such as Mr. Henry Labouchere. And the intrigues now apparently proceeding between the three Powers named will only ensure this result, although they have had the lamentable and incidental consequence of preventing active efforts in behalf of the hapless Armenians.

CHAPTER XIII.

HISTORIC ARMENIA.

The smothered cry of a suffering race which lately came from the plains of Armenia has shocked the conscience of the civilized world. It has practically revealed to Europe and America the existence of a Christian people, who, for nearly two thousand years of struggle and persecution, have kept the faith and fought the fight amid surroundings of almost intolerable gloom and conditions of unprecedented difficulty. It has revived Western memories of the countries in which Christianity had its origin, and in which, despite the absurd practices and strange superstitions gradually incorporating themselves with the system, it has survived the oppressive sweep of barbaric centuries. And as the dim vista of the ages is rolled back, the people of Christian lands can see in Armenia a record of suffering, and an environment of historic struggle, beside which the massacres of to-day become merely one more dreadful incident:

"Dim centuries that darkened and brightened, and darkened again;
And the soul of their song
Was great as their grief, and sublime as their suffering, and strong as their sorrows were strong."

In the very beginning of the Christian era, when the Turk was a wandering nomad in Central Asia; when Russian power was undreamt of; before the English had begun to settle in Britain, or the legions of Rome had overpowered the ancient Druids; Armenia was a rich

Armenian Peasant Women Weaving Turkish Carpets

and powerful kingdom. It has never been the centre of a great Eastern Empire, nor have its people ever swept like a scourage over the other nations and races of Asia. But it has been at times prosperous and extensive, and during more than fourteen centuries has managed to maintain a more or less nominal independence, and institutions controlled by its own sovereigns and nobles. Yet during that prolonged period it suffered, as but few other countries have done, from the inundation of those vast waves of barbarism which poured out of Central Asia upon the wealthier and more civilized nations of the East and West. Mongols and Tartars and Turks, one after the other, over-ran its territory, oppressed its people, and for the time being subjugated its kings.

Then came the Persians and the Romans, the Byzantines and the Russians. But amid all these continued invasions and onslaughts, and, until the rise of the Ottoman power, Armenia retained its national individuality, and a large part of its ancient territory; its kings held a sort of shadowy authority under various conquerors; and its people resolutely, persistently, and nobly maintained their characteristics and their profession of Christianity. Its geographical situation made the country a natural scene of struggle amid contending empires, its beautiful and fertile plains offered a further attraction to aggressive and ambitious rulers, while its people, actuated by unusually peaceable dispositions and commercial instincts, were not as formidable antagonists as might have been desirable in the interest of their own land. Yet the vitality which they showed as a race is simply marvellous, and the Armenian of to-day—like the Jew of all the centuries since Christ—remains the counterpart of his ancient ancestors.

Few countries have been more richly favoured by nature than historic Armenia, and few have been more cursed by the hand of man. An elevated tableland, culminating in the peaks of Mount Ararat, and broken by exquisite glens and valleys, is watered by the Euphrates and the Tigris, and other smaller rivers, while lakes such as that of Van add to the beauty and value of the country. Naturally fertile and capable of producing grain, cotton, tobacco, and grapes, in immense quantities, its prosperity was assured during any passing period of power and peace. In the days of its greatest and exceptional expansion, the Kingdom of Armenia stretched from the Caspian to the shores of the Mediterranean, and was divided into fifteen provinces, containing a large number of flourishing and important towns. For centuries before the Christian era its capital was Armavir, but in the first century following it was changed to the site of modern Ardashad. The ruins of other cities testify to the wealth and magnificence of its monarchs, and indicate one very substantial reason for the frequent inroad of barbarians.

But Armenia as a country no longer exists. It is divided between Russia, Persia, and Turkey. The Russian portion includes about 1,250,000 Armenians, in what is called the Province of Erivan; the Turkish portion embraces some 2,500,000, in the Province of Erzeroum; the Persian portion includes, perhaps, a couple of hundred thousand. Many more are scattered throughout Asiatic and European Turkey, and everywhere they are a distinct people, with a distinct religion and customs. To understand this marvellous survival of a race, it is necessary to comprehend its history. Yet the annals of Armenia go back to such a distant past and include such varied fluctuations and struggles as to make the study very difficult and necessarily limited by an absence of accurate detail. Their traditions point to and claim descent from a grandson of Japhet, but we first hear of them historically as being conquered by Semiramis of Babylon about four thousand years ago. Tigranes of Armenia was a comtemporary and ally of Cyrus the Great of Persia, and his dynasty came to an end under the conquering power of Alexander of Macedon in 328 B.C.

New dynasties and rulers, however, arose after each conquest, and, though the Parthian and Syrian empires subjugated the country, we hear of a later monarch as receiving the exiled Hannibal of Carthage at his court. At the beginning of the first century before Christ, Tigranes II. conquered Syria and many other provinces, assumed the title of King of Kings, and seems to have been in a fair way to found an extensive empire, when he came into collision with the Romans, and was eventually compelled to submit to Pompey. His successor endeavoured to be independent of the Romans, but was subjugated by Antony and carried to Alexandria, where he was afterwards beheaded by Cleopatra of Egypt. Then follow two hundred years of nominal Roman supremacy, and actual anarchy, varied by the rise of strong individuals such as Abgarus and Volagarses. The former, who reigned as King of Edessa, is interesting as being the reputed author of a letter to our Lord, asking Him to repair to the court and cure him of some disease. It is given by Eusebius, Bishop of Cæsarea, the historian of the Church in the fourth century, and while vouched for by him and by Moses of Chorene, the celebrated Armenian writer, is, of course, doubted by many later historians. But it is a striking document, and the translation may be quoted here as being the first traditional mention of Christianity in Armenia:

"Abgarus, King of Edessa, to Jesus the good Saviour, who appeareth at Jerusalem, greeting.

"I have been informed concerning thee and thy cures which are performed without the use of medicine or of herbs.

"For it is reported that thou dost cause the blind to see, the lame to walk, that thou dost cleanse lepers, and dost cast out unclean spirits and devils, and dost restore to health those who have been long diseased, and also that thou dost raise the dead.

"All which when I heard I was persuaded of one of these two things: Either that thou art God Himself, descended from heaven;

"Or that thou art the Son of God.

"On this account, therefore, I have written thee, earnestly desiring that thou wouldst trouble thyself to take a journey hither, and that thou wilt also cure me of the disease under which I suffer. For I hear that the Jews hold thee in derision, and intend to do thee harm.

"My city is indeed small; but is sufficient to contain us both."

The answer is said to have been written by Thomas the Apostle, and to have been a refusal, based upon the fact that "I must fulfil the ends of my mission in this land." But Abgarus does not appear to have adopted Christianity. In A.D. 232 Armenia became subject to the Persians for a time. Then Tiridates was enthroned by the aid of the Romans, and commenced his career by an acute persecution of the Christians, who were now obtaining a foothold in the country. In 274, however, he was converted, and became the first Christian king of Armenia. For a couple of succeeding centuries the country was the arena of an almost ceaseless struggle between the Persians and the Romans. The former eventually won through the decadence of Rome, and, unfortunately, Armenia became subject to a continuous and cruel persecution of its Christian peoples. This period was followed

Armenia became subject to a continuous and cruel persecution of its Christian peoples. This period was followed by one of incessant struggle between the Greek or Eastern Empire, and the rising Moslem power, while the internal rivalries and strife of native princes added further confusion and suffering to the lives of the unhappy inhabitants.

From 743 to 1079 A.D. Armenia was again an independent country, under the Pagratid dynasty, but in the later years was reduced once more, and nominally incorporated with the Greek Empire. Meanwhile, however, other princes rose into some shadow of former power, and maintained themselves, until in 1080 the Rhupenian dynasty came upon the stormy surface of affairs, and founded a kingdom which lasted for over three hundred years, amid every variety of alliance and tribute and dependence. But whether fighting with the Crusaders or against the Knights Templars; with the Turks of Iconium; with the Saracens, or the Sultan of Egypt; it remained practically the last bulwark of Christianity in Asia.

With Leo V., however, the long line of stormy lives on this most precarious and shadowy of thrones was completed, and the kingdom itself lost and almost forgotten. Prior to his accession the nobles of Armenia had elected Peter I., King of Cyprus, to be their ruler, A.D. 1368; but the latter was in Rome at the time and never cared to assume the somewhat uncertain honour, and the very certain obligations of the position. Not long afterwards Leo of Lusignan, the scion of a well-known European family, accepted the crown, and entered upon a career famous only for its misfortunes. For the last time, independent Armenia came into conflict with the Moslems, and was crushed. In the previous century the country had suffered greatly from the cruelties of invading Saracens, and its kings had vainly sought the aid of various other Christian rulers against their foes.

But now it was compelled to face them in final conflict. Leo did his best to hold and defend the provinces and castles, which one by one fell into their hands ; he called the Genoese, who had considerable trading interests in the country, to his assistance, and they rendered gallant service ; but ultimately he had to flee for his life to Cyprus, from whence he passed to Italy and Castile, in the vain endeavour to obtain aid from these Christian princes for one last effort to rescue his country from the power of Islam. In France he was most hospitably received by Charles V., but soon found that a war which was going on with England would prevent any practical assistance being given him. From Paris, in 1378, he passed to London, and there strove to reconcile the King of France and his English rival, Richard II., with a view to persuading the two sovereigns to join in a crusade for the recovery of the Holy Land and his own restoration to the kingdom of Armenia.

In this, as in everything else he atttempted, failure followed, and the unfortunate monarch of a now miserable and conquered country had to live out the rest of his life in Paris as the recipient of plentiful pensions from the Kings of France and England. And it must be admitted that Leo, though an uncrowned king and the last of a royal line, dwelt until his death in a magnificence and comfort which he could never have hoped for in Armenia. To his tomb—just five hundred years ago—he was finally carried, clothed in the royal Armenian robes of white, with an open crown upon his head, and a golden sceptre in his hand. And, though not himself of pure Armenian race, his black marble monument in the Church of the Celestines none the less embodies the death of a national existence which had endured for 5,000 years through every variety of suffering and over-powering barbarism, while it also marks the marvellous vitality of a race which still survives upon the old soil, and still cries to Christian Europe for aid and succour, as did Leo the Fifth five centuries since.

From this time of conquest by the Saracens dates the migratory movement of the Armenian people. Seeing no hope of a renewal of their independence, despairing at last of relief from the spoliation and misery which they had so long endured, the Armenians began, like the Poles, the Jews, and the Irish, to scatter into other lands in pursuit of peaceful prosperity. Some went to various parts of Asia Minor—which seems like stepping from the frying-pan into the fire—others went to Egypt, some even journeyed to Poland, while many migrated to the Crimea and Russia, where they were treated with great kindness by the Empress Catharine. Others settled in Stamboul itself, directly under the shadow of Islam, but, owing to the influence and protection of the Greek Patriarch—who has always been allowed considerable power by the Sultans—received a kind reception, and soon made themselves at home, and perhaps, in a commercial sense, a little more than at home.

Meanwhile, Armenia itself remained on the rack. Tamerlane, the Tartar, over-ran it in 1383, with all the characteristic cruelties of a ruthless barbarism, while the Turks conquered it in 1516, and held it for a time afterwards, only to be driven out again by the Persians in 1534. They reconquered the territory fifty years later; and, finally, after a prolonged struggle, Shah Abbas, in 1604, surrendered Armenia to the Turks. It was during this conflict that the Persians made a desperate effort to depopulate the unfortunate country, when they found themselves unable to retain it, and to this end dragged off some 22,000 miserable families to Persia. Most of them died on the way, and their bones are added to the myriads which already whitened this pathway of Eastern ambition and religious bigotry.

During these centuries, at times when Ottoman power was in the ascendency, the unhappy people of Armenia were frequently persecuted on account of the national and religious coherence which still survived, as it does to-day. Upon one of these occasions a large number of refugees sought shelter with their historic foes, the Persians. They were at first welcomed by the Shah, and settled near Ispahan, but a little later became subject to religious persecutions from these unorthodox Moslems as severe in their way as those their ancestors had encountered from the Persian fire-worshippers, or which their brethren were still enduring at the hands of orthodox Islam. It seems, indeed, as if such conditions were impossible to escape from, and looking over the past fifteen hundred years, from the days of St. Gregory to those of Sassoun, the conclusion must be accepted that no other race in history has ever encountered such continuous and unbroken oppression.

Following the struggles between Turkey and Persia, which from time to time swept over Armenia, came the conquering shadow of Russia, and conflicts between that great Power and the Persian and Turk. The forces of the Czar, between 1774 and 1812, had acquired Crimea, the country around Odessa, all the vast territory from the Sea of Azov to the Caspian, and Bessarabia itself. All this was stripped from Turkey, while Persia, and incidentally Armenia, felt the same slow but sure progress in the loss of the following more or less important territories :

Mingrelia on the Black Sea..........1802
Immeritia...............................1802
Ganga...................................1803
Karabaugh and Sheki.................1805
Shervan.................................1806
Talish...................................1812
Georgia.................................1814
Erivan, Mt. Ararat, and Etchmiazin, 1828

During these years there was prevalent a very general condition of war. As the Russian boundaries approached those of the Turk hostilities were inevitable, and, though sometimes disguised, were none the less constantly present. After the conclusion of the Treaty of Adrianople in 1829, the Russian forces evacuated Kars, Bayazid, Van, Moush, Erzeroum, and Beybourt, which they had occupied during the preceding war. But, previous to doing so, their commanders, by the use of the Czar's name and copious promises of peace and prosperity and happiness under the Russian flag, persuaded some 9,000 Christian Armenian families to leave the admitted miseries of Turkish rule, for the unknown but assumed benefits of paternal Russian goverment, in that portion of Armenia which remained under its control. The result throws a vivid side-light upon the present situation, and, as in the case of Jews, and Poles, and Turcomans, shows the amount of real sympathy and kindness which Russia has for subject races, or suffering Christians. The Hon. Robert Curzon, an English traveller, tells the tale :

" Over their ruined houses I have ridden, and surveyed with sorrow their ancient churches in the valleys of Armenia, desecrated and injured, as far as their solid construction permitted, by the sacrilegious hands of the Russian soldiers, who tried to destroy those temples of their own religion which the Turks had spared, and under whose rule many of the more recent had been rebuilt on their old foundations. The greater part of these Armenians perished from want and starvation ; the few who survived this sharp lesson have since been endeavouring, by every means in their power, to return to the lesser evils of the frying-pan of Turkey, from whence they had leapt into the fire of despotic Russia."

Without attempting any further comparison here between the historic barbarism of Russia, which in a considerable degree must be admitted, and the absolutely unequalled barbarism of the Turk, this incident may be taken, with many others already recorded, to show the wretched condition of a small Christian people lying between, and amongst, three such nations as those of Russia, Turkey, and Persia. Yet despite the continuous condition of war and invasion, alternated with confusion and persecution ; relieved in many individual cases by migration, and finally brought into the latter half of the nineteenth century by division amongst the three Powers named ; Armenia remains a fact, though not a recognized country, and its people still constitute a national unit. The names of its cities and towns and villages are historic, and are becoming once more known to a Christian world which has had opportunity to change in religion, and government, and geographical outline, half a dozen times since they first came into existence. And its bloodsoaked soil is now receiving the attention and sympathy, and should receive the assistance and armed support, which has been for centuries its due.

To the Christian traveller in the East there can, indeed, be only one other country—the Holy Land—which deserves the interest aroused by the scenes of early Christian life in Armenia, where rocked the cradle of that influence which moulds and makes our modern civilization. And, as he walks its soil, memories of that evolution will be aroused on every side by walled cities or ruined villages, mixed, as they will be, with the inevitably painful and harrowing associations of the immediate present. In Etchmiazin, for instance, he will find the ancient fortified monastery within whose walls has resided for os long the successive spiritual heads of the historic Armenian Church. There, under alien Russian control, he will see the man who is looked up to and venerated by the children of the surrounding soil, whether now planted in European Turkey, in Asia Minor, in India, or in commercial and learned centres throughout the civilized world.

Elsewhere in Turkish Armenia is the famed city of Erzeroum. Existing conditions naturally prevent a large population, and it boasts no more than 30,000 or 40,000 people; but, standing at the foot of a mountain, surrounded with its high walls, and with evidences on every side of the wars and troubles it has had to face, Erzeroum remains emphatically an historic city, which no blight of Turkish rule and massacre can entirely efface. At Orfah, which has recently come into such sad and serious prominence, is the seat of ancient Edessa, the traditional "Ur of the Chaldees," the home of King Abgarus, the centre of subsequent Nestorian influence, the scene of a siege, and capture, and frightful slaughter by Moslems in 1144, and the consequent cause of the second European Crusade. Though a small place now, it is therefore none the less interesting—apart altogether from present associations of massacre and Turkish cruelty.

Of a different type is Diarbekr. It has been described as the ideal of a great ancient city. Dark and lofty walls, seemingly uninjured by time, with massive round towers placed at intervals, surround the dimly seen domes and minarets, and rise out of an extensive plain, bounded on the north by a mountain chain, and swept by the waters of the historic Tigris. Such is the surviving fortress and city, famed in Eastern annals as Amida. Its history is perhaps more Syrian than Armenian, but it borders upon both of these ancient countries, and has been more or less connected with the fortunes of the Armenian race, of whom it to-day contains a considerable population. Bitlis, another historical town connected with recent events, is built upon the steep and terraced sites of a rocky gorge rising from the banks of the Bothman River—the ancient Nymphæus, and boundary between the Roman and Persian empires in the days of Propontius. With its paved streets, bold arched bridges, and stone houses, the town presents a picturesque appearance, greatly enhanced by the rugged nature of its location, and the beauty of the plains rolling away along the banks of the river. As in all these cities, the Moslem population is treble that of the Christian, while the latter element has the unpleasant complication of having constant internal divisions to contend against.

The city of Van, lying upon the banks of the lake of that name, bears the reputation of being the most beautiful, as well as the strongest, place in all Armenia. Its local traditions claim the valley of Van as the site of Eden, and there is no doubt that in the days when a numerous population lived in the fertile surrounding plains, with villages embowered in gardens and groves, and hillsides clothed with oliveyards and vineyards, the lake full of boats and galleys, the farms alive with sheep and all the picturesque realities of rural life, it was, indeed, a beautiful place, well worthy of being the scene of man's first happiness and earliest sorrow. But now all is changed. Van, it is true, remains a great fortress seated amid almost impregnable rocks, as it was in the distant period when

Semiramis is said to have founded it. Beneath it has grown up the modern town, with its narrow, dirty streets, but, all around, the country rests under the shadow naturally cast by a Turkish fortress, and presents rather a sweep of desolation, and a population struggling for a miserable and precarious subsistence, than the old-time valleys of beauty and Eastern prosperity.

Another famous city of Armenian location is Trebizond. Originally founded as a Grecian colony on the banks of the Black Sea, then built up in wealth and magnificence as a Roman possession by the Emperor Hadrian, it was for long the centre of a civilization entirely its own, the seat of a Christian empire, small in population, but great in its gold, and almost fabulous splendour, its pride, and romantic history. Eventually, the place fell under the power of the Turk, and sank to its present position of a small seaport, possessed merely of a useful harbour and some beautiful scenery. The climate, however, is still glorious, and in its vicinity lie countless ruins of the successive conquests of Greek and Roman, Byzantine and Genoese. Its connection with Armenian history is only vague and general, but its streets have lately flowed with Armenian blood, and the little commerce it now has owes much to Armenian enterprise.

But this most ancient part of the known world is full of old-time cities, and ruins, and historic places. Erivan, with its over-hanging fortress, its surrounding valley with the Zenqui flowing through its centre, and the ever-present green domes of Moslem mosques in the distance; Batoum, the object of Russian ambition, the scene of its broken promises, and the present centre of great fortifications; Kars, the most famous of Armenian modern fortresses, and the scene of Sir William Fenwick Williams' prolonged defence; Bayazid and Baibourt, and

Akabad, and Ardahan, and a myriad more places, changed alike in condition and name; illustrate the passage of the centuries, and the storms and struggles of the national history.

Yet, with all its disadvantages, Armenia has naturally been so rich a country, so literally and easily made to flow with milk and honey, that the powers of recuperation amongst its people were Providentially great, and have, no doubt, contributed much to the preservation of their nationality. In some considerable districts, maize, wheat, barley, and oats were grown largely, and with a facility only limited by the local impediments of hand-mills, instead of machinery. Grass and clover were particularly rich and luxurious in many portions, while grapes, nectarines, peaches, pears, mulberries, filberts, walnuts, and melons might be found almost everywhere in more or less abundance. Vegetables were generally plentiful and easily grown, and tobacco of a poor quality, was produced in great quantities, while the water supply has been always bountiful, but in constant danger of defilement at the hands of the myriad invaders and the modern Turkish soldier.

This, in brief, is a picture of the Armenia of the past, and, outside of the miserable yet glorious history of his own country, the Armenian has not been undistinguished. In his various migrations, he has, like the Greek, made his mark upon either surrounding trade conditions or upon the literature of the country he has settled in. During the reign of Queen Elizabeth the north of India was over-run and commercially captured by Armenian merchants, who have left their names upon the tombs of Agra and other cities, while their modern successors have impressed their memories upon the churches of Madras, and even Calcutta, and emphasized their usefulness in the roads and bridges of Southern India. In the fourteenth century there were Armenian churches in China, while present-day colonies flourish in London and Manchester, in Paris and Marseilles, in Moscow and Tiflis.

The riches of Armenian literature are as varied and recognized as is the enterprise of its people. M. Felix Nere, in his learned inventory of the subject, divides its history into three periods, the first of which stretches from the fourth century to the time of the Crusades, the second from that period to the eighteenth century, the third from the year 1736, when the Armenian Mechter founded in the island of St. Lazare, near Venice, the celebrated learned community whose influence has been so great wherever Armenians have been met with. To quote another student of Eastern religions—Mr. F. C. Conybeare—the members of this particular body—

"Have compiled dictionaries and grammars of their language which are monuments of erudition; have printed in beautiful form all the leading classical works of the ancient language; have translated into modern Armenian —which differs as much from ancient as Italian from Latin—all kinds of useful modern books, devotional, scientific, historical, and economic. Their versions of Western poets include Virgil, Dante, Milton, and Byron." And he might have added that to them are due the Armenian professorial chairs at Paris, Berlin, Vienna, Munich, Moscow, and St. Petersburg.

The population which remained at home has not grown in numbers, and certainly not in wealth. Apart from the migration already referred to, the constant state of disorder, the crimes of violence, and the dangers of death, are too marked to permit of anything but decreased numbers, or at least a stationary condition. And a great trouble— the main cause of present evils—is the mixture of races and religions. The following table gives authoritative figures, or at least as much so as can be obtained outside of an honest national census:

Turks.............................. 442,000
Kurds............................. 410,000
Christians....................... 398,000

The Mahometans, it will be seen, are twice as many as the Christians, who are nearly all Armenians, and, in the main, members of the Armenian Church. These figures apply to Turkish Armenia only, and, though purely approximate, supply a basis for understanding the condition of the country.

Leaving these considerations for the moment, however, to turn to the equally vital religious record and characteristics of the people, it may be conclusively stated that no race which has ever suffered and struggled through the centuries, since Christianity first cast its light of life and peace over the troubled surface of the world's society, has so thoroughly deserved the study, the sympathy, and the support of civilized nations, as does the scattered population of historic Armenia.

A Bereaved Armenian Family.

Armenian Mountaineer.

CHAPTER XIV.

ARMENIAN RELIGION AND CHARACTERISTICS.

Like the religion of so many other races and countries, that of the people of Armenia, or of Armenian extraction, is an isolated product of circumstances and national peculiarities. It is Christianity, but with an Asiatic embodiment. It has passed through so many crises and has been environed by so many false creeds and complex customs that some measure of heresy and superstition has naturally crept into the originally perfect conception of the Christian faith. But despite criticism of past and present deficiencies, despite divisions in the Church itself, the history of Christianity in Armenia is a magnificent record of endurance, faith, and martyrdom.

Reference has been made elsewhere to the epistle said to have been written by Abgarus of Edessa to Christ at Jerusalem. Tertullian tells us that a Christian church flourished in Armenia during the second century. St. Blaise and others are known to have died for the faith during the persecution of Diocletian, the Roman Emperor, whose far-reaching hand extended into this as it did into so many other countries. And it was about this time that St. Gregory " the Illuminator " came upon the scene, and by his Christian zeal and powerful preaching converted King Tiridates, and with him a large portion of the Armenian race. They were, in fact, the first people to embrace Christianity as a whole, and make it the national faith. St. Gregory was consecrated Bishop by the Archbishop of Cæsarea, and continued his labours for many years in Georgia and other countries on the borders of the Caspian, as well as in Armenia. For half a century after his death, in 336 A.D., there was confusion in the government and the Church, and much persecution at the hands of rulers under Roman dictation.

But about 390, Mesrob, perhaps the greatest man in Armenian annals, rose into power and position. Gregory had founded the new Church, had endured all manner of suffering and hardships, and had established schools as well as Christian temples. But although much had been done, even to the somewhat disgraceful, and certainly very regrettable, destruction of the carefully treasured histories of various heathen dynasties, much more remained to be done. Mesrob devoted himself to the extinction of the idolatry which still existed; to the unification of the doctrines of the Church; to the improvement of the liturgy; and even to participation in the third Œcumenical Council at Ephesus. In this work he was greatly helped by the successor of Gregory in the Bishopric of Armenia—the Patriarch Sahag. During some troublous centuries a part of the people had used the Persian alphabet and part the Syriac characters. Mesrob restored the ancient Armenian letters, and they once more came into national use. He arranged and promulgated a complete Armenian version of the Bible, and distributed it to all the monasteries and churches of the country—a circumstance which greatly helped to preserve the faith and unity of the nation during the terrific persecutions which followed his death in 441.

One mistake he seems to have made. But it was a pardonable one, resulting from the conflict going on all around him in Asia between the civilization and literature of heathen Persia, and the language, religion, and literature of Christian Byzantium and Greece. Naturally the Greek Church and the Greek tongue attracted the sympathy of the Armenian reformer, and he therefore sent the most talented pupils of the community to study in what Moses of Chorene, at this time termed "the mother and nurse of all knowledge"—Athens. Hence the affiliation of much Armenian literature to the mass of Greek writings, and the effort to retain their religious services in the Greek tongue, which, at a later date, made the masses rather pleased at an opportunity to sever their communion from that of the Greek Church.

It was about this time—the beginning of the fifth century—that the Persians made up their minds to suppress this troublesome people and their annoying creed. It was not an easy task. Elisæus, the historian and contemporary of these wars and persecutions, introduces his record by saying that "whenever the hordes of the Persian king made inroads on the country, the knightly band of the Armenians assembled under their leaders and hastened to give the invaders battle; for the fear of God was great and firmly established in the land of the Armenians." The most remarkable of these efforts was that of Yasgerd, who came to the throne of Persia in 440, and belonged, according to Elisæus, "to the accomplices of Satan." He first issued an order depriving Christians in his own dominions of their goods and property. To use the graphic words of the historian in connection with his subsequent torture and execution of Christians: "The king burnt like the fire in the glowing furnace of Babylon, for his friends stirred him as the fire was stirred by the Chaldees."

In Armenia itself he first tried to bribe the princes and chiefs, by means of gold, and presents, and posts of honour, to abandon their religion. For several years this system was maintained, and then he became "wrathful, sullen, and troubled in soul," and commanded that "all people and tongues throughout my dominions must abandon their heresies, worship the sun, bring to him their offerings, and call him God; they shall feed the holy fire, and fulfil all the other ordinances of the Magi." A Persian was now appointed governor over all Armenia, with instructions to tax and plunder the people into a willingness to abandon their faith. And he appears to have done this until " it was a wonder a village could be left standing." But this also was useless, and then came the final ordinance :

" Before the day Navasart shall arrive, the churches of all places in the kingdom of the Great King shall be pulled down, the doors of the houses of God closed and sealed ; the books shall be taken away and sent to the royal treasury ; the sound of psalms shall be hushed and the reading of the prophets be discontinued ; the priests shall not be at liberty in their houses to teach the people. Furthermore, the wives of princes may be brought to the Magi for instruction ; the sons and daughters of the nobles and of the common people shall be instructed by the same Magi in a public assembly. They shall abolish and overthrow the law of holy matrimony which, according the Christian custom, they have received from their fathers ; and shall cause that instead of one wife a man shall take several."

To this curious mandate—translated, it must be remembered, from Persian into Armenian, and thence into Greek—were added other and more infamous clauses embodying the vile morality of the ancient sun-worshippers. The natural result was a war, which broke out in A.D. 450. At first the Armenians succeeded in clearing their country of the oppressive idolaters ; over-ran, under command of the famous Vartan, some neighbouring territories ; made an alliance with certain wild tribes to the north ; and sent a useless embassy to ask the assistance of Byzantium. The Persian King was very angry at this preliminary success, and swore by a tremendous oath : " I will rid myself of this heresy by a great battle, and by means of great torments make it taste of the cup of bitterest death."

But, in his first battle, the Armenians were victorious, and Elisæus triumphantly observes that " men who are armed by the love of God, though they should be ignorant, spiritless, and cowardly, can endure all sufferings ; death as well as the plunder of their possessions." In view of the result of the second conflict this statement proved eminently prophetic. The battle was won by the Persians, and the historian describes in Oriental style the vast number of the invaders; the glancing of the numerous helmets, which rivalled the beams of the sun ; the flashing of swords and spears, which was like the gleam of fearful flames ; the terrible noise of the whizzing of arrows and clash of shields ; the wrath and slaughter on both sides, and the fall of the heroic Vartan. After this defeat the unfortunate Christians fled into the fastnesses of the hills, and lived in caves, or forests, or in neighbouring lands, where they could obtain temporary shelter. Such is the record of one of the many wars and struggles in which the Armenians were involved because of their faith, and their devoted loyalty to its living principles.

A very important result of this particular persecution was the inability of the Armenian Church to participate in the fourth Œcumenical Council at Chalcedon, where the heresy of Eutychius was condemned. His belief—the main principle of which is a vague admission of the contention that Christ had but one nature, the human having been absorbed in the divine—was supposed to be the faith of the Armenian Church. As a result of what turned out to be a mistaken impression, the ordinances of the Council were condemnatory in tone, and provoked the ensuing severance of the churches. The Patriarch of Armenia, in 491 A.D., publicly denounced the hasty action of this Council, and declared in full Synod the complete independence of his Church. Accounts differ as to the exact reasons for failure in afterwards reuniting the churches, as it is known that Armenian Bishops did attend several later Œcumenical Councils and recognize their decrees. None the less, however, did the Church remain a separate body; identify itself more and more closely with the country and the patriotism of the people; and gradually isolate itself from the friendship and help of the still united Eastern Christianity centred in Constantinople, and the Western branch enthroned at Rome.

The schism was not only regrettable, but is very hard to fully understand. The Armenian Bishops claimed at the time that the separation was due to information received by them that the Council had declared in *favour* of the Eutychian heresy, not *against* it. And at the previous Council of Ephesus the representatives of the Armenian Church had bitterly fought Nestorius, who advanced a much more pronounced form of the same heresy, and claimed boldly that in Christ the divine wholly swallows up and absorbs the human character. They had refused, therefore, to accept the Nestorian doctrines which now have such currency in Asia Minor, and which were then being actively carried by missionaries into Siberia, and China, and India.

This doctrine of Nestorius, and the milder forms of Eutychius, divided the Christian Church in the East far more strongly than it does now, and was profoundly hateful to the Greek communion, which contended that Christ had two distinct natures—the human and the divine.

Whether on account of the mistaken separation which then occurred, or because there really is a natural tendency towards Nestorianism amongst the Armenians, is difficult to decide; but they are now unquestionably esteemed heretical by the Greek and Roman Catholic Churches. The following is the clause in their creed referring to this most controversial point, and it would require more than the traditional "bench of bishops" to deal adequately with its polemical capabilities:

"We believe that one of the three Persons, God the Word, was begotten of His Father before all worlds; that in time He descended into the mother of God, the Virgin Mary; that He took from her blood and united it with His Godhead; . . and that He was perfect God and perfect man, in spirit, in intellect, and in body; one person, one aspect, and united by one nature."

Authorities naturally differ in their analysis of this creed, but, upon the whole, the Armenians may be said to rest, because of its phraseology, under the very grave suspicion, if not condemnation, of the orthodox Roman and Greek Churches. Aside from this matter of theoretical belief, the Armenians have seven sacraments. Baptism involves immersion of the child, and is immediately followed by Confirmation—anointing all over by the Priest with chrism, or holy oil, blessed by the Bishop—and also by the administration of the Eucharist. This is given with pure wine, in which the unleavened bread is steeped, and the words of administration are considered to transubstantiate the elements. Penitence is a sacrament, as also auricular confession according to an ancient and special form of catalogued offences. Ordination of priests, marriage, and extreme unction, are the remaining sacraments, administered as in the Greek Church. And so with the custom, common to both communions, of rigorous and frequent fasts—in which even eggs, butter, milk and cheese are forbidden. Prayers for the dead are permitted—that they may be relieved of their sins—but there is no purgatory or system of indulgences.

The Hierarchy consists of bishops, priests, and deacons. Priests must be married when ordained, but may not marry a second time. These ordinary priests, it must be remembered, are not allowed to preach in the churches, and are dressed in white to distinguish them from the black-gowned celibate bishops and doctors, or teachers of religion. In the monastery of Etchmiazin dwells the Catholicos of the Armenian Church, and from thence come the orders and influence which control the devotees of Armenianism in all parts of the world as effectively as do the mandates of the Pope in the vast circle of Roman religious power. Besides this spiritual head, there is a Patriarch at Constantinople and another at Jerusalem, who have much to do with the national objects of the Church—the holding together of the scattered Armenian people in a religious organization, which strives to retain its ancient liturgy and principles, and almost national form of government.

To return for a moment to the question of heresy. The Nestorian principles do not seem to have greatly divided the Armenian Church, perhaps because its own views were rather loose in that connection. But the creed, or heresy, as it is called, which, of all others, has most divided European Christendom—the Paulician—arose in Armenia during the eighth century and thence swept over Asia Minor into Bulgaria, where it was known as Bogomilism, and into Europe generally, where the Albigenses made it long afterwards famous in the annals of persecution. Armenia itself would have none of it, and succeeded, by the then common method, in persecuting it out of local existence. But elsewhere it throve in forms of various development, and became the predecessor of that radical religious spirit which made the Reformation possible, and inevitable.

Named after St. Paul, because of the stress laid upon his epistles, the sect believed in a God who was the creator of all that was good, and in an evil spirit who had written and inspired the Old Testament in opposition to the principles laid down in the righteously-inspired New Testament. They rejected Mariolatry, did not believe in the physical personality of Christ, and considered the Eucharist, as well as the rite of baptism, to be a mere symbolical function. The importance of such a propaganda, amidst the governing religious elements of that time, can only be understood by a broad outlook, which sees in the bitter ensuing persecutions and the spirit of religious free-thought thus aroused the first seeds of Protestantism, and of those future struggles led by Luther, Knox, Wycliffe, and Huss.

But an influence which had a far greater direct effect upon the Armenian Church than Paulicianism was that of Rome. From the time of the Crusades, pronounced efforts were made to draw the Armenians into the fold of the Western Church. The works of St. Bernard and St. Thomas Aquinas, and other mediæval writers, were translated into the native language, and in 1307 the Armenian King of Cilicia was induced to recognize the Pope, and to fight against the Saracens under a banner which he had blessed. In the eastern part of Armenia a long line of bishops recognized the same spiritual authority through the middle ages, while during the fifteenth and sixteenth centuries a number of Jesuits settled in the country, and finally converted a portion of the population, entered into pronounced rivalry with the national Church, and precipitated several persecutions of its votaries, and consequent reprisals when the opportunity offered. But the weight of Roman Catholic influence was ultimately seen more amongst the migratory Armenians than with those at home. Mechtar was a convert to Rome, and his famous institution at Venice was founded in the faith. In Constantinople, Tiflis, and Etchmiazin i. ., there are Catholic Armenians, as also throughout the entire Turkish Empire. They only number about 80,000 all told, but hold high position through their general wealth and intelligence.

As might be expected under Moslem rule, the more modern history of the Armenian Church is that of suppressed and silent struggle. The fate of the individual under the sword of Islam was always bound up with his religion, and the consequent strength of the national conviction in this case is seen in the fact that persecution of every kind has been endured for centu ', and is still experienced, without shrinking or shifting the part of the people, and despite the fact that acceptance of Mahomet would at any moment lift the individual Armenian into personal freedom, facility for obtaining wealth, and capability of attaining power. And under present as well as past conditions the Armenian Church is not allowed—except at rare intervals—to manage its own affairs, or to build new churches; while the people can hardly be said to have freedom of worship, or the right to educate their children in the Christian faith. It is, of course, a question whether the Turk considers that they have the right even to live.

Meanwhile, as good sometimes results from apparent evil, this process of painful evolution has strengthened the intellectual and competitive qualities of the Armenian, while it does not appear to have influenced his physical qualities. Observers do not all agree in their opinion concerning the race, but the majority are decidedly favourable. The men are strong, well built, and hardy, fond of mechanical arts, but specially devoted to commerce and banking. Crafty they undoubtedly are, and have to be, while submissive and pleasant in manner to the Turk, even though their hearts may blaze with hatred and contempt. But, as Mr. S. S. Cox, for some time American Minister at Stamboul, has said, with much truth, " The Armenians are the sharpest people in the world." He also declares them to be the Yankees of the Orient —with much additional acuteness. And there is a common saying in the East that it takes the wit of four Turks to over-reach one European ; two Europeans to cheat one Greek; two Greeks to cheat one Jew; and six Jews to cheat one Armenian ! An English traveller, the Rev. E. A. Cutts, writing some twenty years ago, after a studious tour through this part of the world, is still more complimentary :

"The Armenians are very highly endowed race ; physically a tall, slender, h ·h-bred-.ooking race, with a very fine type of face ; I was very much struck with the finely-cut features and pleasing expression which was quite general amongst the young men. They are intellectually acute, and of an energetic, enterprising, ambitious disposition. They are the great commercial race of the East. It is said of them that the three degrees of comparison in commercial acuteness are, positive Jew, comparative Greek, superlative Armenian. From a religious point of view they are the most enlightened of all the Christian communities of the East."

He adds the interesting statement that there is a reforming party in the Church which looks with hope to the sympathy and co-operation of the Anglican communion. However that may be, and, to judge by the national weakness of character—jealousy and proneness to fight or quarrel with each other—ecclesiastical differences are always possible, it would be the worst of all policies to encourage any such discord. Persecution and misery have helped to hold the Armenians together in a religious sense despite this tendency, but, had they only been united to the same degree in national objects and loyalty, some at least of their historic sorrows might have been averted. Not very many perhaps, but sufficient to make a difference in the sum total.

In appearance the Armenians are generally dark in complexion, with large heads, and black, coarse, but plentiful hair. Their eyes are black and almond-shaped, with thick eye-brows meeting over the nose, which is large and hooked. The mouth also is large, the lips are thick and the chin prominent, while the bearing is dignified, marred, however, by a frequent want of grace. The women are, upon the whole, good-looking, but amid the unfortunate circumstances of their lives have not learned the value of cleanliness or neatness. They are practically compelled to dress in much the same way as the Turkish women, except in centres like Constantinople and Smyrna, where they mix in European society, dress in the European garb, and bear a considerable reputation for beauty.

Mr. Grattan Geary, who has seen much of Asia Minor, tells us that the Armenian ladies whom he saw in Bagdad were remarkably handsome, and would be deemed exceptionally so even in Western Europe. And he adds the statement that " most Europeans who settle in Bagdad, while still bachelors, fall victims to their charms, and marry Armenian wives." It is certainly an unusual thing in these countries for Europeans to marry the women of surrounding races, and this fact is undoubtedly a substantial compliment to the culture and beauty of these isolated members of a subjugated nationality :

"Lonely and sweet, nor loved the less
For blossoming in the wilderness."

Two-thirds of the Armenian people are devoted to agriculture, or, in other words, to that simple, patriarchal life which the peasant in the fruitful East might so delightfully enjoy—if only his rulers and the surrounding nationalities would permit him peace. They all possess more or less of the ability which makes the other third of the race masters in Asiatic commerce and banking. It is a sort of native shrewdness which finds expression in personal bargains, in conversation and the acquisition of knowledge, and too often in the endeavour to escape from Turkish exactions, oppression, and outrage. To attend a village gathering of Armenians means the hearing of a voluble conversation—not limited to politics, as is the Greek fashion—but dealing with political economy, literature, history, or religion; the crops, the taxes, or the condition of farming; the telegraph, the steam-engine, or some new machinery.

And, despite all that has occurred in the past, the Armenian has not, up to the painful present, really hated his powerful taskmasters. This, perhaps, is his great national weakness. Although individual hostility would only result in personal destruction, yet the race itself is strong enough, extended enough, rich enough, to make itself felt, if every Armenian abroad, as well as at home, would unite in the single aim of obtaining national independence. There are many and great difficulties, but the people is, upon the whole a united one in religion, and language, and spiritual allegiance. And in regard to its possible financial power, a Rothschild is reported to have once said: "Shut up all the Jews and all the Armenians of the world together in one Exchange, and within half an hour the total wealth of the former will have passed into the hands of the latter."

Despair is always foolish, while energy and ambition may make any cause hopeful. Given, therefore, a just and national appreciation of the bearing of these two facts, and the future position of Armenia, with all its splendour of historic endurance and religious sacrifice, is by no means as black as the imagination is prone to paint it, in view of the lurid pictures presented by the sufferings of to-day.

Armenian Monastery near Van.

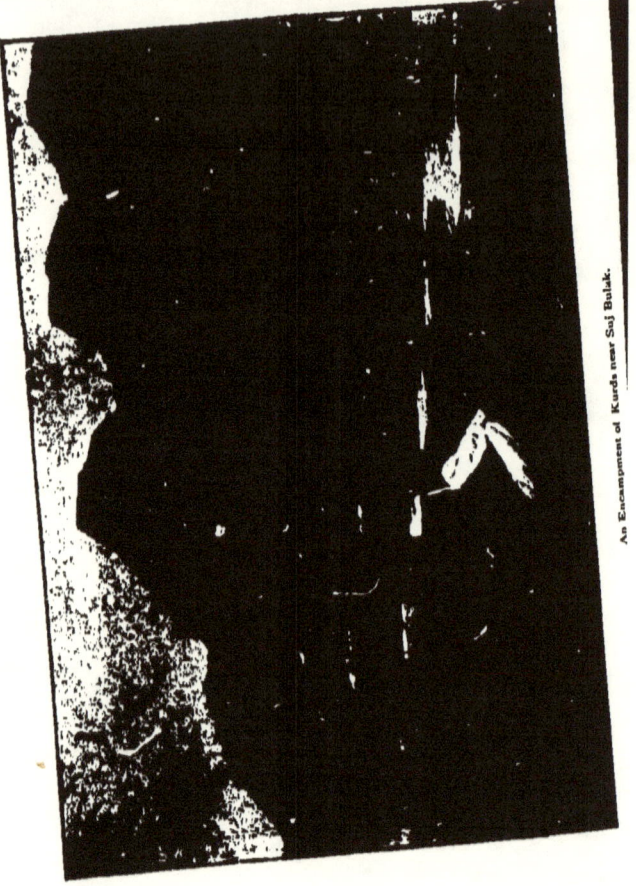
An Encampment of Kurds near Suj Bulak.

CHAPTER XV.

A GLANCE OVER ASIATIC TURKEY.

Around Armenia lie some of the most fruitful and beautiful countries of the Eastern world. Partly to the north and east are Georgia and Persia; to the south and west are the varied territories of Asia Minor, Syria, Mesopotamia, Arabia—all under Turkish sway; to the north also is the Black Sea, from which the Turks of Constantinople claim that everything bad comes—the plague, the Russians, the fog, and the cold. Touching its more immediate borders, as now defined, are Russian Armenia, Persian Armenia, and Kurdistan.

The latter country of mountains and hills possesses a population of wild tribes which seem to be uncontrolled to any great extent by the nominal rule of Turkey in the north, or Persia in the south. They hold the land famed in history as ancient Assyria, and from their fierce Mahometan ranks come the savage hordes which sweep down upon the hapless Armenians, or settle, in a sort of nomadic way, around and upon the Christian villagers in the valleys of their unfortunate neighbouring countries. In 1834, the Turkish Government first succeeded in establishing its sovereignty over a large portion of their hitherto inaccessible territory, and it was then found—somewhat to the surprise of Europe—that there was a considerable body of Nestorian Christians living in and amongst the Kurds. A few years later a Kurdish chief, Bedir Khan Bey, perpetrated the most horrible massacres amongst these helpless people, and served to present to the world the first international illustration of the character and ferocity of the Kurd. It was in 1843 and 1846 that these events took place, and, from what could afterwards be learned, they constituted a determined attempt to annihilate a learned and devoted body of Christians; and, if not actually arranged by Turkish authorities, were certainly condoned and appreciated.

Sir Henry Layard, in his elaborate work on Nineveh, gives us a carefully prepared history of the massacres, in which more than 10,000 Christians, of every age and sex, were murdered in cold blood. Fully half of the Christian population of Kurdistan was thus distroyed, their villages burned, their gardens turned into a desert, their churches pulled down, their learned men specially sought out and killed. In one case a large number had fled to an almost inaccessible place, where they hoped the Kurds might not find or be able to molest them. This is what followed:

"Women and young children, as well as men, had concealed themselves in a spot which the mountain goat could scarcely reach. Bedir Khan Bey was not long in discovering their retreat; but being unable to force it, he surrounded the place with his men, and waited until they should be compelled to yield. The weather was hot and sultry; the Christians had brought but small supplies of water and provisions; after three days the first began to fail them, and they offered to capitulate. The terms proposed by Bedir Khan Bey, and ratified by an oath on the Koran, were their lives on the surrender of their arms and property. The Kurds were then admitted to the platform. After they had disarmed their prisoners, they commenced an indiscriminate slaughter, until, weary of using their weapons, they hurled the few survivors from the rocks into the river below—the Zab. Out of nearly 1,000 souls who are said to have congregated here only one escaped."

Sir H. Layard describes one of the scenes of massacre through which he passed. Upon all sides were skeletons, bones, garments, and other sickening remains of victims, who seemed to be so numerous that the horses' feet trampled over the bones, and he had to give up counting even the skeletons which still continued hanging to the dwarfed shrubs and trees upon which they had fallen from above. "This is nothing," explained the guide, " they are but the remains of those thrown from above, or who sought to escape the sword by jumping from the rock." Many were the melancholy and true stories of these horrors. In one case, ten girls of the village of Serspeetho, as they were being led by the Kurds over a bridge crossing the Zab, threw themselves into the river, preferring death to the terrible fate of Kurdish slaves. And so with many others.

Not long after these eminent achievements a son of Bedir Khan Bey visited the Sultan in command of a detachment of Kurds, and undertook to transform his father's very satisfactory forces into regiments of cavalry which should each be six hundred strong, and should, presumably, "protect" the interests of local and neighbouring Christians, besides further promoting the strength and reputation of Islam. In response, however, to the very vigorous protests of England, and the fact that at this moment he required European aid against Mehemet Ali, of Egypt, the Sultan felt impelled to punish the father—whom he had meanwhile created a Pasha—by sending him for a period to live in the beautiful Isle of Crete. Some years afterwards the Kurdish irregulars were duly organized, and the Kurd brigands transformed into the official and State guardians of the helpless Christians of Armenia and Kurdistan. And the Nestorians have continued to live in constant terror of a repetition of these massacres. In 1888 a band of Kurds did overpower one of the villages, murdered the men, and ill-used the women. The Christians at once tried to prepare for what seemed inevitable, while 8,000 Kurds assembled to defend the marauders, and made another slaughter seem unavoidable. Fortunately, quick action by the foreign consuls and their ministers at Stamboul forced the Porte to bring the necessary pressure to bear upon its amiable subjects and soldiers. Further trouble was averted for the moment, though, of course, no justice was done the hopeless villagers, or perhaps even thought of.

The Kurds are naturally a healthy and hearty race. They live much in the open air, do little or no work, and depend mainly upon local plunder or the products of marauding expeditions. But they are not a brave, or in any sense honourable, people. There have been gallant races of robbers who almost merited the epithet of " honourable," but the Kurd is a cowardly, cruel, unprincipled brigand, with no stomach for a real fight, and no mercy towards the weak or helpless. Yet these men are allowed to prey almost at will upon the Armenian people and other neighbouring Christians, and are dignified in many cases with an official military standing, under the nominal control of civilian Turks who at least sympathize with almost any outrage upon the Christian population. And this, aside from the Nestorians at home in Kurdistan, whose appeal to the Archbishop of Canterbury in 1868 is such pathetic reading in the same connection:

"Moreover, the rulers who govern us are corrupt, and by their careless administration foster violence and oppression. The judges, too, treat the daughters of our people wrongfully. Plunder is committed with impunity; robbers steal, and no one dares to remonstrate; outrage is perpetrated, and the criminals are allowed to escape; felony is rife on the highways, and the felons are screened; evil-doers bear sway throughout the land, and no one ventures to resist them. To such an abject condition has oppression reduced our people that the living among us are led to envy the unmolested dead."

Language of this kind may be said to apply, without exaggeration, to the condition of the great bulk of the two or three million Christians now scattered through Asia Minor, and its historic neighbouring countries. Arabia, with its small, nomadic, and mainly Moslem population, may be excluded from consideration in this regard. But elsewhere, the overpowering mass of ten or twelve million Mahometans, ignorant, brutal, and fanatical, as they are, holds absolute sway over those of alien religion. Of course, there are complications, and some, at least, of the Christian weakness and subservience to oppressors is due to unfortunate internal divisions. The Gregorian, or orthodox and original Armenian Christian, bitterly dislikes the Greek Church. So does the Nestorian of Syria and Kurdistan, while the Phanariot Greek, living upon and through the Turkish Government, hates the Greek who sympathizes with Russia, or affects the policy of looking to Russia for help in the future aggrandizement of Greece. The former class, however, though now influential, is small and intensely unpopular.

Then the Melchite, or Uniat Christian, professing obedience to the See of Rome, and dividing, to some extent, the Armenian, the Syrian, and the Greek Christians, is imbued with strong hostility toward the rival communions. With this class, despite some differences, may be included the well-known Maronites of the Lebanon. Other sects of peculiar Christian types are the smaller bodies of Yezidees in Mesopotamia, Amseyruyehs in Northern Syria, and Sabæans in Chaldea. None of these divisions will work together, and it is questionable if some do not hate each other worse than they do the Moslem. From the true Christian standpoint this is all very sad, and explains in part the absence of progress in Eastern Christendom, while it undoubtedly enhances the contempt with with which the proud follower of Islam looks upon these " infidel dogs."

Yet, they surely have enough to guard against, and sufficiently vital reasons for some kind of friendly combination. The following table gives a sort of bird's-eye glance over the Turkish massacre record of the present century, although figures are unattainable in many of the cases mentioned, and in others an estimate only can be given—under, rather than over:

1822 Greeks in Chios	70,000
1822 Cretans	3,000
1821-28 Greek war (non-combatants)	200,000
1846 Nestorians in Kurdistan	10,000
1860 Christians in the Lebanon and Syria	11,000
1866 Cretans	——
1876 Bosnians	——
1876 Bulgarians	25,000
1877 Armenians	——
1892 Yezidees in Mesopotamia	——
1894-5 Armenians	100,000

The Syrian massacres of 1860 are fairly well known in Europe, and they bear a very distinct family likeness to other Moslem atrocities. The situation in the mountains of Lebanon, where they began, is an historical one, with many peculiarities of its own, but typical, in a general sense, of the war of races and religions prevalent in some form or other throughout Asiatic as well as European Turkey. The Druses, who occupy the southern slopes of the Lebanon, are a brave, hardy, but ruthless race of fanatical Mahometans. Originally, they came from Egypt during the tenth century, and, though the principles of Islam still retained amongst them are few, they none the less are fiercely devoted to the name of Mahomet and the nominal profession of his faith. Their opponents and rivals in settlement, and religion, and race, are the Maronites, a body of some 50,000 Christians, who, during the fifth century, were converted to the doctrines of Nestorius, were afterwards in the service of the Christian kings of Jerusalem, and have since been reconciled to the Church of Rome.

In history the Druses do not appear unfavourably. They have been a gallant race, prone to quarrel with their Maronite neighbours, but fighting for centuries with various invaders, and preserving, in the main, a sort of wild independence. For nearly a hundred years they resisted the Turk—Mahometans though they were—and defeated the armies of the Sultan upon more than one occasion. Many of their Emirs—notably Fakreddeen—were able men and skilful generals. Others, under the Turkish supremacy which eventually came, obtained extended territories and titles. It was not until about 1840 that the rivalry of the Druses and Maronites broke into really active hostility. Eventually, however, a state of desperate civil war developed, in which the Druses were worsted, and finally compelled to migrate some distance from their homes and settlements.

But they waited, and in time their revenge came and was taken to the fullest extent. In this massacre of the Maronites, however—which took place in 1860—the Druses were really only the tools used by the Turkish governor to exterminate the Christians of the Lebanon. Mr. (afterwards Sir) Cyril Graham, who was subsequently asked by the

British Foreign Office to report upon the subject, describes the massacre as a "premeditated and carefully planned scheme" laid by this Pasha—a man known to have long been in the confidence of the Sultan. It was most systematically done. The Druses, who were not already armed men, were supplied with all necessary weapons; the Maronites were disarmed by Turkish regular troops; and the precious combination then commenced their work of wholesale slaughter.

It is not altogether easy to understand how the Druses could have consented to do this awful work. They must have been inspired with the most profound desire for revenge upon their enemies, and the fanatical Mahometanism which permeated their character must have acquired complete control over the nobler instincts which their history reveals. Yet they were not so bad as their allies. Mr. Graham says, in his official report concerning one of the massacres—that at Hasbeya, a large town resting under the shadow of Mount Hermon:

"Many Christians whom I have examined have sworn to me that they saw the soldiers taking part in the slaughter, and the subsequent behaviour of these brutal troops to the women was savage in the extreme. From the wounds I have seen, both on the living and the dead, it would appear that they went to work with the most systematic cruelty. . . . . Women the Druses did not slaughter, nor, for the most part, I believe, ill-use; that was left for the Turks and Moslems to do; and they did it. Little boys of four or five years old were not safe; these would be seized from their mother   d on the ground, or torn to pieces befor   f her grasp was too tight, they would   ia   nd in some cases, to save further tro   , m   r . d child were cut down together. Many women ve assured me that the Turkish soldiers have taken th r children, one leg in each hand, and torn them in two."

Deir-el-Kamar was another scene of tragedy. It was a repetition of the above massacre in all its horrible details. The inhabitants were disarmed by the governor, the men killed, without a thought of mercy, by the Druses and the troops, and the women dealt with as only Turkish soldiery can conceive possible. Mr. Graham says that "almost every house was burnt and the streets crowded with dead bodies, most of them stripped and mutilated in every possible way. My road lay through the town, and through some of the streets my horse could not even pass, for the bodies were literally piled up." His further description is too gruesome to be quoted. In the town of Sidon occurred events which Captain Paynter, of H.M.S. Exmouth, describes in a despatch given in one of the British blue-books. After saying that he had succeeded in saving some 2,200 women and children from the awful fate prepared for them, through the potency of his national prestige, the Captain continues :

"The whole of those wounded were shot or sabred flying from the town after their husbands and *male* children had been slaughtered. . . . The conduct of Osman Bey really appears in this age without a parallel. He first of all induced the Christians to surrender their arms. He then crowded the poor creatures in the courts of the Serai, and for eight days kept them with barely sufficient food to keep life together. And then, when unable to resist from physical debility, he opened the gates and allowed the Druses to rush in and massacre them to the number of 800 men, women, and children. The few that escaped owed their preservation to crawling under the bodies of the dead, and escaped under the cover of darkness."

It was here that the Druses, who, speaking generally, had shared in the killing of the men, but had refrained from the more brutal butcheries, embodied their thoughts in the remark made by one of their leaders—words that should live and burn in Eastern annals: "After all, the Turks understand this work best." Yet, just as Chefket Pasha in Bulgaria; the hero of the Kurdish massacres; and the still more recent exponent of Moslem rule in Armenia; have been rewarded by their Sultans, so Osman Bey, the fiend who directed the events in Hasbeya, Sidon, and elsewhere, was received at Damascus with all honour and triumph, while his chief, Ahmed Pasha, was far, indeed, from losing favour with the authorities at Constantinople.

These massacres in the Lebanon extended to some one hundred and fifty-one villages and to thousands of persons, but they did not close the record of death. A sort of religious fury seized the Mahometans throughout Syria, and the result was a general massacre of Christians, including the slaughter of about 3,500 in Damascus alone. One pleasant incident there was, when Abd-el-Kadir, the famous African chieftain of other days, exerted his wide influence to protect and save many of the hapless Christians. He was successful in numerous cases, and followed up his good work by acts of kindness which won from his old enemy—Napoleon III. of France—the gift of the Legion of Honour.

Such, then, is the general position of the Christian in Asiatic Turkey. As in Damascus and the mountains of Lebanon, so it is amongst the hills of Kurdistan or the elevated plains of Armenia, the streets of Trebizond or the isolated villages in Asia Minor. Life is nowhere secure; honour is of no value; property belongs to the strongest; brigandage is universal; respect for the law—outside of the Mahometan's regard for the precepts of the Koran—is unknown; the rich resources of the land lie uncultivated; and Asiatic Turkey remains little more than a paradise for the Pashas, a home for usury and fraud, a seething hotbed of rival races and religions crushed under the iron-clad foot of the contemptuous Turk.

Yet this cradle of Christianity, and of the modern civilization which has grown out of it, is a veritable mine of natural wealth—a storehouse of golden possibilities. The fertile soil bears from twenty-five to one hundred fold, the climate as a whole is exquisite, the rivers run in every direction through marvellous valleys of natural richness, the mountain ranges teem with coal and copper and other minerals. Almost literallly true are the poet's lines:

> "Whatever fruits in different climes are found,
> That proudly rise, or humbly court the ground ;
> Whatever blooms in torrid zones appear,
> Whose bright succession decks the varied year ;
> Whatever sweets salute the Northern sky
> With vernal lives that blossom but to die ;
> These, here disporting, own the kindred soil,
> Nor ask luxuriance from the planter's toil ;
> While sea-borne gales their gentle wings expand
> To scatter fragrance round the smiling land."

This is indeed the nature of a chief part of the country which stretches in undulating beauty and richness from the Sea of Marmora to the furthest borders of Armenia. But there seems no chance of it being utilized, developed, or made subject to the comfort of its population, under the existing rule—or misrule. It is true that some of the cities boast considerable wealth, that many of the Pashas and higher-class Turks live in great magnificence and that a large trade is done in certain products of Eastern skill and handiwork. Broussa, for instance, has a population of 100,000, is celebrated for the fertility of its surrounding plains, and for the manufacture of silks and carpets and velvets. But it is the seat of a Greek Metropolitan and an Armenian Archbishop, and of many enterprising merchants of those nationalities.

Smyrna is also a large and beautiful town; the head of Asiatic commerce with Europe in raisins, figs, carpets, rhubarb, and silk. But at least one-half of its 200,000 people are Europeans. Konieh boasts large carpet and morocco manufactures; Tokat is famous for the gathering of caravans, and its copper manufactures, dye works, and Turkey leather; historic Bagdad maintains an extensive trade in caravan goods; Bussorah is the emporium for East Indian products; Tripoli, in Syria, possesses a good harbour and a considerable commerce; Beyrout is the prosperous Syrian port on the Mediterranean, and stands on the edge of a plain covered with mulberry and fig plantations.

Damascus is, of course, one of the most interesting of all the cities in this part of the world. Historically famous, it still boasts a population of 140,000, chiefly Mahometans of the most fanatical type, and including a number of Turks who live in unusual splendour. Visited every year by 50,000 Moslem pilgrims, situated upon one of the most beautiful and fertile plains in all Asia, the centre of considerable commerce, the seat of the most famous bazaars, khans, and hospitals in the East, the rendezvous of caravans for Mecca, Bagdad, and other Mahometan cities, it should, indeed, be a great metropolis. And amongst any other people its population would be counted in millions.

St. Jean d'Acre and Jerusalem are mainly known historically. The former is the famous seaport and fortified place at the entrance of the valley which leads into the heart of Palestine, but has only 20,000 people within its present bounds. Jerusalem contains the beautiful Mosque of Omar, built upon the foundations of Solomon's temple, and some thirty years ago contained but a small population, of whom nearly one-half were Turks. It is now increasing, however, through the influx of many Jews.

Meanwhile, numerous ancient cities have become villages, and of those already mentioned very few are growing in size or importance. Nicodemia, on the Sea of Marmora, was one of the largest cities in the Roman Empire, and has now some 30,000 of a population. Tarsus, once so great in wealth and power, is a poor place, with about the same number of people. Trebizond is a mere wreck of the past; Aleppo, though still a large place—as they go in the East—was once second only to Constantinople and Cairo. And these are all the centres worthy of mention in a population of some 15,000,000, placed amidst the richest of Oriental countries, and surrounded or touched by the seas which control the commerce of Europe, Asia, and the distant East. The Mediterranean and the Black Sea wash the shores of Asiatic Turkey, while dependent Arabia, though not included in this general consideration, brings them into touch with the Red Sea, the Persian Gulf, and the Indian Ocean.

Such are the Asiatic lands which have been marred, and stunted, and well-nigh destroyed by the sword of Islam and the rule of the Turk. Development is impossible where every animal and shrub, every bushel of grain or crop of figs, every olive grove or vineyard, every productive possibility or attempted enterprise, is almost taxed out of existence, or prevented from coming into profitable shape by the desire to avoid almost inconceivable burdens. And when universal disorder and individual oppression are added to these difficulties, the backward condition of the countries which environ the supposed Garden of Eden, and include the admitted gardens of the East, is easily comprehended.

CHAPTER XVI.

CHARACTERISTICS OF THE TURK.

Upon the present characteristics and nature of the Turk depend the future of Ottoman power in Europe, the possibilities of progress in Asia Minor, the hope of liberty and life in Armenia, the security and happiness of all the Christians now suffering under the banner of the Crescent. What his characteristics have been is written upon every page of Ottoman history, and upon many leaves of Christian annals. As thus exhibited, the leading features of the Turkish character have been religious fanaticism, intense pride, dogged bravery, a curious fatalism, an almost boundless corruption, and apparently uncontrolled sensuality.

To his religion the Turk has been, and is, profoundly devoted. It matters not that his conception or point of view has entirely changed, and that qualities, such as military aggressiveness and conquest, which Mahomet made paramount, he has now rendered distinctly subordinate. To him Islam is still the great religious force of the world; its dictates, as understood in the face of present necessities, are absolutely final; its sacred book is still the miracle of the ages. Yet in his sombre sentiments he hardly does justice to the better elements of his faith. Mahomet himself was not altogether intolerant, was inclined to treat Christians with respect and consideration, and was certainly a believer in the benefits of literature and learning. And this may be said without

Types of Armenian Refugees from Sassoun

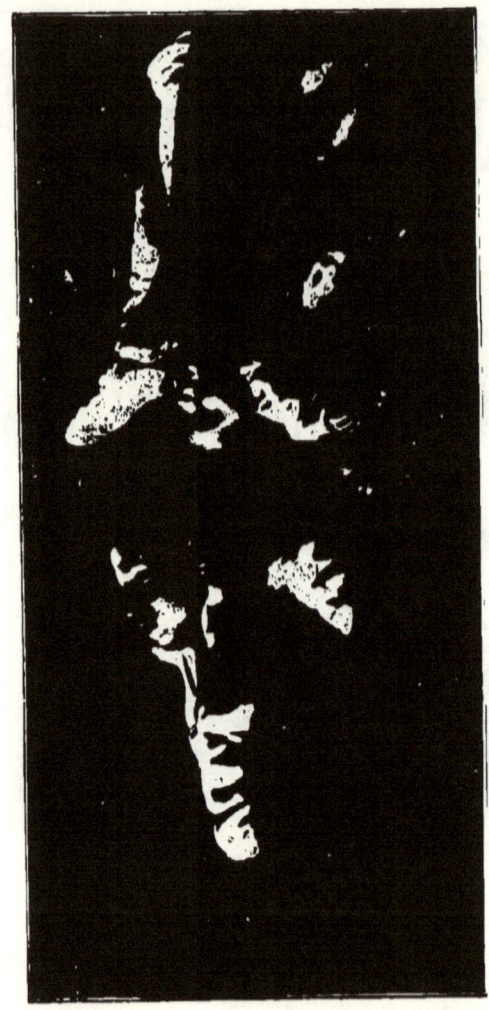

accepting Carlyle's greatly exaggerated conception of him as a Hero-Prophet.

To Arabia, it must also be admitted, Mahometanism has been a blessing rather than a curse. Though dead in the eyes of the modern world, and without the most fitful signs of a national existence, the Arab of to-day has still many noble instincts and qualities, while the Arabs of Moslem history present the picture of a roaming shepherd people becoming, to quote Carlyle, world-notable and world-great. Within a single century after Mahomet' appearance, "Arabia is at Grenada on this hand, hi on that; glancing in valour and splendour and of genius, Arabia shines through long ages over at section of the world." All the products of Islam, :fore, have not been bad. The Moors of Spain, and lovely buildings and gardens of the Alhambra; even many features of the Turkish reign of Solyman the Magnificent, prove the contrary.

And this despite the fact that Mahomet gave way in his curious mingling of sincere conviction and ambitious design to some of the worst elements in the Arabian character, and—as it turned out—to some of the most dangerous qualities of their Ottoman successors. He encouraged the Arab's contempt for human life; sympathized with his personal and extreme vanity; encouraged his free-booting tendencies by preaching war, which might be religious in nature, but must inevitably be predatory in result; promoted the slavery which Arabians loved by giving them the victims of conflict, whose lives might be spared; encouraged by his domestic system the natural licentiousness of an Eastern race.

Yet although this creed might be "a sentence of perpetual barbarism," as some modern writer has termed it, and really did contain within itself all the seeds of tyranny, cruelty, immorality, and national death, such results were not clearly visible upon the Arabs or Saracens, and are hardly discernible in the Bedouins of to-day. This statement, of course, must be taken with a clear recollection of the difference between the people and customs of Europe and Asia, both then and now.

But upon the Turk and the majority of the Mahometan races under his government the influence of this religion has been in the main evil—hopelessly evil. There seems to have been something in the nature of the Ottoman which developed the worst characteristics of Islam, just as some soils will grow weeds in rank luxuriance and refuse to give more useful or beautiful plants the slightest root. His fanaticism became cold and cruel and cowardly in its application, while that of the Saracen was hot-blooded and sincere, but, as many memories of the Crusades have indicated, neither studied in practice nor dishonourable in its nature. Hence the almost unbearable characteristics of modern Turkish massacres—the natural successors of a long series of forgotten but deliberate efforts at the destruction, rather than the mere conquest, of Christianity.

The intense pride of the Turk is another clear development of his creed. There is, according to the Koran and his own profound belief, but one God, with Mahomet as his Prophet, and the Turks as his chosen people. Similar beliefs, in varied detail, have actuated other nations; but in none has the feeling of religious pride so completely dominated the individual life and been so absorbed into the personal character. The pride of the old-time Jew, and the haughty manner of the Spaniard in his days of greatness, were undoubtedly affected by religious sentiment; but in neither case did this pride become so completely a part and parcel of the daily life and action. It is a deep-rooted, instinctive, national, and personal disdain of all other peoples, and contempt for all other religions.

> "The race of Mussulmen
> Not oft betrays to standers-by
> The mind within, well skilled to hide
> All but unconquerable pride."

It is felt by the most apparently liberal Turk, as by the openly bigoted one. A Christian of any type or country is to him merely "a dog of an infidel." For the sake of policy he may treat him graciously, and converse with him in that courteous manner which most Oriental peoples of culture possess in rare perfection, but he will at the same time mumble prayers for pardon of his sin in thus communicating with an unbeliever. In this connection an amusing, but characteristic, and no doubt true, story is told of one of Lord Stratford de Redcliffe's secretaries, and the Sheik-ul-Islam of the period. The Secretary was a somewhat original character, and on being sent one day to have an interview with the great official of the Moslem world found that individual at his devotions. He therefore sat down and waited patiently until the Grand Mufti had finished his prayers, with the request to Allah that he might be forgiven, as a true believer, the sin of holding direct communication with a Giaour. Then rising from his knees the Turk smilingly welcomed his guest. But the Secretary, in his turn, begged permission to perform his devotions, and then and there gravely went through an Arabic formula, ending by begging Allah to forgive a good Christian the crime of visiting "a faithless dog of an infidel." With Turkish impassiveness, the venerable official accepted the insult, but he was obviously and naturally nettled.

This pride takes many forms besides that of comtempt for the Christian. It makes the Turk pleasantly condone, or admire, or commit crimes against the persons of those professing other religions, at which Christendom fairly shudders. But, at the same time, it occasionally promotes a devotion to his faith amongst the humbler classes of the people which might be worthy of even Christian emulation. The long, weary, painful pilgrimages to Mecca and Medina are well known, and travellers in Asiatic Turkey are equally familiar with the bands of thinly-clad, pale-faced youths, struggling and starving in the endeavour to reach some distant and renowned seat of learning. " There is no god but God. I bear witness that there is no god but God," lay gasping one of these young men whom Mr. William Gifford Palgrave found by the dusty roadside, in southern Analotia, on a hot summer day. " Dying," he continues, "of sheer exhaustion, amid half a dozen companions, travelling students like himself, unable to afford any help but the support of their own lean arms and repeated assurance of Paradise. One of our attendants hastened to fill a leathern cup from a neighbouring fountain, and put it to the mouth of the lad, if that might revive him. ' There is no god but God' repeated he, as the water trickled back from his lips ; a few instants later he was dead."

Yet such is the curse of Islam that had this honest and devout youth lived to become a Mollah, or Mufti, or Cadi, he would have encountered every conceivable temptation to iniquity and corruption, to say nothing of the mental narrowness, and hardening of the very soul, which accompanies a complete course of Moslem "higher" education. The pride, therefore, which in a Christian or civilized European helps to promote personal morality and develop individual culture, whilst encouraging national sentiment and patriotism, finds its chief expression in the Turk through the medium of indifference to the sufferings of others, cruelty of conduct, gross injustice to inferiors and aliens, falsehood and duplicity in his international affairs, ignorance of any patriotism outside of his own religion. It is this pride also which finds expression in the unchangeable canons of the Multka—a book which ranks higher in Moslem law than Coke or Blackstone in British courts, and, in following the Koran, emphasizes its precepts, and rules the legal decisions and appeals of the Turkish Empire. It is this pride which the following mandate or principle so fully embodies:

"And the tributary (or Christian) is to be distinguished in the beast he rides, and in his saddle, and he is not to ride a horse; he is not to work at his work with his arms on; he shall not ride on his saddle like a pillion; he shall not ride on that except as a matter of necessity, and even then he shall dismount in places of public resort; he shall not wear clothes worn by men of learning, piety, and nobility. His women shall be distinguished in the streets and at the baths, and he shall place in his house a sign or mark so that people may not pray for him or salute him. And the street shall be narrowed for him, and he shall pay his tribute standing, the receiver being seated, and he shall be seized by the collar and shall be shaken, and it shall be said to him, 'Pay the tribute, O tributary! Oh, thou enemy of God!'"

Of Turkish bravery history leaves no doubt, and its military expression has come down to the war of 1877 and the exploits of Omar Pasha. But since the days of Mahomet II., and Solyman the Magnificent, when a declaration of war would ring through the Moslem world from the Euphrates to the Danube, from the Crimea to the Peloponnesus, and bring under the green banner of the Prophet vast hordes of splendid soldiers—trained in battle and kept in the finest condition—its efficiency has vastly decreased, and even its quality has become deteriorated. Turkish courage in these days of massacre is hardly the same as when the sword of Islam was handled by men prepared to devote property, and person, and life to the cause. Massacres were committed then as now, and atrocities perpetrated which make the blood of modern peoples run cold, but it was done when the passions of a conquering and barbarous race were aroused—so far as they could be—by war and battle and the words of the Prophet, "In the shade of the crossing scimitars there is Paradise."

Even in those days, however, when the Turk is seen at his barbaric best, there was something inhuman in his brutality. Mahomet, the conquering Sultan, with all his brilliant qualities, was as cruel in his Hungarian campaign, as was Selim afterwards in Egypt, or Solyman at Vienna, or Amurath in Persia. Certainly, it would be hard to equal in all history the following enactment by Mahomet II.:

"The majority of my jurists have pronounced that those of my illustrious descendants who ascend the throne may put their brothers to death, in order to secure the repose of the world. It will be their duty to act accordingly."

Barbarism of this nature is not true courage, any more than the massacres in Bulgaria or Armenia were acts of bravery. But it indicates a certain boldness of character, derived from profound bigotry of faith, and capable, under certain conditions, of being transmuted into great deeds and brilliant qualities. Christianity might have made the Turks a noble nation, but, unfortunately, they came too soon under the malignant effects of a religion which changed their strong and masculine barbarism into a cruel and merciless fanaticism.

The fatalistic ideal implanted in Islam has had much to do with this. As worked out in the practice of centuries upon the character of an Oriental race—which originally seems to have been docile to its leaders, but ferocious towards its enemies—the principle of belief in the over-ruling decrees of a Providence said to have ordained everything from the beginning,and to have created immutable future conditions which no man can change of his own volition, has apparently developed every Turkish defect and smothered almost every beneficial aspiration. Under the Eastern conception of things, this doctrine has grown into a feeling that everything depends upon Allah; nothing upon man. Outside of the forms, and ceremonies, and observances ordained by the Prophet, it is therefore felt that exertion is useless, ambition to do good absolutely fruitless, obedience to the Koran only of service. The rest must be left to fate, to "Kismet," to the one God.

Under such a code of life, character, morals, and energy alike decayed, and became merged in the fatalistic Turkish personality, and conduct, and government of past and present experience. This feeling, as well as the word Kismet, permeates, indeed, the private condition and national position of the Turk. It has lost him battles before they were really lost. It has made him brave under the most desperate circumstances, but with a dogged, unreasoning sort of bravery which has been more useless than beneficial. It has been the cause of prejudices fatal to health, of indolence in conditions which created disease and sweeping epidemics, of ignorance and industrial stagnation. It makes him rely upon the rain to keep his streets clean, upon the dogs to act as scavengers, and the sun to make the roads passable, in countries which, above all others, require acute and active human agencies to avert pestilence and promote the comfort of the wayfarer.

It has made the common people submit to the exactions and rules of an endless series of corrupt Pashas. It has made both masses and classes accept the government of Sultans such as Amurath the Manslayer, or Ibrahim the Cruel. It has enabled a Turkish writer, Rycaut, to say, at the close of the seventeenth century, that "the Grand Seignior can never be deposed or made accountable to any for his crimes, while he destroys causelessly of his subjects under the number of *a thousand* a day." It has made very many victims submit with utter impassiveness to death at the Sultan's hand or by his orders, in the hope of consequent eternal felicity and a heaven of houris. It has made the masses idle, lazy, and gradually impoverished, and the upper classes equally idle, entirely unenterprising, and naturally corrupt.

Of this corruption there is hardly a page in Turkish history since the reign of the great Solyman without disgraceful and injurious evidence. What has been already said upon the past in these pages and in this connection need not be amplified, but the present requires some consideration. Nassau W. Senior, an acute English writer and observer, after travelling through the Turkish Empire, declared that "all the faults of the Asiatic are exaggerated in the Turk. Whatever be his purpose, he uses the means which require the least thought. If he has to create a local government, he simply hands over to the Pasha all the powers of the Sultan. If he wants money, he takes it wherever he can find it; and if he cannot get it by force, he puts up to auction power, justice, the prosperity, and indeed the subsistence, of his subjects."

From the Sultan down everything festers with corruption. The recent Caliphs of the Moslem world have been as much purchased by Russian gold, or English loans, or European promises of aid, as are their own local honours and high positions by obsequious Pashas and rich intriguers of the present moment. The Turkish national income is obtained from customs dues—wide corruption in the collection; from tithes upon all agricultural produce—subject to unlimited corruption and oppression; from the sale of certain articles, such as salt, which become Government monopolies; from innumerable petty imposts, and from capitation and exemption taxes levied upon Christian subjects. All these means of revenue are more or less "farmed out" to collectors who embody every possible element of corruption and dishonesty, of evasions and petty persecutions. Salaries in Government departments are always in arrears, the compensation being fees—and a further development of the same public disease.

The Pashas and governors in most cases buy their posts, and have naturally no code of fiscal honour in dealing with their subjects. The people, therefore, have frequently to pay not only Government legal taxes—a part only of which ever reach their destination—but also the special demands of their precious local rulers. Even the best known Turkish statesmen, men who have had reputations in Europe as would-be reformers, were jobbers to a greater or lesser extent. Reschid Pasha, for instance, is said to have sold himself, while acting as Grand Vizier, large tracts of public land at low prices. He was thus enabled to build a palace costing a million dollars and to sell it to the Sultan, who afterwards made his daughter a present of it, and married her to Reschid's son. One good turn deserved another.

The result of all this is apparent in the Turkey of to-day. Mr. Blunt, for twenty years Consul at Salonika, has stated that "the poorer, the humbler, the Turk is, the better he is; as he mixes with the world, and as he gets money and power, he deteriorates. In the lowest class I have *sometimes* found truth, honesty, and gratitude; in the middle classes, seldom; in the highest, never. Even the lowest classes are changed for the worse." Sir Henry Lytton Bulwer (Lord Dalling and Bulwer), writing in 1858, declared that:

"Wherever the Turk is sufficiently predominant to be implicitly obeyed, laziness, corruption, extravagance, and penury mark his rule; and wherever he is too feeble to exert more than a doubtful and nominal authority, the system of government which prevails is that of the Arab robber and the lawless Highland chieftain."

Intimately associated with this corruption, with the general condition and future of the Turk, with his domestic system and religious code, is the question of morals. Upon this subject, perhaps the less said the better. What must be stated in order to understand that the race is deteriorating in physical power, endurance, and fighting strength, year by year, is the conclusion—forced upon the student of Moslem affairs by a host of independent writers*—that immorality in its worst forms is engrained in the whole structure of Ottoman life, private as well as national.

Every one in Christian lands is aware how much the well-being of a nation, the progress, and strength, and happiness of a people, depend upon the elevation, and education, and character of its women. Under the laws and customs of Islam, however, woman is hopelessly degraded into the mere slave of the man who calls himself her husband. Absolutely ignorant, unutterably frivolous, naturally incapable of thought, and untrained in any principle of honour or Christian morality, she is yet the custodian and constant companion of her children until

*Sandwith, Denton, Porter, Nassau Senior, MacColl, Barkley, Badger; Leveson, Bianconi, Burton.

they arrive at maturity. Amid such surroundings—further contaminated, in the case of the well-to-do, by complete control over the slaves of the household—it is little wonder if the youthful Turk grows up without principle, or knowledge of any right or wrong, outside the Koran and the dictates of his own will.

There is, unfortunately, no doubt as to the consequences of this system of polygamy, slavery, and female degradation. The modern Turk is immoral beyond description, and vice has reached down until the whole nation is permeated with it. The late Earl of Carlisle, in writing his diary of Turkish travel, had to say that, upon this subject, "I debar myself from entering." And so it must be here. But, naturally, a condition of things worse than that which once prevailed in the ancient Cities of the Plains is having a grave effect upon the present and future of the Ottoman Power. It is this which has really been the chief, though least known or understood, cause of Turkish decadence and weakness. Other factors have been outlined, but they were practically collateral to the unpleasant and apparently hopeless evil, caused by a combination of Mahomet's domestic injunctions with natural Eastern profligacy.

Hence the present condition of a race which is decreasing in numbers year by year; which is gradually giving way in wealth, and influence, and power, before other peoples—only kept in control by historic terror, recurrent massacres, and armed force ; which is becoming more and more effeminate in expression and character ; which, while retaining a fine appearance, is none the less physically weak, and lacking in that elasticity and vitality so necessary in either individuals or nations—the living, breathing force which makes them factors in the whirling work and achievements of the modern world. To quote Lord

Carlisle's summary and survey of the Turkish situation as he saw it is to embody the national result of this decadence of a race:

"When you leave the partial splendours of the capital, and the great State establishments, what is it you find over this broad surface of a land which nature and climate have favoured beyond all others, once the home of all art and all civilization? Look yourself—ask those who live there; deserted villages, uncultivated plains, banditti, torpid laws, a corrupt administration, a disappearing people."

Of course, the Turk in many individual cases, in some sections of the empire, in some special occupations, in some given direction or achievement, has good qualities, and is free from vice, is averse to cruelty, is not corrupt. Amongst some classes of certain communities, avarice or stinginess is rare. Amongst many, hospitality is a common virtue, and courtesy is delightfully embodied. But these qualities are largely limited in application, and mainly confined to Moslems and influential visitors. Content in his position, and absence of the restless dissatisfaction which marks Europe or America, may also seem a good quality, but it is too often based upon natural indolence or religious fatalism. An excuse for lack of enterprise may, of course, be found in the laws of the Koran, which prohibit the receipt of interest or percentage; which limit exchange, contracts, and bargains; which prevent insurances, annuities, and speculation; which restrict commerce and business, so far as all devout Moslems are concerned.

But, taken altogether, the Turk has been singularly unfortunate in his religion; the religion has been equally unfortunate in being too adaptable in its worst and lowest elements to the character of the Turk. As already pointed out, Islam has not had this fatal effect upon the Arab.

It has left the Mahometans of India a rather noble race of men, and infinitely superior to the Hindoos and other natives. It has not destroyed the capabilities and industry of the Turcomans. On the other hand, it has had an injurious effect upon the Persians; has brutalized the Kurds and the Circassians; has turned the natives of the Soudan into ruthless slave-drivers; has degraded the Hungarians, Poles, and other Europeans who have been, from various causes, perverted or converted; has made the Bosnian Beys cruel beyond belief.

The Turk, however, is now the principal product and representative of Islam. By his character it must, in the main, be judged, and to judge it in this cas its fruit is to almost wholly condemn both, and to ⌐aim the Turk an individual curse and an interr ational ⌐isgrace.

CHAPTER XVII.

GREAT BRITAIN AND THE OTTOMAN EMPIRE.

It is one of the apparent marvels of history that any tie of sympathy, or element of friendship and alliance, should have subsisted during nearly three hundred years between the Turk and the Briton. To the ordinary observer in these later days, there seems an utter absence of substantial basis for such a sentiment or united action. The dark creed of Islam, with its domestic institutions and national attributes, is absolutely antagonistic to the light of British Christianity and the beautiful home life of the English people. The despotism inherent in the Turkish government and character is entirely opposed to every principle and action of the average Briton. The natural cruelty, fatalism, and sensuality of the Turk finds no counterpart, nor the slightest chord of sympathy, in the character of the British race.

Yet Great Britain has supported Turkey upon many occasions. She drove the forces of Napoleon out of Egypt; encountered all the terrible evils of the Crimean war; compelled the French to give up Syria in the early forties; faced the danger of war with Russia in 1878; and has lately declined to intervene at the point of the sword in Armenia—all for reasons connected with the maintenance of Turkish power. On the other hand, she has made commercial treaties with Turkey; has practically taken Egypt out of its hands; has devoted an enor-

Stratford Canning, Lord Stratford de Redcliffe.

Rt. Hon. George J. Goschen, M.P.
First Lord of the Admiralty—Special Ambassador to Turkey, 1880-81.

mous amount of diplomatic toil and strenuous exertion to attempts at reforming its internal government; has helped the freedom of Greece, and increased the territory of that power at the expense of the Turk; has supported the extension and independence of the Bulgarian state.

The reasons for this curious condition of affairs are threefold in their nature, and include the question of British trade in the Levant and waters bordering upon Turkish territory; British hostility to Russia and its known designs upon Constantinople; British interests in India and the far East. It was long before England had any territorial foothold in the Mediterranean, or much territorial interest in Asia, that the natural enterprise and trading spirit of her citizens brought her goods and ships along the shores of Turkey, and into the rich waters of the Levant. In 1579 it was found that the British commerce in that part of the world required some protection and recognition against the innate violence of Turkish power, the cupidity of Turkish authorities, and the prejudices of a Moslem population. Hence a treaty of commerce between the land of Elizabeth and the country of the debauched Amurath III. A couple of years later the charter of the first great Levant Company was given in London, and resulted in the rapid growth of a trade which for a time rivalled in importance that of the more famous East India Company. For the protection of this commerce other arrangements were entered into from time to time with the Turk under the name of capitulations.

British trade with Persia and the countries of Asia Minor; with Turkey and the countries lying within its fluctuating European borders; with Hungary and parts of Austria, and the rising Russian power; was all more or less affected by these arrangements, and by the fact that Turkey was then, and has ever since been, a believer in low customs duties. An English minister was for the first time appointed to reside at the court of the Grand Seignior—as the Sultan was then frequently termed—and in a treatise published in 1621 it is stated that England maintained the most profitable trade of all the countries of Europe in those seas. But in view of the considerable commerce of Venice at this period, it is probable that the writer referred to the profit of the trade and not its value in bulk. Since then, with the various fluctuations incidental to such a commerce and to the rise and fall of important corporations like that of the Levant, its growth has been well maintained. In 1854 British imports from Turkey, Moldavia, Wallachia, Egypt, and Syria amounted to £6,131,000, and the exports to £4,475,000. In 1889, with the exception of Syria, which has but little external commerce now, these imports were £17,372,000, and the exports £10,746,000.

While this commerce was, and is, of value to England, it did not in itself afford much of a basis for co-operation between the powers. But in times when commercial hostility to England was at the root of a great number of international complications, the fact that Turkey went out of its way to open its ports, and to act generally on the principles of free trade, undoubtedly served as a means of bringing the two otherwise antagonistic peoples into friendly relationship. And in these later days, when European and American and Asian rivalry has taken the natural form of high protective tariffs, the attitude thus maintained by the Turkish Empire has helped in continuing a friendly feeling which might otherwise have developed into one of intense hostility.

It certainly afforded an opportunity for the establishment of diplomatic intercourse, and, as far back as 1621, we hear of Sir Thomas Roe arriving at Constantinople as ambassador from King James the First. The following extract from his speech to the Sultan explains the import of his mission:

"His Majesty hath commanded me to offer himself as a mediator of peace to accommodate the late breach with the Kingdom of Poland . . . which if your Majesty shall hearken unto me rather for his sake, as your royal ancestor has done in the like occasion, His Majesty will accept it as a respect of your love. which will assure and increase the commerce and friendsi ϸ of your dominions."

The Sultan, in his reply, declares that " all matters shall be pacified and ended " whenever a Polish embassy should appear to request favour and amity. He concludes with an expression of confident expectation that between His Britannic Majesty and the Sublime Porte "the ancient, perfect, and acceptable course of friendship will be always observed and maintained." Some seventy-five years later England gave a still more practical illustration of her friendliness. For a couple of decades the Turks had been engaged in war with Austria and Russia, as well as Poland and the Venetians, and was now visibly getting the worst of it. Peter the Great of Russia had lately prosecuted the campaign with great vigour, and had alarmed the British, for the first time, by giving very definite indications of his ulterior intentions. At any rate, England intervened through her ambassador at the Porte—Lord Paget—and suggested a pacification on the basis of each Power retaining what it had seized or successfully held. This involved the loss of considerable Turkish territory, and the Sultan took the then unprecedented step of embodying a counter project in his own handwriting, and sending it with a letter from his Grand Vizier to the King of England. But Peter of Russia did not want peace, even on these terms, and he visited

**IMAGE EVALUATION
TEST TARGET (MT-3)**

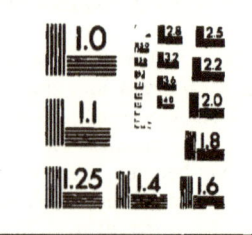

Photographic
Sciences
Corporation

23 WEST MAIN STREET
WEBSTER, N.Y. 14580
(716) 872-4503

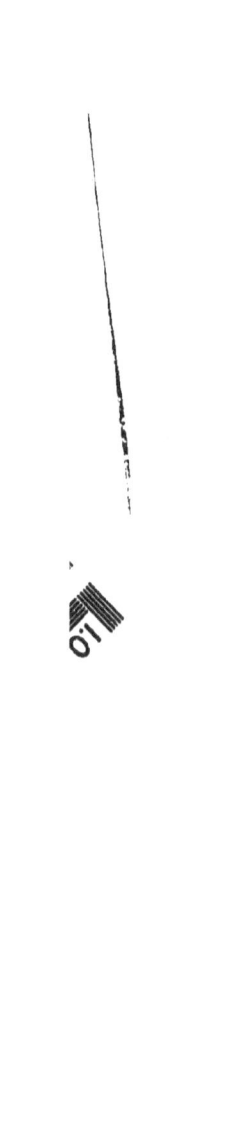

Vienna in order to persuade the Emperor Leopold not to accept the proposals.

That ruler, however, told the great Russian that he agreed with England in the matter. "Beware," said the Czar in reply, "how you trust what the Dutch and the English say. They are looking only to the benefit of their commerce; they care nothing about the interests of their allies." But the result of this first intervention of Great Britain in the affairs of Turkey was not only immediately successful as checking the designs of the Muscovite, and procuring the Peace of Carlowitz (1698); it was the beginning of its modern policy, and of the long record of diplomacy and war which surrounds the annals of the Eastern Question. In 1712, according to an historic letter from Sultan Achmet III. to Charles XII. of Sweden, England offered to mediate once more between the Russians and the Turks, in the interest of a lasting and beneficial peace. The Sultan here speaks of the British Government as an "ancient ally" of the Porte. Again, in 1787-91, England was on the verge of war with Russia upon questions connected with the proposed independence of Moldavia and Wallachia—the Roumania of to-day. She offered to mediate between Turkey and Russia in the war then going on, and, as Lord Stratford de Redcliffe somewhere says in dealing with the subject, "displayed a very remarkable consideration for the interests of the former."

In these negotiations we find the full indication of the second and greatest reason for British protection of Turkey. The mutual relationship had commenced in the necessities of commercial intercourse. It was soon cemented by the more potent factor of mutual hostility to Russia--to the early ambitions and later schemes of the Muscovite power. About this time—the end of the eighteenth century—Catharine II., in all the brilliance and plenitude of her Asiatic power and Oriental qualities, was intent upon transforming the Turkish provinces of Moldo-Wallachia and Bessarabia into a nominally free kingdom. Under some circumstances this proposal would have been an unmixed blessing to the inhab... is of those countries. But England and all Europe we... aware that this suggestion was a perfect farce, and the mere preliminary to their annexation to Russia after a brief period of internal disturbance and popular misery. The Crimea had recently gone through a similar experience, and the wishes of the great Czarina were therefore promptly rejected by the courts of Prussia and England as being incompatible with the maintenance of the balance of power—that cherished creation of William III. of Great Britain.

Then Russia wanted to annex certain territories reaching up to the Dneister, and Pitt, rather than permit it, and despite the vigorous protests of Fox and others against any assistance being given the Turkish barbarians, prepared to send a fleet up the Baltic. Eventually the British Premier had to give way, and Russia upon this occasion held its own, and a little more. During the debates which followed in the House of Commons the Liberal attacks upon Turkey were very pronounced, and their defence of Russia equally so. It was the Eastern Question of 1878 in an earlier form. Mr. Whitbread, for instance, said : " Suppose the Empress could realize all her imputed views of ambition and get possession of Constantinople, and expel the Turks from all their European provinces, would any unprejudiced man contend that by such an event mankind would not be largely benefited ? "

Between 1821 and 1831 occurred the British intervention on behalf of Greece, and the stripping of Turkey to a moderate extent—much less than desired by Russia—in order to establish a free and independent kingdom. Following this event, in 1840, came the curious complications in Egypt and Syria; the British interference in support of the Sultan against his rebellious vassal; the danger of war with France upon the question; the defeat of Ibrahim's troops and capture of St. Jean d'Acre by the British; the commission of Lord Dufferin, his proposed reforms, and the usual deceptive acquiescence by the Porte; the harmonious co-operation of Russia and England in defence of Turkey. This was indeed carrying out to the full the then English idea of preserving the integrity and independence of the Ottoman power as a rampart against Russian ambition.

In the Crimean war this policy was more fully developed, and for a quarter of a century afterwards remained the pivot upon which the Eastern Question turned. It is one which some critics like to condemn in the full glare of modern developments. But such condemnation is clearly unreasonable, and is usually based upon a prejudice against England, upon ignorance of the original international situation, or upon a desire to promote some personal aim by creating public misapprehension regarding British policy and statecraft. Of this latter character appears to be Mr. Goldwin Smith's recent statement in a Canadian paper* that, " forty years ago, I was one of a political minority in England which was overwhelmed with obloquy for opposing wars with Russia *in defence of Turkish dominion over the Armenians and other Christian races* beneath that sway."

*Toronto Telegram, February 10th, 1896.

Whatever the motive for this statement—and the only visible one is the desire to promote annexation sentiment in Canada by arousing dislike against England— it is absolutely untrue. Every one who understands history knows—and Mr. Goldwin Smith better than most—that this war was fought primarily to check Russian aggression; to prevent the Emperor Nicholas from carrying out his avowed policy of partitioning Turkey; to avert the danger of another and stronger military despotism being established upon the banks of the Bosphorus; to protect the rising Christian nations of Turkey from the despotic rule of the Czar; to guard the countries of Europe generally from the permanent menace of a great semi-barbarian Power, beside which the Turk, even in the days of Solyman the Magnificent, was a comparatively insignificant European factor.

Under Russian rule at Constantinople countries such as Bulgaria and Servia would have met the fate of Poland, or been crushed, as was Hungary in 1848, by the troops of the Muscovite. In 1853, as Mr. Goldwin Smith must be aware, there was no Armenian question, and the people of that country had hardly yet made themselves felt or known to European diplomacy. To preserve the semi-independence of Bessarabia, or of Moldavia and Wallachia, from the aggression of Russia was then as important a part of British policy as it was to prevent them from being crushed by Turkish rule. Moreover, although little was then known in England regarding the customs and character of the Turk, the Crimean war was, at the outset, an immensely popular one, and was waged in the opinion and intention of almost the entire British nation against unjust and dangerous Russian aggression, and not " in defence of Turkish dominion over Christians." Upon its necessity, Lord Stratford de Redcliffe, the great diplomatist, who was arranging the constitution of new Christian nationalities, and battling with the Sublime Porte in defence of Eastern Christian peoples and individual Armenian victims of the Turk, before Mr. Goldwin Smith had left school, is sufficiently explicit:

"Where is our alternative? At Adrianople the Emperor (of Russia) seemed to be satisfied for life. He was satisfied before at Akkerman. But the Greek war was tempting; he stole a march on his friends, and took another meal. . . . Then came the generous era—forbearance, protection, patronage, fraternal sympathy, and *Unkiar Skelessi*. The Sultan gradually discerned that hugging was pressure, and pressure coercion. He betrayed his alarm by an occasional struggle, but . . . the Porte was still feeble, and Russian influence continued to predominate. The seeming moderation which blinded Europe might, therefore, yet go on without danger or escape. But the uneasiness excited at St. Petersburg by the Porte's independent conduct regarding the Hungarian and Polish refugees (whom it refused to give up to Austria and Russia) assumed a more alarming character, when at one and the same time appeared the question of the Holy Places and a crisis, intimating that Turkey must either sink into hopeless decrepitude or make a new start by the enforcement and expansion of its reforming policy. Russian susceptibility now found itself in presence of a danger and a temptation—the danger of losing a permanent influence, the temptation of a dismemberment. Hence the secret overtures to Sir H. Seymour; hence, on their failure, the Menschikof requisition; hence a determination to rule the roost in Turkey, either by a concerted division of the empire, or through a recognized protection at Constantinople."

The war was therefore necessary, and in defence of the general interests of Europe and England; but it may be admitted that mistakes were made not only in its military conduct, but in the prior arrangements between England and the Turk, to say nothing of the general views of the ensuing Treaty of Paris. The struggle was entered upon without any guarantees from Turkey as to its future internal government; without coercing it into a practical—instead of nominal—acceptance of Lord Stratford's proposed reforms—from the future success of which he hoped so much, and upon which he seems, in some degree, to have based his defence of the war; without a proper knowledge of the Ottoman character or appreciation of Turkish history; without taking care afterwards to retain the power and right of intervention which this defence of Turkish "integrity and independence" should have given England.

And the unfortunate, yet glorious, events in the Crimea changed the colour of British diplomacy in Turkey, though the net result was a success, so far as the crushing of Russian rivalry for some twenty years was concerned. Amongst a few, however, who knew something of the Turk, there had at first been a natural aversion to this war, in spite of its evident necessity. The Queen, for instance, in one of Her Majesty's statesmanlike letters to the Cabinet—in this case through Lord Clarendon—spoke of the "hundred and twenty fanatical Turks constituting the Divan at Constantinople"; referred to the necessity of binding Turkey to defined conditions; and even declared that "it may be a question whether England ought to go to war for the defence of so-called Turkish independence." But later events somewhat changed this view, and the Queen's letters to the King of Prussia and others, in 1854, present a strong defence of the war, and of its absolute necessity. The Prince Consort, in a most able memorandum, looked, however, to the future, with a very clear knowledge of the nation with which he was dealing. The conflict, he declared, ought to be carried on "unshackled by obligations to the Porte, and will probably lead . . to the obtaining of arrangements more consistent with the well-understood interests of Europe, of Christianity, liberty, and civilization, than the re-imposition of the ignorant, barbarian, and despotic yoke of the Moslem in the most fertile and favoured portion of Europe."

But, unfortunately, neither Palmerston nor Gladstone nor the other leaders of the time except, perhaps, Lord Aberdeen himself, saw eye to eye with the Prince in this matter of the future. Of course, none of them, least of all the Prince himself, regarded the war at any time as being fought in defence of Turkish dominion over Eastern Christians. They were fighting for the independence of Turkey, against the dominance of Russia, a country which could not apparently rest in peace. Its aggressive policy has been frequently referred to in these pages, and was described by many of the leaders at this time. But by no one was it dealt harder blows, in better terms, than by the Earl of Derby—afterwards Prime Minister—in 1854:

"For the last 150 years it has been a policy of gradual aggression—not a policy of conquest, but of aggression. It has never been preceded by storm, but by sap and mine. The first process has been invariably that of fomenting discontent and dissatisfaction amongst the subjects of subordinate states—then proffering mediation —then offering assistance to the weaker party—then declaring the independence of that party—then placing that independence under the protection of Russia; and, finally, from protection proceeding to the incorporation, one by one, of those States into the gigantic body of the Russian Empire. I say nothing of Poland or of Livonia, but I speak of Mingrelia, Imeritia, and the countries of the Caspian—even as far as the boundaries of the Araxes; and, again, the Crimea itself."

The general result of the struggle, so far as Turkey was concerned, failed to achieve the hopes expressed by Prince Albert. The Ninth Article of the Treaty of Paris, in 1856, communicated to the Powers a firman issued by the Sultan at the practical dictation of Lord Stratford, and providing for the protection of his Christian subjects; accepted it in the name of each and all the great Powers; and then proceeded: " It is well understood that it (the firman) does not, in any case, give a right to the said Powers, either collectively or separately, to interfere with the relations of the Sultan to his subjects, or in the internal administration of the empire." And the further fatal mistake was made of admitting the Ottoman power into the concert and public law of Europe. No wonder, if, after all this, Lord Stratford found his influence in Stamboul greatly weakened, and the pledges regarding Christians issued by the Sultan to be so much waste paper. Little wonder, also, if the Porte became more prone to violence than before, under the impression that its miserable rule, to quote the Grand Vizier in 1855, " is forever necessary to the balance of power in Europe."

Of course, it is easy to look back now and say that, while the war was a necessity under the circumstances, the conclusion was mismanaged, and the result blameworthy. But myriads of lives had been sacrificed, and five hundred million dollars expended ; France was anxious to get away from the Allies, and the war ; the English people, though still willing to carry it on, were disgusted with the sufferings of their soldiers ; and finally, when it appeared that Russia was willing to accept the conditions for which the struggle had been originally entered upon, the Treaty of Paris was hastily made, and ratified without, perhaps, much regard for what then seemed very minor issues, but which to us of to-day, and in the light of sad experience, loom so largely and luridly. Ignorance of Turkish fatuity and cruelty was then very complete, and even Bright and Cobden, the two isolated leaders who opposed the Crimean war, did not do so as much on the general ground of dislike to Turkey as on that of antagonism to all war and love for peace at almost any price.

During the succeeding twenty years much happened to blind still further the eyes of England. The Ottoman Empire for a long time presented two shields, one of promised reform and progress to Europe, the other of black and silent oppression to its helpless subject Christians. Lord Stratford had retired from diplomacy, and with him had gone much of British prestige and power over the hypocritical Sultans and their submissive Ministers. Abdul-Aziz visited England in 1867; was fêted in every direction; made the most lavish protestations as to his home policy of conciliation and kindness; received a return visit of the Prince and Princess of Wales—and then, in half a dozen years, increased the national debt from $15,000,000 to $900,000,000. With the loans thus cleverly obtained he crushed the insurrections in Bosnia and Herzegovina, built great palaces at Constantinople, and ran a riot of wild and reckless dissipation.

The Bulgarian massacres followed, and opened the eyes of Great Britain to the nature of the Turk, as his progressive national bankruptcy had already done with the investing public. With the Russo-Turkish war of 1877, the previous opening of the Suez Canal, the immense development of British trade in the East, and of British interests in India, began the third phase of the Eastern Question and of England's relation with the Ottoman. That relationship had commenced in commerce, had continued in a common autagonism to Russia, and now changed primarily to a question of guarding trade routes. Of course, there was, and must remain, the ever-present necessity of preventing Russian access to Constantinople, by which, in the momentary turn of the international kaleidoscope now on view (1896), that Power, allied with France, might sweep the Mediterranean. And there will always be the complication of guarding the independence of the Balkan States against an aggression from Russia more dangerous to their independence—though not perhaps to their individual comfort and well-being—than ever was the nominal sovereignty of the Sultan.

Meanwhile, Lord Beaconsfield had checked Russia as effectually without war as Lord Palmerston and Mr. Gladstone did, in 1856, with war. And by the Treaty of Berlin he forced the Turk to give liberty and practical independence to several Balkan countries which, under the superseded Russo-Turkish Treaty of San Stefano, would have been merely transferred from the Turkish yoke to that of the country whose memory is so pleasant to the Pole, the Jew, the Hungarian, and the Turcoman. But none the less was there now a complete change in British treatment of Turkey. The Ottoman power might still be retained as a buffer against Russia, but the policy of various British ambassadors in succession to Lord Stratford—Sir Henry Bulwer, Lord Lyons, or Sir H. Elliot—was altered, and the principle of non-intervention enjoined by the Treaty of Paris, and practically waived by the arrangements at Berlin, was entirely given up at Constantinople. The massacres in Bulgaria, the international crisis, and the financial condition of the Porte had revived Lord Stratford's policy of direct interference in the internal affairs of the country, combined, however, with a total lack of that friendship and sympathy which had once—based upon English ignorance of the Turk—really existed.

Three representative men, between 1876 and 1880, were sent out to Stamboul. Lord Salisbury attended an abortive Conference in the first-named year, and had to face the diplomatic statecraft with which Prince Gortchakoff so well understood how to blind the Turk to Russian intentions. In the next year Sir Henry Layard appeared upon the scene as a friend of the Turk, and one naturally inclined to disbelieve the stories of his vicious government, even though he knew something of Moslem cruelty in Asiatic Turkey. But, with others, he might have argued that a Kurd was not a Turk. After three years, however, he wrote home a despatch dealing with existing abuses, misdeeds, and general corruption (April 27th, 1880), and concludes as follows:

"I have exhausted every diplomatic resource in endeavouring to bring the Sultan and his advisers to a sense of the danger to which the Empire is exposed, in consequence of the state of things I have described. I have used every representation and remonstrance—I may almost say menace—to induce them to put in execution and to carry out loyally and fully the promised reforms. I have made incessant personal appeals to the Sultan himself. I have placed before him, even in writing, without reserve, the condition of his empire and the consequent disaffection of his subjects. I have exposed to him the incapacity and corruption of his ministers, and of his high public functionaries. I have pointed out to him the inevitable consequences of his disregard of the warnings which he has received, the forfeiture of the sympathy and friendship of England, and the possible further dismemberment of his empire."

But, as he said, these protests were of no avail unless backed up by force, and the ensuing missions of Mr. Goschen, of Lord Dufferin, of Sir Edward Thornton, and

Sir William White, found the same impassive but powerful obstacle to all real reform, amendment, or change. And, as the years passed on, to the time when the present ambassador assumed office, and the Armenian horrors first loomed upon the horizon of diplomacy and intrigue, the Sultan and his satellites have maintained the same attitude of absolute indifference to promises, contempt for Christian advice, and for any intervention short of ships and soldiers and cannon.

CHAPTER XVIII.

THE SHADOW OF THE SWORD IN ARMENIA.

With the incidents surrounding the inception and progress of the Russo-Turkish war of 1877 came the first warning and shadow of what might ultimately be expected in Armenia. The horrors perpetrated in Bulgaria at that time not only roused England from end to end, and shocked the sense of the civilized world, but indicated the worn and slender thread by which Christian lives and homes were protected throughout the Turkish Empire. In Armenia, which became the Asian theatre of the war, evidences of misgovernment and oppressive cruelty had already been so numerous as to prove only second in extent and volume to what had transpired in the miserable European province.

Every now and then throughout the present century stories have reached civilized Europe concerning the state of things in Armenia, as well as in Bulgaria, and Bosnia, and Greece. Mr. Robert Curzon, for instance, writing in his journal on August 2nd, 1843, tells us of an incident which came under his own observation at Erzeroum. A Turkish soldier had been seen stealing and concealing some merchandise. He was arrested, but only one-half of the goods were found. The rest, he alleged, had been taken by an Armenian named Artin. The latter, on the word of this admitted thief, and against the evidence of several Christians—which was of no avail under Moslem

Erzeroum looking South from the Bell Tower of the Armenian Church

law—was dragged before the local Mahometan tribunal. The result may be left to Mr. Curzon to describe :

"The Pasha ordered him to be tortured. A metal drinking cup of hot brass was put upon his head; afterwards a cord was tied around his head, two sheep's knuckle-bones were placed upon his temples, and the cord tightened till his eyes nearly came out. As he would not confess, his front teeth were then drawn one at a time; pieces of cane were run up under his toe nails and his finger nails. Various tortures have been inflicted on him in this way for the last twelve days, and he is now hung up by the hands in the prison of the Seraskier."

This occurred fifty years ago, and is given, in passing, merely as an ordinary illustration of the treatment meted out to Christians in many parts of Turkey under the auspices of local governing bodies. What can be expected under such circumstances from lawless bands of Bashi-Bazouks or Kurds? When the law itself is thus utilized and administered for purposes of cruel oppression, it is not difficult to understand what lawlessness must mean. During 1876 the condition of Turkish Armenia became more and more deplorable. It had always been in a state of more or less disorder, but in this year matters seemed to get worse—if that were possible. Perhaps it only appears so because of the evidence given us in a British Blue Book dealing with the condition of the Christians in Turkey during this period. The oppression, therefore, looms up more distinctly and vividly. Just as the lurid flash of 1894-5 lit up the Eastern sky and revealed the Armenians in their desolation and suffering, so in a more limited degree we are able, from the pages of those reports, to see the state of affairs twenty years ago, and perceive its preliminary bearing upon the massacres of to-day.

The first witness who may be quoted is Mr. Consul Zohrab of E eroum. He draws a graphic picture of the crushing taxation under which the population groaned, and which included arrears of taxes impossible to collect in any court of modern law, current taxes, taxes in advance, aid in money for the coming war, contributions in kind for the army, means of transport for munitions of war and provisions, besides various exactions of the most unscrupulous nature. This "systematic spoliation of the people," which extended, so far as taxation was concerned, to the Moslem peasant as well as the Christian, was intensified by the personal demands of the corrupt officials, until thousands of families were so reduced as to live only by public charity. But the plundering in this extreme degree was not limited to taxation, and was directed far more against the Armenian than the Turk. In a fire, for instance, which took place at Van in December, 1876, the officials and soldiers openly broke into the burning houses and carried off any property they could conveniently seize. It was, indeed, nothing unusual. During the Damascus massacres of years before, the officers of the Sultan had been seen by Europeans returning from the Christian quarter laden with plunder.

There appears to have been a perfect reign of terror at this time. On January 30th, 1877, Consul Zohrab telegraphed Sir Henry Elliot, the British Ambassador in Stamboul, to the following effect: " Panic in Bitlis district, several murders, many villages devastated, others deserted by inhabitants from dread of Kurds, who threaten the towns." On the 14th of March he telegraphed that 175 Turkish Redifs, or troops, on their way to Erzeroum, had stopped in three villages of the district of Bunis, desecrated the churches, maltreated the priests, beaten the Christians, and brutally ill-treated the women. He adds significantly: " Christians begin to suffer severely. Acts of oppression and cruelty occur daily." It must be remembered amid all these occurrences, and the chronic condition of the country, past and present, that no Christian was allowed to carry arms, while the Christian oath was of no value against a Mahometan. This in itself is sufficient to reveal the horrible helplessness of the Armenian inhabitant as regards himself, his family, and his goods.

Mr. Consul Taylor, in his reports, covers wide ground. He gives details of the condition of the Western Armenians in the range of heights occupied by the Kurds between Turkish and Persian Armenia. Cruelty and outrage were, of course, common occurrences, plunder was the ordinary method of transacting business, several villages he had seen were pillaged of literally everything, and a varied array of crimes had been committed by the Kurdish "Government Police." On more than one occasion the Turks or Kurds yoked Christian women to their ploughs. In the district of Moosh, he describes a society of holy men called Sheiks, who preached war incessantly against the infidels or Christians, and represented every outrage as being lawful and meritorious. As far back as 1868 these people had stormed and plundered the venerable church and convent of Moosh, which dates from the time of Gregory the Illuminator. Of course no redress was possible, although the injury had been intensified by the wanton destruction of an invaluable manuscript library. In the country around the collection of hovels which represented the once splendid Armenian city of Klat, Mr. Taylor saw nothing at the time of writing but "deserted villages, ruined churches, crumbling mosques, abandoned fields." "The ruthless conduct," he adds, " of these ruffian Kurds have rendered what ought to have been a paradise a desert." Here, as elsewhere in unfortunate Armenia, " great crimes always unpunished, grievous oppressions unredressed," developed into a condition of lawless wickedness which the Kurds seemed to consider warranted by custom, and entirely permissible.

As an illustration of what might occur in any populous place where Mahometans and Christians live together, the Consul gives us the following incident. Khachatoor Effendi was a wealthy Christian of Erzeroum, living in an Armenian district, and under the shadow of a British consulate. He was, like a few opulent Christians in other lands, anxious to improve the material condition of his fellow-beings, and therefore purchased a portion of the city covered with mean and poverty-infested buildings, and erected in their place rows of excellent houses, shops, and public buildings. Their completion, including repairs to a ruined mosque, was signalized by an evidently incendiary fire, in which the whole quarter and $100,000 of capital went up in smoke and flame. During the conflagration not a Moslem offered aid, though many plundered wherever the opportunity offered. But Khachatoor Effendi was a determined as well as a rich man, so he set himself to the work of rebuilding his quarter. Shortly afterwards, however, while seated in a café, a Mahometan rode up and shot him dead. Not a finger was raised against the murderer, and the Consul states that he was known to be one of a gang to which the important official in the Vilayet—or administrative province—corresponding with a British Chief Justice, himself belonged.

Such was the state of affairs in Armenia when the Russo-Turkish war began, and it became once more the battle-ground of struggling nations. To the miserable Armenians the war offered neither relief, nor prospect of relief. It enhanced the exactions of the Turks and the power of the Kurds. In periods of Russian success it gave an additional burden for local towns and villages to carry, and where they had before to feed the Moslem they had now to purvey for the Russian. The invaders were kinder and less addicted to individual acts of cruelty than the Turks, but the weight of armed men proved almost crushing to the unhappy population.

It was on the 24th of April, 1877, that the forces of the Czar entered, simultaneously, the territory of the Turk in European Roumania and in Asiatic Armenia. Under the Grand Duke Michael and General Loris Mekoff, they invaded this latter and historic region of Eastern warfare, defeated the Turks, stormed Ardahan, invested Kars, and were in turn defeated at Kizel-Tepe. After prolonged battles, advances and retreats, successes and failures, they took Kars by storm, entered Erzeroum, and became masters of Armenia about the time the Russian armies in Europe had reached the hills around Stamboul and forced the Treaty of San Stefano from the now helpless and beaten Turk.

The net result of the war to Armenia and its suffering people was the transfer of a portion of their territory and of several important fortified or strategic places, such as Kars and Batoum, to Russia. It may be said here that the condition of the Armenian Christian in the land of the Czar is infinitely better than it is upon Turkish soil. It could not, of course, be worse. But the kindness shown by Russia in this case is purely political. Neither its government nor its people have any fondness for sectaries, and some of the most cruel religious persecutions in history have taken place upon their soil. Had the Armenians been of the orthodox Greek Church the situation might be somewhat different, but even then they would be used simply to forward Russian ambitions.

Years ago, Armenians, as elsewhere mentioned, suffered considerably at their hands, and it was not until the occupation of the entire country—the ancient Asiatic path to Stamboul—loomed into view as a possible future policy that this kindly treatment of resident Russian Armenians became apparent.

One deplorable consequence followed the cessation of the struggle. The Kurds, to the number of fifteen thousand or more, had been freshly armed and uniformed by the Sultan during the war, and had signalized their services by blood-curdling atrocities upon all enemies, or suspected enemies, who fell into their hands. Without discipline or object, aside from plunder and lawless liberty, they had been a curse to the country while hostilities lasted, and, now that they were over, became a still greater and more pressing infliction. Unable to obtain their full and regular pay, many of them became scattered through the land in bands of disaffected and ruthless robbers—nominally soldiers, but really thieves and murderers.

Aside from this terrible fact, the Armenians, in the ten or fifteen years preceding the immediate present, have had to face a majority of armed Moslems; a system of absolute helplessness in the Mahometan courts; a weakness intensified by the inability to carry arms; an absolute lack of privacy, comfort, or safety in their homes; the confiscation of all works by their national authors; the proscription even of leading English books; the destruction of their cherished printing processes; the imprisonment of their young men for reading a poem or singing a song; the constant and indescribable dangers to their households and families at the hands of either Turk or Kurd, soldier or Moslem civilian.

Upon this latter subject something must be said, unpleasant as it is to either discuss or read. During these years no Christian woman could depend upon preserving either honour or life. They were both at the mercy of travelling Turks, visiting officials, or marauding Kurds. The husband who endeavoured to protect his wife, the brother who sought to save his sister, were alike slaughtered without mercy. Helpless, unarmed, and cowed, what, indeed, could the men do, and what had the women to hope for? Writing on January 30th, 1891, three years before the recent massacres, Mr. Charles S. Hampson, British Consul at Erzeroum, narrates the following amongst a long list of similar instances:

"A band of thirty mounted police which were on the march were billeted for the night in a small Armenian village of ten houses, a few miles distant from Bitlis. Four of them were quartered in the house of a young married Armenian. Overhearing them discussing plans against his wife's honour, he secretly sent her to the house of a neighbour. When the Zaptiehs learnt this they ordered him to send for her, and, on his refusing to do so, beat him most cruelly. He fled to a neighbour's house, but two days later died from the effects of the ill-treatment he had received. In the houses where the other Zaptiehs were quartered their designs against the female members of the family were carried out without resistance."

A few months later, the same Consul reports that Hussein Agha, the district Governor of Patnos, with his nephew, had entered by night the home of a local Armenian named Caspar, in order to carry off the latter's beautiful daughter-in-law. On the people of the house being aroused and crying for help, this Turkish governor drew his revolver and shot the young woman dead. A little later he was raised to high rank in the Hamidieh forces. Under date of September 19th, Mr. Hampson describes a case in which several Turks entered the village of Havar and seized and outraged a number of Armenian women in broad daylight. So also in Zartarich, a village near Kharput. The Consul gives numerous similar instances of brutality and violence. But the evidence of Dr. E. J. Dillon, who has spent months on the spot, and dealt in detail with the whole subject—especially with this most horrible feature of it—in the columns of the *London Daily Telegraph*, is as ghastly as it is reliable. He gives a large number of cases where Kurdish police have taken possession of some village, seized and dishonoured the women, and killed any men who opposed them. Dr. Dillon sums up his statements in this particular connection by describing the manner in which these fiends levy taxes upon a community, give a receipt, and return again in a week to seize another instalment or anything they can lay their hands upon. " Then they demand the surrender of the young women and girls . . . and refusal is punished with a series of tortures over which decency and humanity throw a veil of silence. Rape, and every kind of brutal outrage conceivable to the diseased minds of Oriental profligates, varied, perhaps, with murder or arson, wind up the incident."

Torture and robbery, murder and outrage, have, indeed, been the lot of Armenian men and women for years before the last lurid light was let in upon their conditions. Tahsin Bey, the late Governor of Bitlis, used, for instance, to imprison scores of wealthy Armenians, and then torture them until they surrendered such of their money or goods as he might desire. His methods were as ingenious as they were cruel. " Some men," says Dr. Dillon, "were kept standing up all day and all night, forbidden to eat, drink, or move. If they lost strength or consciousness, cold water or hot irons soon brought them round, and the work of coercion continued. Time and perseverance being on the side of the Turks, the Armenians generally ended by sacrificing everything that made life valuable for the sake of exemption from maddening pain."

This species of financial pressure was naturally hard to resist. In 1890, the village elder of Odandjor was a wealthy man in local estimation. He owned fifty buffaloes, eighty oxen, six hundred sheep, besides horses, etc. In 1894 he was a poverty-stricken peasant, familiar with misery and accustomed to hunger, while his once prosperous village and the entire surrounding district had been plundered and stripped absolutely bare, under the smiling approval of the Turkish authorities. As an illustration of Mahometan justice, the following incident is also instructive : During August, 1893, the Kurds attacked and plundered the village of Kaghkik, wounding a merchant named Oannes in the course of their raid. The latter went next day to the Deputy Governor of the district and lodged a complaint, but was promptly put in prison—a hotbed of typhoid and filth—for "lying." A week later his neighbours brought a Kurd (their own oaths being valueless) to prove that the unfortunate prisoner was not lying. Then the authorities actually consented to let the people pay a bribe of fifty dollars for the release of the wounded man.

This same village of Odandjor, and several neighbouring ones, were flourishing and prosperous places in 1890, but in 1894 did not contain a single sheep, or buffalo, or horse. The stables were empty, the houses in ruins, the stacks of corn in ashes. Yet during all this period two hundred cavalry of the regular forces were stationed at half an hour's distance. But these Imperial troops are as bad as the Kurds. In 1893 a couple of hundred entered one of the villages, under the command of Rahim

Pasha. After being quartered with reckless brutality upon the people, they remained there some forty days. The following incident of their stay is a striking but not uncommon one: "Rahim Pasha, angry with his host, Pare, for grumbling, had a copper vessel hung over the fire, and, when heated, ordered it to be placed on Pare's head. Then he had him stripped and little bits of flesh nipped out of his quivering arms with pincers."

The tale of the village of Avzood in the Moush district sounds incredible, but has been fully verified. In 1892 a young Armenian who had been working, and was now settled in Russia, came back on a visit. Hearing of this, Isaag Tshaush was sent to arrest him. Entering the house alone, while his troops guarded the entrance, pistol shots were shortly heard, and Isaag and the young Armenian were both found lying dead. The authorities in Bitlis at once sent a Colonel of the Zaptiehs, or police, to Avzood to see that justice was done—in Turkish style. The Colonel sent for the men of the village and threw them temporarily into prison. All the girls and the young women were then dealt with in the way characteristic of Zaptiehs and Turks. Some of the prisoners were permanently retained, and it was decided to charge a young Armenian named Markar, belonging to another village, with the murder of Isaag. There was, of course, no evidence, but the prisoners were tortured in order to obtain some. "They were stripped, and burned in various parts of the body till they yelled with pain. Then they were prevented from sleeping for several nights, and tortured acutely again, till, writhing and quivering, they promised to swear anything, everything. A document declaring that Markar was in the village when Isaag arrived there, and had shot Isaag in their presence, was then drawn up in their names."

Meanwhile, Markar himself was being tortured in another part of the prison. When the trial came on the signatories to the document stripped themselves in Court, detailed the torture to which they had been subjected, and declared the statements a lie. Markar swore that he had not been in the village that night at all, but was none the less hanged for his alleged crime, while some of the women in the village died about the same time, from the brutal treatment received at the hands of the Zaptiehs. Such are some of the preliminaries to the recent massacres.

But they do not fully illustrate the responsibility of Constantinople, and the share taken in this organized harrying of the Armenians out of Armenia by the Turkish authorities. It will be remembered that Bedir Khan Bey had, in the early fifties, organized some regiments of irregular Kurdish troops in Kurdestan. These had expanded during the Russian war, but had afterwards been more or less disbanded, or been quartered upon the miserable Christians as " police," or Zaptiehs. In 1891, however, it was resolved to organize them into a military force of cavalry under the generic name of Ertoghrul regiments; and the subsequent official announcement stated that "the initiative of this happy idea, and the great success which will certainly crown its execution, are due to the wisdom and foresight of His Imperial Majesty the Sultan." This "happy idea" was received with unmixed terror by the Armenians, while the British Foreign Office was advised by the ambassador at Stamboul that he " received it with apprehension." And Mr. Hampson reported to the latter from Erzeroum regarding the proposal that:

" This measure of arming the Kurds is regarded with great anxiety here. This feeling is much increased by the conduct of the Kurds themselves, many of whom openly state that they have been appointed to suppress Armenians, and th at they have received assurances that they will not be called to answer before the tribunals for any acts of oppression committed against Christians.

"The Armenians in this town are very uneasy, and very many of those who are in a position to be able to do so have expressed their intention of leaving Erzeroum as soon as the roads are open."

On March 30th, the interesting announcement was made that a contingent of the new Kurdish cavalry had embarked on board a special steamer for Constantinople, in order to be presented to the Sultan. Along the route they were everywhere fêted, and at Trebizond were greeted with civic and military honours. It was also stated that that this " new auxiliary force of the Ottoman army is to find its own equipment and depend on the State for its arms and ammunition only," which meant that some 30,000 Kurds, after being armed by the Government, were to live upon the Armenian Christians. Then comes the further official description of their reception by the Sultan, their welcome by Dervisch Pasha, and the Caliph's orders that "their smallest wants are to be attended to."

The general result of this new military formation was the organized effort at destroying the Armenians; the immediate consequence was an increase of outrage and crime. In July, 1892, a captain of the Hamidieh cavalry, Idris by name, went with his brother to demand a contribution of fodder from the villagers of Hamsisheikh. They accosted two of the local head men, and ordered them to provide the hay. "We do not possess such a quantity in the whole village," was the reply. "Produce the hay or I'll shoot you dead," said Idris. They replied that it did not exist, and that they could not create it. "Then die," said the captain, and shot them both on the spot. The people were, however, lucky if the village was spared, or their families and property were allowed to remain safe from destruction and outrage. It did not often happen so, even before the massacres of 1895. For instance, five villages east of Kara Kilisse had a population of some 3,000 Christians. But, in 1893, Eyoob, a general officer in the Hamidieh, sent his three sons—also officers—to take possession of these villages. To-day they have not an inhabitant, and their houses are ruins.

But it is not necessary to say more. At a moment when the horrors of Sassoun were beginning to reach Europe, 306 of the principal residents of the district of Khnouss signed the following statement, addressed to the " humane and noble people of England " :

" We now solemnly assure you that the butchery of Sassoun is but a drop in the ocean Armenian blood shed gradually and silently all over the Empire since the late Turko-Russian war. Year by year, month by month, day by day, innocent men, women, and children have been shot down, stabbed, or clubbed to death in their houses and their fields, tortured in strange, fiendish ways in fetid prison cells, or left to rot in exile under the scorching sun of Arabia. During the progress of that long and horrible tragedy no voice was raised for mercy, no hand extended to help us."

And this pictures truly, though sternly, the situation which had grown by official encouragement and natural Turkish and Kurdish depravity, until it burst into the flaming atrocities of the recent Armenian massacres.

CHAPTER XIX.

THE SWORD OF ISLAM FALLS.

From 1878 onwards, there had been little of peace, happiness, or security in Armenia. Its Christian population lived under the shadow of that awful prayer breathed daily from millions of Moslem throats throughout Turkey, and which embodies the creed of Islam, and the condition of Christians under its control, as no amount of learned exposition or fierce denunciation could possibly do:

"I seek refuge with Allah from Satan, the accursed. In the name of Allah the Compassionate, the Merciful! Oh, Lord of all Creatures! Oh, Allah! Destroy the infidels and the polytheists, thine enemies, the enemies of thy religion! Oh, Allah! Make their children orphans, and defile their abodes, and make their feet to slip; and give them, and their families, and their households, and their women, and their children, and their relations by marriage, and their brothers, and their friends, and their possessions, and their race, and their wealth, and their lands, as booty to the Moslem. Oh, Lord of all Creatures!"

It is true that during many centuries the Armenians, as well as other Christians in Turkey, have lived and suffered and been slaughtered in isolated batches under this Islamic injunction. It is true that in an extract from a private letter, dated April 3rd, 1894, five months before the first of the recent massacres, the writer stated that there was "no computing the lives that are going, not in open massacre, as in Bulgaria, but in secret, silent, and secluded ways." But as yet the Armenians had not been revealed to a world which seemed to have forgotten them

A Group of Americans who escaped from the Mission at Iguassu

and their Christian heroism and endurance, in the full glare of the national holocaust upon the altar of Mahometan cruelty.

To those who followed British Parliamentary proceedings, or were interested in the Eastern Question, or read Blue Books, or sympathized with the exertions of Eastern missionaries, something was known of the dangers menacing the suffering Armenian race. Mr. Clifford Lloyd, at one time Consul-General at Erzeroum, summarized in an official despatch, as late as October, 1890, the condition of the country under the following heads:

I. The insecurity of the lives and properties of Christians.

II. The insecurity of their persons, and the absence of all liberty of thought and action.

III. The unequal status of Christian and Mahometan in the eyes of the Government.

But the instructed inaction of European Consuls; the delicate and difficult position of the missionaries under a despotic government, and amid a hostile, ignorant, and all-powerful Mahometan population; the absolutely false reports of the Turkish authorities; combined to keep Armenia in the shadow of the Moslem sword, and away from the help and countenance of international Christianity. When, therefore, late in 1894, rumours reached Constantinople from distant and mountainous Sassoun of some terrible massacres and cruelty to the Armenian Christians in that district, the news was at once suppressed, so far as the Sultan's Government could do so. But, gradually, intelligence of the frightful nature of the occurrences crept into English and American newspapers; private letters began to come to hand by messengers who had eluded Turkish surveillance; missionaries, though afraid to give their names, described incidents coming within their own experience; British Consuls reported concerning the atrocities they had heard of, and, in some cases, seen. Isolated as Sassoun was; despairing as were the miserable survivors of the massacres; emphatic as was the denial of Turkish Ministers, the truth could not be long concealed.

At first the reports were disbelieved in England. British newspapers, of Conservative complexion, did not wish to amplify or dwell upon stories which gave another hard blow to the British friends of Turkey. The Liberal press was not particularly anxious to add another foreign complication to the many which Lord Rosebery then had to deal with. The terrible news was therefore minimized and discredited, and, even when reliable information came to hand, it was thought that Armenian revolutionists might have had a considerable hand in provoking the massacres. And British political leaders were still more limited in their expressions of belief or sympathy, with the notable exceptions of Mr. Gladstone, the Duke of Argyll, and the Duke of Westminster. But eventually conviction came to every one that a great national crime had been committed. To quote the *London Times*, early in December, 1894;

"There seems to be no longer any possibility of doubting that revolting cruelties have been committed on a very large scale, not by fanatical villagers or savage Bashi-Bazouks, but by regular troops, acting on the express orders of a Turkish general, and regardless of the protest of a Turkish district-governor. Worst of all, the conduct of the general has been not only condoned, but rewarded by an imperial decoration, while the humane protesting official has been summarily removed from his post."

The first massacres seem to have risen out of a temporary alliance between the lamb and the wolf—the Armenian peasant and his Kurdish oppressor—for the purpose of enabling the former to refuse payment of certain additional Turkish taxes. The Armenians in this isolated Sassoun district, having to pay the almost intolerable exactions of the Kurds, seem to have thought that through the latter's help they might defy their Ottoman oppressors, and thus let wolf eat wolf. Hence the driving away of the troops sent to collect certain taxes, and the immediate representation to Constantinople that a serious Armenian rebellion had broken out. Orders were at once sent to Zekki Pasha, the military commander at Erzinjan, to proceed to the disturbed district with a force sufficient to suppress the alleged troubles. What his orders were will perhaps never be exactly known, but they were enough to inspire the commander with a brutally unique vigour, and to draw to his aid the Kurds themselves. Both the troops and Kurds seem to have then fallen upon the villagers—unarmed, it must be remembered, as a rule—and to have murdered, tortured, and pillaged to the very extreme point of Moslem cruelty.

Such, at least, was the immediate origin of the troubles, according to what the London *Times* termed "the best authenticated account." But refugees have since stated that for eighteen months prior to the massacres the district of Sassoun was surrounded by Turkish troops, who allowed no one to pass their lines. Upon one occasion, however, they learned that people in the village of Vartimis, just outside the district, had managed to smuggle some food through the lines into the neighbouring village of Dalvorig. For this offence Vartimis was raided, and the majority of its inhabitants slaughtered—25 Armenian houses out of 325 being left standing as memorials of mercy. There have, of course, been many other and varied versions of the first cause of the massacres, outside of the generally accepted belief amongst local Turks, and Kurds, and Armenians, that they formed part of an official scheme of prearranged extermination. One story is that the Armenians fought and drove away the Kurds in 1893, and that the latter came back with the regular troops in 1894, and performed the horrible work they had before attempted.

But whatever the exact origin of the occurrences, there is no doubt as to their nature. The details indeed are too horrible to be more than briefly indicated. A letter dated Bitlis, October 9th, declared that some of the Turkish soldiers actually shrank back shuddering from the picture and record of what they had themselves done, and claimed that the Kurds had committed the worst of the crimes. "No compassion," says the writer, "was shown to age or sex, even by the regular soldiery—not even when victims fell suppliant at their feet. Five to ten thousand met such a fate as even the darkest ages of darkest Africa had hardly witnessed." The torments which were inflicted on the helpless women and children are as indescribable as they are inconceivable to Christian minds. The letter concludes by saying that the writer could not further prolong the sickening tale. "There must be a God in heaven who will do right in all these matters, or some of us would lose faith."

Another letter declares that twenty-seven villages were annihilated in Sassoun, and six thousand men, women, and children massacred by the Turks and Kurds. It adds—October 31st—that "the awful story is only just beginning to be known in Constantinople, though the massacres took place early in September. The Turks have used infinite pains to prevent the news leaking out, even going to the length of sending back from Trebizond many hundreds from the Moush region who had come this way on business." An epistle published in the "Artzakank" of Tiflis, and written by one whom the *Times* described as an " able and careful correspondent in Armenia," gives the following account of a portion of the slaughter :

" Zekki Pasha, that prowling enemy to the peace and life of mankind, who was quite recently rewarded with the Osmanieh of the first class, marched against Sassoun with the troops under his orders, consisting of regulars and the Hamidieh rabble, and, having been repulsed, could only attack the eleven villages in the Shadakh district between Sassoun and Moush. . . . The inhabitants of these villages consisted of unarmed, defenceless, decrepid old men, old women, housewives, boys and girls. The Pasha has pitilessly hacked to pieces and stabbed these people with swords and bayonets, some 900 souls, and about 150 of them were led as prisoners— horribly maltreated and half dead, in heavy chains—and incarcerated in the central prison at Moush. . . . The villages were given up to pillage and fired."

These Turkish-Armenian prisons, by the way, have been described by Dr. Dillon as the home of filth, disease, deformity, pain in forms almost inconceivable to civilized peoples, torture, and madness—" the whole incarnated in grotesque beings whose resemblance to man is a living blasphemy on the Deity." Reports such as the above continued to pour in upon private individuals at Constantinople, in London, and in New York, from men of undoubted position and probity, the use of whose names, however, would have placed them in the greatest danger. One letter, for instance, states that the details which had then reached Bitlis—a few miles from the scene of massacre—indicated a repetition of the sickening horrors of 1876 in Bulgaria. Another adds the statement that the massacres, even as reported by the regular soldiers themselves, were " most fiendish." Many of the latter admitted to him, without any particular shame, of having disposed of a hundred persons each—by torture, outrage, and the bayonet. "Twenty to thirty villages were wholly destroyed; people were burned with kerosene in their own homes." The London *Times'* correspondent reported a number of individual cases of Turkish cruelty which illustrate the horrors of the more general massacres.

In the village of Semal, for instance, a Kurd commander of regular troops, named Selo Bey, took the local priest from his church, placed him and the sacred vessels upon a donkey, and then, going a little distance away, shot the man dead. Selo also forcibly seized a number of Armenian girls in the village, and sent them to his harem at Quitzoum. The village of Kelichuzen was set on fire by a body of troops in the early dawn, before its people were stirring, and a priest named Margos, with twenty other persons, were burned alive in a single house, not one being allowed to escape. The chief of the village—Cheneg by name—was bound up with his two daughters, and all three scalded to death. A man named Arakiel and his wife were tortured with red-hot irons and then killed. Ibo Bey, another Kurd brigand and a Colonel in the regular army, took his troops to the villages of Bahlow, Hatzgent, and Komk, and there committed outrages of the most abominable and indescribable nature. In one case two hundred women were collected together, brutally maltreated, and then shot or bayoneted.

A number of letters, necessarily anonymous, but written by Americans resident in Turkey whose standing has been vouched for by the Governor of Massachusetts and others, have been recently published, and throw considerable detailed light on these scenes of horror. In some cases small companies of troops entered the villages, declared their intention of protecting the people, and then, in the middle of the night, "arose and slaughtered the sleeping villagers, man, woman, and child." Upon one occasion a priest and some leading men went out to meet the officer, declared their loyalty, presented their tax-receipts, and pleaded for mercy. But " the village was surrounded, and all human beings put to the bayonet." A large and strong man, the chief of another village, was captured by the Kurds," who tied him, threw him on the ground, and squatting around him stabbed him to pieces. " By this time," says a correspondent :

" Those in other villages were beginning to feel that extermination was the object of the government, and desperately determined to sell their lives as dearly as possible. And then began a campaign of butchery that lasted some twenty-three days, or, roughly, from the middle of August to the middle of September. The Ferik Pasha (Marshal Zekki Pasha), who came post-haste from Erzinjan, read the Sultan's firman for extermination, and then, hanging the document on his breast, exhorted the soldiers not to be found wanting in their duty. On the last day of August, the anniversary of the Sultan's accession, the soldiers were especially urged to distinguish themselves, and they made it the day of the greatest slaughter."

The details of torture and death are awful. At Galo-gozan, for instance, many young men were tied hand and foot, laid in a row, covered with brushwood, and burned alive. " Others were seized and hacked to death, piecemeal." The men of another village, when fleeing, took the women and children, some 500 in number, and concealed them in a sort of cave. " After several days the soldiers found them, and butchered those who had not died of hunger." Children were massacred without mercy, sometimes literally torn to pieces. In one instance a little boy ran out of the flames of his burning home, but was caught on a bayonet and thrown back. A portion of the doomed population, about 1,000 in number, sought refuge on Mount Audoke, and for fifteen days, despite almost continuous attack by fresh relays of Kurds, managed to hold their own. But food and ammunition gave out, and exhaustion finally enabled the enemy to capture their position. Hardly an Armenian survived to tell the tale of the result.

The troops and Kurds then turned their attention to the Dalvorig district, where some 4,000 survivors still clung together. They were soon decimated, however, by rifle shots, and the remainder slaughtered with sword and bayonet. The fate of the women during these occurrences cannot be described. But in nearly every case they refused to accept Mahometanism and a Turkish harem as the price of life. In one village 400 women, in another 200 women, in another 60 girls, and hundreds of isolated individuals throughout these districts, accepted their dreadful fate, rather than repudiate Christianity. The Armenian estimate of the total number slaughtered in these preliminary massacres is 16,000; the Turkish admission is about 1,000; the probable number is about 10,000.

As soon as these facts became reasonably substantiated and publicly known, steps were taken in the English-speaking countries to express sympathy, proffer aid to the survivors, and urge international action. In London the Armenian Relief Committee was formed, with the Duke of Argyll as President, and the Duke of Westminster and the Archbishop of York as Vice-Presidents. Amongst its members were the Bishops of Salisbury, St. Asaph, and Hereford, Lord Edmund Fitzmaurice, Mr. James Bryce, M.P., Canon McCall, Rev. Dr. Guinness Rogers, and Mr. Edward Atkin (Secretary and Treasurer). Thousands of pounds were soon collected and sent out to the starving people still scattered

over the Sassoun district, and wandering amid the ruins
of their homes and the wrecks of household happiness.
In the United States a large Committee was also organized, to which New York contributed its leading
men, and the great republic many thousands of dollars.
The Hon. Seth Low, Mayor Strong, Bishop Potter, Rev.
Dr. Lyman Abbott, General Horace Porter, and many
others took an active interest in the work, which was supervised by Mr. Bleecker Miller, the chairman; Mr. C. H.
Stout, the treasurer; and an earnest Armenian resident,
Herant Mesrob Kiretchjian, as general secretary.
Canada was not behindhand in its aid, and through the
energetic efforts of Dr. Walter B. Geikie, of Toronto, as
treasurer of a large Committee, it contributed as much
proportionately as the richer and more populous countries.

But, naturally, this work of sympathy and Christianity did not have immediate effect. Many delays occurred
in the organizing of relief, owing to Turkish deception and
intrigue, while the funds themselves did not grow as rapidly
as was the case when, a year later, there came the news
of still more awful massacres—if such were possible.
Meanwhile events and knowledge alike progressed. At a
mass meeting in New York, Mr. Varton Dilloyan, a survivor and witness of the Sassoun horrors, explained the
nature of the occurrences, and pleaded for aid to the starving remnant in that once beautiful district. " I saw wi h
my own eyes," said he, " how the soldiers rushed through
our village—Dalvorig—and picked up the little children
and cut them to pieces, and then rushed on to slay others,
calling to those behind them, "Come on! Come on!"
After going into some other details, he went on to describe how the Moslems had desecrated their churches,
murdered their priests, tied the Cross to the necks of
dogs, and tortured and killed the women.

In January, 1896, more than a year after these events, two large British blue-books were issued dealing with them, so far as it was possible for the Consular Delegates accompanying the farcical Turkish Commission of Inquiry to do so. They were, of course, hampered by the presence of the Turkish officials, and prevented from obtaining any really serviceable information by the fact that no Armenian could dare to tell the truth, while all Moslems felt bound to tell the reverse. They, therefore, found hundreds to have been slaughtered where the private evidence of myriads of witnesses—European and American residents, missionaries and Armenian refugees —proved thousands to have been openly massacred. Still, they found that the details were sufficiently atrocious, and Mr. H. S. Shipley, the British Commissioner, in a report which was presented to Sir Philip Currie and Lord Salisbury, says:

"I do not think, seeing as I did, in company with my colleagues, the entire ruin of a whole district, not a house being left standing, the fields even having been wantonly devastated, as well as the abject misery and destitution to which these Armenians have been reduced, that the epithets applied to the conduct of the Turkish soldiers and Kurds by the press are in any way too strong. We have in our report given it as our conviction, arrived at from the evidence brought before us, that the Armenians were massacred without distinction of age or sex, and, indeed, for a period of three weeks—August 12 to September 4—it is not too much to say that the Armenians were absolutely hunted like wild beasts, being killed wherever they were met."

He goes on to say that the story of revolt on the part of the Christians is false, and that all indications favour the belief that the Turkish authorities desired the extermination, pure and simple, of the Christian population of these districts. And he adds his own conviction that "whether they instigated the above attack or not, they were responsible for it; it took place with their knowledge and consent, as is shown by the fact that the soldiers sent nominally to keep order sided with the Kurks, and so contributed to the ruin of the Talori Armenians." It might well be asked where in all Armenian, or, indeed, Turkish history was the Moslem soldier ever known to side with, or defend, his Christian fellow-subject? In addition to the analysis of the evidence received, the Consular Delegates had been instructed to take depositions from certain reliable Armenian witnesses, and six of these sworn statements are included in the blue-books. They furnish the most horrible accounts of outrage and massacre, describe events which have either been already referred to, or the nature of which may be easily understood from what has been previously stated.

To return to an earlier stage of the subject, and when news had reached the authorities at Constantinople concerning the suppression of this "rebellion," the Sultan at once despatched a special officer to Zekki Pasha, the "hero" of Sassoun, and chief representative of military power in that division of the empire, with a message of thanks, and a very high decoration set in brilliants. Accompanying this were new flags to be given, as a special token of honour and appreciation, to the Kurdish cavalry, or Hamidieh. This action was in reality a challenge to Christendom, and a more open approval than even that accorded to Chefket Pasha for the Bulgarian massacres of twenty years before. And it should have been accepted as such, when the proofs came fully to hand of the atrocities which it practically approved and praised. But, although universal sympathy in all English-speaking countries was aroused, this sentiment did not assume the form of a sufficiently acute indignation to make the Sultan feel that he had gone too far—or let his myrmidons go too far. The result was seen in the massacres of 1895. Yet these events, even so far as they had gone in December, 1894, amongst the valleys and hills of Sassoun, were worse than any recorded of the Reign of Terror or the Sicilian Vespers. These latter occurrences are famous amongst the tragedies of history, although the estimated direct deaths in neither case exceeded 2,000 in number, and were certainly unaccompanied by the unique brutalities of the Kurd and Turk. True, indeed, is the sentiment of William Watson in those forceful lines:

> "The panther of the desert, matched with these,
> Is pitiful; beside their lust and hate
> Fire and the plague-wind are compassionate,
> And soft the deadliest pangs of ravening seas."

Still, Abdul-Hamid denied the massacres, and made great protestations in appointing his Committee of Inquiry, when their truth was publicly forced upon him. And England, as well as America, hoped that he would prove not only innocent of all complicity, but determined in the prevention of further crime. Events and investigations already described have, however, indicated how greatly the authorities at Constantinople were in reality responsible, and even at that time thoughtful persons must have seen and felt the strength of the ties binding the Sultan and his officials, to say nothing of the significance of his having so speedily rewarded the chief criminal. The light of many other occurrences have, since then, shown the Sultan's true position in these Sassoun horrors.

He was, in fact, directly responsible through his creation of the Hamidieh or Kurdish cavalry, and the share of his officered and regular troops in the deepest depths of murder and outrage. He was indirectly responsible through the general disarmament of the Christians over a long term of years; through his knowledge of preceding and multitudinous crimes against the Armenians; through his memory of many historic Turkish massacres, especially the Kurdish one of 1846; through his refusal to accept the advice and requests of Christian ambassadors regarding Armenian reform; through his intimate knowledge of the character of Turkish officials, and the particularly villainous character of those in Armenia. And these proofs of responsibility were enhanced a thousand times by the circumstances surrounding Turkish policy and the Eastern Question during the ten or twelve months which succeeded Sassoun, and preceded the still more widespread slaughter.

CHAPTER XX.

THE EASTERN CRISIS.

To be adequately understood, the critical international situation which developed during 1895 as the result of the first Armenian massacres, and became so greatly accentuated during those of the ensuing year, must be studied in the dry light of the Berlin Treaty, in the complexities of British national politics, and amid the rivalries of European powers.

It is easy enough, in these days of newspaper predominance, to read and comprehend the bare terms of the famous treaty which Lord Beaconsfield and Lord Salisbury forced down the throat of Russia at Berlin. It is a very simple matter to condemn those portions which have not turned out exactly as was hoped and expected at the time when Great Britain was told that peace had been preserved with honour. It is easy to forget the enormous difficulties surrounding the whole problem, then as well as now, and the success which followed many of the arrangements made. And very few seem to remember the political circumstances which surrounded or succeeded that treaty in England, and the connection of those political issues with the present disastrous situation in Armenia.

When the war of 1876-7 broke out between Russia and Turkey as the consequence of undoubted aggression on the part of the former, England did not interfere further than by diplomatic protest. But under the terms of the

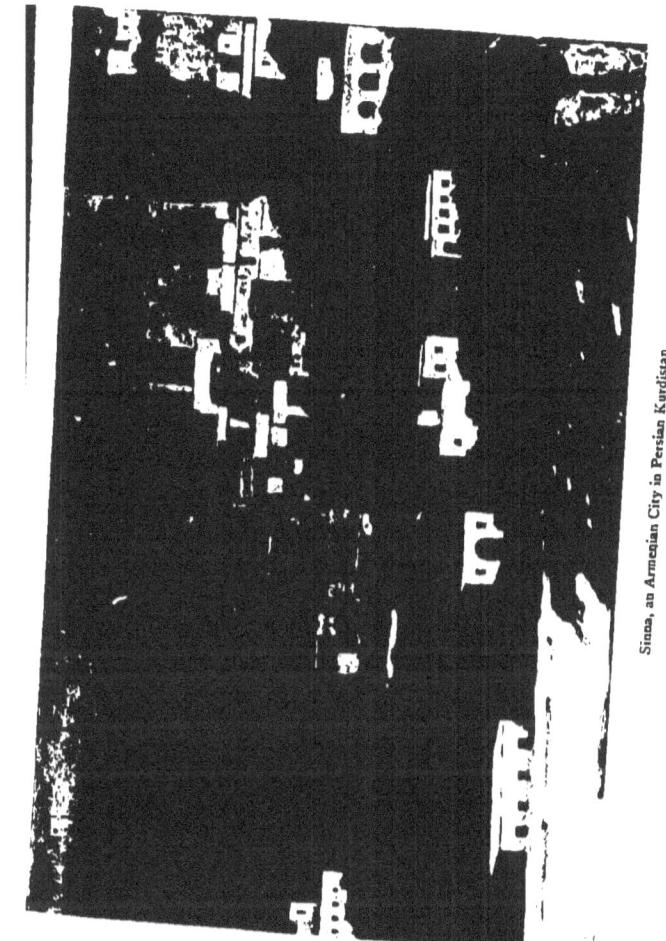

Sinna, an Armenian City in Persian Kurdistan.

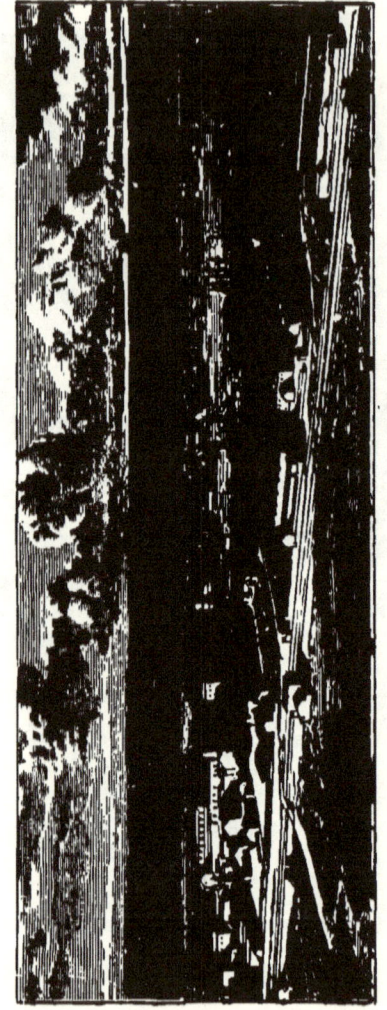

Batoum, a Russian Fortress on the Borders of Turkish Armenia.

Treaty of Paris (1856) France, Austria, and Prussia were pledged, with Great Britain, to preserve the integrity and independence of the Ottoman Empire; and when the war was concluded by the Treaty of San Stefano and the practical placing of Constantinople under the control of the Czar, the British Government forced the Powers to take action. The Berlin Treaty was the result of this intervention, which Lord Beaconsfield would have carried to the point of war, rather than leave the Russians omnipotent in Turkey. By the terms of the arrangement which thus aggrandized Greece, and freed Bulgaria, Servia, Montenegro, and Roumania, while maintaining the national position of the Turk, a paragraph was given to the affairs of Armenia. Article 61 declared that "the Sublime Porte undertakes to carry out without further delay the improvements and reforms demanded by local requirements in the provinces inhabited by the Armenians, and to guarantee their security against the Circassians and the Kurds. It will periodically make known the steps taken to this effect to the Powers, who will superintend their application."

This particular clause was the veriest farce. Not one of the Powers, excepting England, took the slightest real interest in the Armenians, or entertained any genuine sympathy with their religious sufferings. And even in England their position was largely overlooked amid the darkness of better known conditions in Bulgaria. Russia, of course, had a territorial interest in the matter. She had acquired a large amount of Armenian territory and a number of Armenian, or rather Turkish, fortresses by the treaty, and was not disinclined to obtain more. But she had not the slightest desire or intention of helping to improve the condition of any subjects of the Ottoman power anywhere. Nor has she now. The more they suffered or were oppressed, the better for Russian designs and intrigues. And aside from Great Britain, the other Powers were far too willing to let sleeping dogs lie; far too desirous of seeing the Eastern Question in a condition of atrophy to permit of their taking any active steps in forcing reforms to the front. This the Sultan knew just as well as they did.

But Lord Beaconsfield was honestly anxious to effect something—if not purely in the interest of Christianity, at least in the interest of those historic Christian lands which he loved so well, and about which the innermost sympathies of his curiously romantic nature were intertwined. A second and semi-secret treaty was therefore made with Turkey. If reforms could not be carried out under the auspices of the Powers, they must be realized under the orders of England. If Asia Minor had no hope of improvement or development under the dominance of the Turk, and the neighbouring shadow of the Russian, it should have some chance under the protectorate and guidance of Great Britain. The scheme was a bold one, worthy of the great Premier's genius and broad sympathies, and it found expression in the following clause of the Anglo-Turkish Convention:

"Article I. If Batoum, Ardahan, Kars, or any of them, shall be retained by Russia, and if any attempt shall be made at any future time by Russia to take possession of any further territory of His Imperial Majesty the Sultan in Asia, as fixed by the Definitive Treaty of Peace, England engages to join His Imperial Majesty the Sultan in defending them by force of arms.

"In return, His Imperial Majesty the Sultan promises to England to introduce necessary reforms, *to be agreed upon later between the two powers*, into the Government and for the protection of the Christian and other subjects of the Porte in those territories; and in order to enable England to make necessary provisions for executing her engagement, His Imperial Majesty the Sultan further consents to assign the Island of Cyprus to be occupied and administered by England."

In making this arrangement with Turkey, Lord Beaconsfield was actuated by a statesmanship which now seems clearly apparent. He was quite aware of the futility of Turkish promises, and the strength of Moslem prejudices. To meet the difficulty in part, he had taken Cyprus as a hostage. He must also have been well aware of the British aversion to Turkey then existing in many quarters, and of the force of this public opinion as shown in Mr. Gladstone's agitation regarding the Bulgarian horrors of 1877. But, no doubt, the expectation was that as soon as the protectorate of Asiatic Turkey became a recognized fact, and a growing influence for good in the administration of Eastern affairs, this feeling would gradually die away, and be replaced by satisfaction at the existence of a potent force for the protection of Turkish Christians; the steady development of this marvellously rich Turkish territory; the natural and consequent growth of British interests and commerce. And it seemed evident enough to his far-sighted political judgment that a defined British position in these countries toward Russian aggression and Russian intrigues—even at the expense of a defensive alliance with the Turks—would be greatly better than existing vague and indefinite responsibilities, and be in itself a preventive of war by enabling England to more or less control the Ottoman policy. It was, in fact, a noble idea, and a plan which might have averted many succeeding international troubles, to say nothing of the sufferings of the Armenians during the last twenty years.

Speaking, with Lord Salisbury, at the famous Conservative banquet in Knightsbridge, upon their return from

Berlin, the Premier declared in words well worthy of recollection in these latter days, and in connection with this particular branch of the general question:
"We thought the time had come when we should take steps which should produce some order out of the anarchy and chaos that had so long prevailed. We asked ourselves, was it absolutely a necessity that the fairest provinces of the world should be the most devastated and most ill-used, and for this reason, that there is no security for life or property so long as that country is in perpetual fear of aggression and invasion? It was under these circumstances that we recommended the course we have taken, and I believe that the consequences of that policy will tend to, and even secure, peace and order, in a portion of the globe which hitherto has seldom been blessed by these celestial visitants. I hold that we have laid the foundation of a state of affairs which may open a new continent to the civilization of Europe, and that the welfare of the world, and the wealth of the world, may be increased by availing ourselves of that tranquillity and order which the more intimate connection of England with that country will now produce."

But, unfortunately, he under-estimated the strength of Mr. Gladstone's opposition, and the force of the public sentiment which that great orator had aroused against the Turk. He did not see the shadow of the miserable little wars in Afghanistan and Zululand, nor the complications which in less than two years were to sweep him from power and destroy the prospects of British administration in Asia Minor—under stress of party pledges from which the Liberal leaders could hardly withdraw. Mr. Gladstone had been consistent enough in his policy of bitter antagonism to this Anglo-Turkish arrangement, and to the Eastern schemes of the great "Asian Mystery," as *Punch* once dubbed Lord Beaconsfield. From its first announcement he had protested vigorously and fiercely against the Cyprus convention as an "insane covenant." He had declared it to be unwise, unwarrantable, extravagant, unconstitutional, dangerous, and shameful, and had afterwards supported Lord Hartington's motion in the House to condemn the Government for entering into "undefined engagements in respect to the better administration of those provinces." Of course the resolution was not carried, but it none the less committed the Liberal party to a reversal of the whole policy involved in what Mr. Gladstone once more denounced as "an unheard-of, mad undertaking."

And amongst other severe critics of the arrangement was the Duke of Argyle, who is now so generously working for the welfare of the Armenians. Speaking in reply to him, on May 16th, 1879, Lord Beaconsfield referred to the noble Duke as having laughed at the idea of any beneficial change ensuing in Asia Minor from British protection and intervention. He then expressed his own belief that "there was nothing difficult or great that was not laughed at in the beginning," and looked hopefully forward to what he termed the "regeneration of Asia Minor."

In fact, all his speeches at that period teem with references to the proposed policy in the East. And one more extract may be given as illustrating the strength of his views. "My Lords," said the Conservative Premier, in addressing the Peers upon the Berlin Treaty, "it seemed to us that as we had now taken, and as Europe generally had taken, so avowedly deep an interest in the welfare of the subjects of the Porte in Europe, the time had come when we ought to consider whether we could not do something which would improve the general condition of the dominions of the Sultan in Asia; and instead of these most favoured portions of the globe every year being in a more forlorn and disadvantageous position, whether it would not be possible to take some steps which would secure at least tranquillity and order." When that had been done, he pointed out, the next and natural step would be to try to find some mear "to develop the resources of a country which nature made so rich and teeming."

Although opposed so strenuously by the Liberals, this policy was generally supported by his own party. Lord Sandon—afterwards Earl of Harrowby—has been since described as "descanting in most glowing strains upon the cornucopia of blessings that England was about to shower on the Armenians." He had travelled years before in Asia Minor, and found everywhere a feverish expectation of British intervention on behalf of better government, and protection for Christian populations. Mr. Grattan Geary, in a work pub 'hed during 1878, went even further in this last conne , and stated that he was more than once asked con..dentially by good Mahometans why England did not come in and take possession of the country as a whole. "If England, they said, took over the country, it would soon prosper; trade would expand at once; and there would be no conscription."

Mr. Geary goes on to speak of the influence which the wealth and magnificence of the cities in British India had upon Arab and other traders, and the consequent glowing opinion prevalent in many quarters concerning British supremacy. "I found that the splendour and civilization of Bombay filled a large place in the popular imagination of Bagdad; and that the trade, and prosperity, and fine buildings of that city were attributed to the fact that the port of India was under British rule." And there was undoubtedly a general belief in Asiatic Turkey, and in Russian diplomatic circles, as well as in

British political and Parliamentary life, that something efficient and strong was to come out of the Anglo-Turkish arrangements. It would indeed have been a blessing to Asia and the world had such been the case, and would long since have partially anticipated the recently written lines of Lewis Morris:

> "Let the new-coming age, a happier birth,
> Bless these waste places of the suffering earth;
> Let peace, with law, the tranquil valleys fill,
> And make the desert blossom as the rose."

But it must be remembered that in addition to all the other objections entertained by the Opposition, for the terms of the Anglo-Turkish Convention, there was the vital one—to them—that it reversed the policy of united action by the great Powers in regard to Turkey, which had been so lamentably embodied in the Treaty of Paris, and so consistently carried out by the governments of Lord Palmerston and Mr. Gladstone. The one little clause about necessary reforms "to be agreed upon afterwards between the *two* Powers" meant the breaking up of European combined action—or rather inaction—regarding Turkish matters, and a complete change in British Foreign policy. Continuity in the conduct of Foreign affairs had not yet become a principle in British public life, and, unfortunately, it did not do so until Lord Rosebery's appearance upon the national stage. As it turned out, the Liberal party refused to accept this reversal, and in 1880 Lord Granville returned to the old scheme of joint international operations, and put in practice once more a policy which resulted in such farcical scenes as the demonstration at Dulcigno.

Meanwhile, Lord Salisbury, as Foreign Secretary in the Beaconsfield Administration from 1878 to 1880, had acted in the very fullest sympathy with the new Conservative policy in Asiatic Turkey. Speaking with his chief at the Knightsbridge banquet upon their return from Berlin, he had declared that the party was "striving to pick up the thread—the broken thread—of England's old Imperial position." He strongly denounced the men who disdained empire, objected to the colonies, and grumbled at the responsibilities connected with India. He pointed out the pleasure with which the people of Cyprus had accepted transfer to the Crown of Great Britain, and the enthusiasm with which the Queen's name had been received. He spoke of England as having won her spurs in the cause of civilization and good government, and claimed that where British rule prevailed peace and order revived, while prosperity and wealth increased. Then, having prepared the way, and criticized those who wished to hide this light under a bushel, or minimize the extension of British influence, he continued and concluded:

"I am told that in the task of aiding and counselling the Ottoman Empire to bring the blessings of civilization to some of the fairest portions of the earth, we shall be hampered by the jealousy of other Powers. I utterly refuse to believe it. When they find what our policy really is; that we are there merely to extend to others the benefits we ourselves enjoy; when they find that we welcome their competition, that we invite every trade, that we grudge success to no nationality, that the one object we have in view is that peace and order should be restored, and that races and creeds which for centuries back have lived in feud should henceforth live in amity and good will, then I believe that all idea of jealousy will vanish, and they will heartily co-operate with us in our civilizing mission. At all events, *we will not recoil* from such a task because it may seem to add to our responsibilities or increase our labours; and if we are able, in even so small a degree, to accomplish these results, we at least shall have no cause to repent of the labours we have undertaken, and you will have no cause to be ashamed of us."

Something was at once done to carry out this policy. Of course, permanent action would depend upon the result of the elections which were to take place within a year or two, and in which this whole Turkish arrangement was to be one of the issues forced on the country by the eloquent voice of Mr. Gladstone. A number of military consuls were appointed in Asia Minor, to reside there and supervise the promised reforms. Their reports came duly to hand, but by that time the Government was plunged in matters of war and home politics, which made immediate consideration impossible. And, within a few months, Mr. Gladstone was in office and Lord Granville in control of Foreign affairs. Hence the gross injustice of a recent Radical speaker in England, who intimates that because these reports were pigeon-holed, and the consuls one by one withdrawn, the Conservative party was therefore responsible for what followed.

The fact is that this was done under the new Government, and by virtue of their well-known intention and pledged policy. For five years thereafter, the whole course of action regarding Turkey was one of combination with the other Powers. England seemed unable to do anything or obtain anything without a European Concert—which usually resulted in nothing. The Anglo-Turkish Convention, so far as Asiatic Turkey was concerned, appears to have been absolutely ignored—where it was not reversed in petty matters. Cyprus was still retained, and one would suppose that, in common honour, the two concurrent and inter-dependent arrangements—Turkish reform in Asia, and British protection over the territory and its Christian population—should have been also retained and enforced.

But by his European "Concert" Lord Granville did several important things. He repudiated the right of England to act alone in Asia Minor; he renounced the one possible chance of successful interference by thus introducing into the question the animated discord of Europe; he brought Russia back into Turkish affairs as an intriguing, troublesome factor; he introduced the necessarily indifferent, vague, and dilatory views of many nations into the consideration of a problem which, above all things, required concentrated, prolonged, and positive treatment; he made it morally certain that nothing would be done for countries about which European Powers—aside from the selfish motives of Russia—felt no genuine concern; he increased the dangers of the local situation by giving the Sultan an object lesson of divided counsels amongst his European advisers, whom—being a Turk and a Mahometan—he naturally regarded as his enemies.

Hence the failure of the policy which replaced that of Lord Beaconsfield and Lord Salisbury. Hence the difficulty, not generally appreciated or understood, encountered by the latter statesman when in power from 1886 to 1892, and again in 1895. In the first-named year, Lord Salisbury faced an international situation very different from that which presented itself in 1878. Then, Russia had been diplomatically defeated at Berlin, and driven back from the very walls of Stamboul to the far side of the Balkans. England was the friend who had saved the Turk, while safeguarding the Christians in Bulgaria, Greece, Roumania, and Armenia. Russia was the discredited foe of both Powers, and the specially determined enemy of Islam. Turkey was not only, therefore, dependent upon England—who was backed up by Austria and Germany—but had received a pledge of defensive alliance for the future.

British influence was consequently paramount in Constantinople, and a few years of vigorous policy would have ensured reforms in Asiatic Turkey, the safety and comfort of its people, and the fruition of some at least of Lord Beaconsfield's cherished plans for its well-being and development. But in five years everything had changed. Germany was now jealous of England's colonial progress, and had been coming into constant collision with her in connection with schemes of territorial extension in Africa, New Guinea, Samoa, etc. France was bitterly hostile owing to Egyptian and other matters. Austria, which has never been popular with English Liberalism, certainly did not like Mr. Gladstone. The European Concert had proved an unmitigated farce, but was still the recognized method of dealing with Turkey. Russia was once more in the full fling of diplomatic intrigue at Stamboul, and had just come out of the Pendjeh affair, on the borders of Afghanistan, with some accession of prestige. And, above all, the Anglo-Turkish Convention was an absolute deadletter; practically repudiated by the late British Government; altogether disregarded by the Sublime Porte; considered by Russia and the other Powers as superseded by their plan of combined action.

To revive the dormant arrangement in the teeth of general European indifference or hostility, and the more specific and active antagonism of Russia, was to not only throw the Turk into the arms of England's old-time enemy, but to combine the two Powers with France in a determined effort to get the British out of Egypt—besides rendering really useful action in Asia Minor impossible. So the Anglo-Turkish Convention remained inoperative, although one of its chief framers was in power, while the so-called concerted policy of the great

Powers was continued. Lord Rosebery, in 1892, came to the front at the Foreign Office, and announced, with all sincerity, his intention of adopting "continuity of policy" as the most dignified, safe, and wise system for British diplomacy to pursue. He was right and patriotic in the general statement and principle—one which Lord Salisbury fully endorsed and ratified when he succeeded him two or three years later.

Such, in brief, has been the record of British parties and leaders upon this question, and its details should be most carefully studied before condemning the Government of Lord Salisbury for not intervening in Armenia, or denouncing its members for having broken the terms of the Anglo-Turkish arrangement. Certainly, such denunciations come very badly from Liberal leaders. Lord Rosebery, in the main, has refused to join those who have heartily shared in demonstrations along this line, and so, to his honour be it said, has Mr. Gladstone. Sir William Vernon Harcourt, however, has not hesitated to try to make political capital out of the sufferings of Armenia; but, in doing so, has made the strange admission—February 11th, 1896—that "we were to defend Turkey in Asia Minor. We were to hold Cyprus, and Turkey, in consideration of that undertaking, covenanted to protect the Christian population in Armenia."

True; but if that Convention was a bad and dangerous and insane one, as Mr. Gladstone claimed at the time with the entire approval of his party, then Lord Salisbury should not be condemned now for having failed to revive it, amid very different conditions, and after the lapse of eighteen years. If, on the other hand, it was a wise Convention, as Lord Salisbury believed at the time he signed it, and an arrangement calculated to protect the Christians, and develop the countries of Asia Minor, and strengthen the beneficent influence of England, then the Government to which Sir William Harcourt belonged from 1880 to 1885 was more than blameworthy in having repudiated England's obligations under that treaty, while retaining Cyprus—the price paid for services which they practically proclaimed their intention of never giving.

When the Sassoun massacres occurred, however, a crisis came which really tested the merits of these two opposing policies—the one a single-handed, responsible, and persistent British control in Asiatic Turkey; the other a continuance of the old system of combined, concerted action by the allied, but bitterly antagonistic, great Powers. Lord Rosebery might perhaps, by a daring *coup*, have returned then to the Beaconsfield policy of 1878, but the difficulties were so great that it was probably impossible. Failing this, he followed the rut of international practice, and the united protests of an absolutely indifferent Austria; a France which was only anxious to join Russia in tripping up England; and a Germany which cared nothing about the Armenians, and has never troubled itself about Turkish reform; were sent in to "support" Great Britain in its sincere desire to effect something beneficial.

It is not difficult to imagine the smile with which the Sultan would receive the ambassadors bearing the protests, or demands, which their "united" Governments might make under such circumstances. Had Great Britain retained, or been able to re-assert, the Beaconsfield idea of a protectorate over Asia Minor, how differently would he have received the single representative of a Power which knew its own rights and responsibilities, which knew how far it was prepared to go, and was willing to carry out the threats which might be necessary! Under the existence of that protectorate, the Kurds would never have been organized into military divisions; the preliminary miseries and murders in Armenia would have been long since checked; the brigands themselves would have been driven back into their mountain recesses. If it could have been re-established in even the most modified form by Lord Rosebery, the second series of massacres could not have occurred, and the present terrible issue would not have been troubling the Salisbury Government and the conscience of the civilized world.

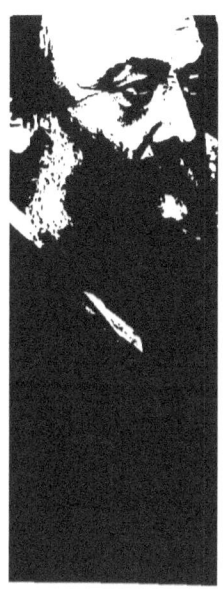

The Marquess of Salisbury, K.G.
Prime Minister of Great Britain

Rt. Hon. W. E. Gladstone in 1893.

CHAPTER XXI.

MR. GLADSTONE AND ARMENIA.

From the time when news first crept into public European channels concerning the massacres in Armenia, and while the shadows of a still greater slaughter were growing more dark and ominous, many in England looked to Mr. Gladstone for the inauguration of a strong campaign against the unspeakable Turk. They felt in a vague way that the aged statesman was an enemy of Turkish rule; that he had been a fierce critic of Turkish cruelty in Bulgaria and Greece; that he had upon one famous occasion urged the expulsion of the Turks from Europe; and that his sympathies with the oppressed would be more powerful than his sentimental adherence to a retired life, and his very practical objections to sacrificing considerations of personal health and comfort. To a certain degree they were right, but it was in a very modified way that the intervention eventually came.

The former Liberal leader found himself in a rather difficult position. So far as antagonism to Turkish power, or even sympathy with Russian interference in Ottoman affairs, was concerned, he remained on sure and consistent ground. At the commencement of the Russo-Turkish war he had urged the British Government to support Russia, and had claimed that the inveterately ambitious and aggressive power then invading Turkey was actuated by the purest and highest motives. "I believe," he said, that " it is the pulse of humanity which is now throbbing almost ungovernably in her people." He had joined in a public meeting to denounce Lord Beaconsfield's policy of resistance to Russia, and had supported Prof. Fawcett's declaration that the Turkish Government was the most detestable one that had ever afflicted mankind. In another speech he had expressed the hope that "the knell of Turkish tyranny" would soon be sounded.

Of the British effort to support or reform Turkey, and the determined invasion of Russian armies, he declared in the House of Commons that "we are engaged in a continuous effort; we roll the stone of Sisyphus against the slope, and the moment the hand shall be withdrawn down it will begin to run. However, the time is short; the sands of the hour-glass are running out. The longer you delay, the less, in all likelihood, you will be able to save from the wreck of the integrity and independence of the Turkish Empire. If Russia should fail, her failure would be a disaster to mankind, and the condition of the suffering races, for whom we are supposed to have laboured, will be worse than it was before." So far, he would have been consistent in denouncing the Turk, or in supporting Russian intervention. But just as in 1878 the ghosts of the Crimean war came to disturb his passionate and vivid arraignment of the Ottoman power at the bar of history, so now the shadow of the Cyprus Convention threatened to mar the effect of any attack he might make upon the present policy of Great Britain.

But Mr. Gladstone has always been an impulsive and sympathetic leader rather than a cautious and reasoning statesman. And this has been at the root of many of his most brilliant oratorical triumphs. He had been a prominent member of the Government which, in 1853, declared war against Russia on behalf of Turkish autonomy. But he was eager twenty-five years later to join Russia in absolutely destroying that autonomy, because of the Turkish barbarities in Bulgaria. So, in 1895, sentiment would have made him anxious for England to intervene on behalf of Armenia had he not so bitterly denounced, in 1878-9, the arrangements by which that unfortunate country might have been made, under British protection, the home of peaceful happiness—the garden of the fruitful East. And, as if to add to the perplexities of the situation, it soon became evident that Russia—selfish as usual, and indifferent to the dictates of humanity unless they subserved her own ambitious purposes—would not help in any serious intervention on behalf of the suffering Christians. She would only zealously hamper the exertions of England.

To the appeals made him, therefore, Mr. Gladstone would at first only respond in the vaguest generalities. But in the following letter to Mr. F. S. Stevenson, M.P., dated 14th December, 1894, he gave a hint to the Government of Lord Rosebery that it should now, at last, carry out the terms of that Anglo-Turkish Convention which his party, and he himself, had so long denounced and repudiated:

"The terrible statements concerning Armenia have riveted the attention of the world, and I heartily wish well to you and to every effort at bringing out the truth. Should the allegations be sustained, they will prompt the civilized world now to ask how long these things are to be endured. I will not anticipate the results of the examination, but I feel morally certain that the Administration will not rest without the most thorough examination of the matter, in which, under the Cyprus Convention, we have a separate, deep, and painful interest. It is my present duty to hope that the Ottoman Government will, for its own honour, concur in the most searching examination."

Mr. Gladstone was, in fact, the one man who could have taken hold of such a question and stirred the heart and conscience of England into a recognition of its own great mission in the East, and vast opportunities for beneficial action. Unfortunately, what had been practicable in the years immediately following 1878, when the great Powers were, nominally at least, behind Great Britain in the policy of protecting Turkey against Russian aggression, was no longer easy, or perhaps even possible, in the face of European alliances with the Czar, and European hostility to British interests. What Beaconsfield's statesmanship might have effected during a renewed lease of power had been prevented by Mr. Gladstone and Lord Granville, and was now no longer capable of achievement short of war with Russia. The ex-Premier's just hatred of the Turk had long since prevented him from seeing that a defensive alliance with that Power, coupled with a direct British control over its policy toward the Christians in its territories, was infinitely better than any will-o'-the-wisp phantasm of European joint action.

But apart from all these considerations—which might perhaps have been forgotten in the fiery blast of such a campaign as he had started in 1876 over the Bulgarian horrors—the old statesman's health would hardly permit of so extensive an incursion into generous and lofty politics. What he could do under the circumstances he did. Without attempting to embarrass t'   ent of Lord Rosebery or the succeedi   ilisbury, he once more denounced the   w.   ost unmeasured language, urged the   rible   ature of the crimes which had been committed in t   name of Mahomet, charged the Sultan with responsibility, if not complicity, and pointed out certain steps which he thought fe   ble

Following his letter to Mr. Stevenson came the reception of a deputation from the National Church of Armenia at Hawarden. It arrived at Mr. Gladstone's home on December 29th, while he was celebrating his eighty-fifth birthday, amid showers of congratulations and friendly wishes. The deputation included a number of Armenians from London and Paris, who first presented the Rev. Stephen Gladstone with a silver chalice for the use of Hawarden Church—in memory of the ex-Premier's sympathy with the Christians of Bulgaria and Greece—and then listened to the speech of the latter in response.

Mr. Gladstone explained that the feelings of intense indignation which stirred him when he first heard of the atrocities in Armenia had been necessarily controlled by the possibility of great exaggeration in the stories; by the limitations of British power in such a connection; and by confidence in the Government of the Queen. He added his belief that, great as the influence and power of England might be, the country could hardly undertake to represent humanity at large, or, in other words, to be the policeman of the world. And then, having sufficiently guarded himself, the veteran speaker warmed to his theme, and gave the Turks one of those old-time scathing denunciations which had once rung through Europe like the blasts of a trumpet. If, as it now seemed, the abominations of Bulgaria had been repeated in Armenia, then he thought:

" It is time that one general shout of execration, not of men, but of deeds, one general shout of execration directed against deeds of wickedness, should rise from outraged humanity, and should force itself into the ears of the Sultan of Turkey, and make him sensible, if anything can make him sensible, of the madness of such a course. The history of Turkey has been a sad and painful history. That race has not been without remarkable, and, even in some cases, fine qualities, but from too many points of view it has been a scourge to the world, made use of, no doubt, by a wise Providence for the sins of the world. If these tales of murder, violation, and outrage be true, then it will follow that they cannot be overlooked, and cannot be made light of.

"I have lived to see the Empire of Turkey in Europe reduced to less than one-half of what it was when I was born, and why? Simply because of its misdeeds—great record written by the hand of Almighty God, in whom the Turk, as a Mahometan, believes, and believes firmly—written by the hand of Almighty God against injustice, against lust, against the most abominable cruelty. . . . If allegations such as these are established, it will stand as if written with letters of iron on the records of the world that such a Government as that which can countenance and cover the perpetration of such outrages is a disgrace to Mahomet, the Prophet whom it professes to follow; a disgrace to civilization at large ; and a curse to mankind."

Not long after this ringing utterance, the massacres dealt with were proved to be facts, and were subsequently repeated with tenfold violence and criminal wickedness. The situation, however, seemed bad enough as it was, and writing again to Mr. Stevenson in June, 1895, the ex-Premier declared that " the conduct and Government of Turkey has in this question been even worse than it was as to Bulgaria in 1876." Meanwhile, the Duke of Argyle, who had stood shoulder to shoulder with Mr. Gladstone upon this latter subject, but had long since parted with him upon the Home Rule issue, came vigorously to the front on behalf of the Armenians, and was soon as earnestly and enthusiastically engaged in the work as though he had been a young man, instead of a veteran verging on fourscore years. And *Punch*, which so often hits the political nail on the head, promptly portrayed these two old-time friends as once more united upon this question, and as starting out on a new crusade, armed in coats of mail and mounted on fiery chargers. To the Duke, Mr. Gladstone had written on May 6th that "the danger lying ahead is that we may be tempted in the abandonment of all useful action by plans and promises of reform." "Mere words coming from a Turk," he added, "are not worth the breath spent in uttering them."

In this denunciation he was absolutely justified, but unfortunately the mere statement did not have much weight. Turkish denials and diplomatic schemes for delaying investigation, or preventing the obtaining of definite proofs as to the massacres in Sassoun, were all that the Governments of Europe and the successive Cabinets of England could obtain, until the grudging appointment of an absolutely useless Committee of Inquiry. The results of this "investigation" have been referred to elsewhere, and, as might have been expected, were farcical in the extreme. Meantime, by letter and public appeal, Mr. Gladstone was being urged to do or say something more for the wretched Armenians, whose general condition and prospects were now becoming better known. The work of the Relief Committee; the unceasing labours of a number of earnest men, headed by the Dukes of Argyle and Westminster; the publication of pamphlets and letters by Canon MacColl, whose literary denunciations of Turkish rule and cruelty had for years been as strong as pen could make them, were having their natural effect in an aroused public interest.

And, on August 6th, Mr. Gladstone at last addressed a public meeting in the Town Hall of Chester. It was a wonderful speech to be delivered by a man of eighty-five, and it dealt with the grave issues involved as earnestly and eloquently as the speaker might have done twenty years before. Mr. Bryce, the Liberal politician, so well known upon this continent for his work dealing with "The American Commonwealth," wrote the chairman that it was to be feared the Turks had resolved upon exterminating the Armenians of Armenia, and that the safety of all the Christians in the Turkish East was virtually at stake. The Duke of Westminster presided, and in his opening speech declared that, " on good authority, it was believed that a mass of inoffensive and defenceless Christians of the appalling number of 10,000—men, women, and children—had been massacred, in many cases after untold barbarities had been inflicted on them." He spoke of this as having been done by the police and soldiers of the Sultan, while the statements of local Consuls indicated that "there were thousands left whose all had been destroyed, living in abject destitution and calling for help."

Mr. Gladstone commenced his address by referring to the Ottoman authorities as constituting " an intolerably bad government—perhaps the worst on the face of earth." And, after speaking briefly of the sympathy felt in the United States as being greater even than that in the United Kingdom, he moved the following resolution, by way of serious introduction to the main part of his speech :

"That this meeting expresses its conviction that Her Majesty's Government will have the cordial support of the entire nation, without distinction of party, in any measure which it may adopt for securing to the people of Turkish Armenia such reforms in the administration of that province as shall provide effective guarantees for the safety of life, honour, religion, and property, and that no reforms can be effective which are not placed under the continuous control of the great Powers of Europe."

The resolution was, in a sense, good, but it held within itself the fatal weakness of past Liberal policy, and the obviously enhanced difficulty of present Conservative diplomacy—the appeal to united action by the great Powers. Indirectly, of course, it embodied a condemnation of the Cyprus Convention and of British independent action in Asiatic Turkey, and, so far, was a warning to Lord Salisbury not to attempt a revival of England's responsibility in that direction. Aside from this indirect political reference in the resolution, Mr. Gladstone avoided, with one exception, all partisan statement or language. He, first of all, spoke of the evidences now pouring in as to these latest Turkish horrors, and the details of indescribable crime and outrage which were being daily perpetrated, since the events of Sassoun, in other parts of Armenia.

He referred to the work which had been done by Canon MacColl in exploiting the evils of Ottoman rule, and then described Dr. Dillon, from whom several quotations have been given in these pages, as one who had taken his life in hand and investigated the massacres upon the spot; in the midst of imminent and continuous danger of discovery and the death which would have probably followed. After speaking of the horrible details of plunder, murder, rape, and torture, thus revealed, he dealt with the Kurds, the Turkish soldiers, and the police and Government tax-gatherers, as being engaged in the deadly competition of which should excel in the infernal work before them. The Kurds and the Sultan were equally bad. "These (Kurds) the Sultan and the Government at Constantinople have enrolled, though in a nominal fashion, not with military discipline, into pretended cavalry regiments and then set them loose with the authority of soldiers of the Sultan to harry and destroy the people of Armenia."

Mr. Gladstone here quoted a passage from an interview held by Dr. Dillon with one of these fiends, which is remarkable for the fact that it not only exhibit no shame, but rather positive pride in the dreadful deeds spoken of. This Kurd, Montigo by name, after observing that they had done great deeds—deeds that would astonish the Powers to hear of—said : " We attacked villages, killed people, gutted houses—taking money, carpets, sheep, and women. Daring and great were our deeds, and the mouths of men were full of them." The classification of women in this statement with other chattels conveys a whole volume of brutal meaning and crime. The speaker then passed from the victims to the criminals, and declared falsehood and fraud in such cases to be the invariable policy of the Ottoman Government. It had allowed months to pass before appointing the Sassoun Commission, and other months had gone by since that Commission submitted its report—such as it was. He might well have quoted those old and very apt lines in description of the Sultan's shuffling procedure :

"Promise, pause, prepare, postpone,
And end by letting things alone."

There was no doubt, he thought, that the best and most ideal course would be to "tell the Turk to march out of Armenia." Ottoman rights there had long since been forfeited. No Turkish promises should be accepted. They were not only "absolutely and entirely worthless," but eminently delusive, while no guarantees of reform were of the slightest use unless supported by some factor "outside of the Turkish Government." And then the speaker made a reference which was most extraordinary in view of his own past policy, and speeches, and principles. Referring to the general right of intervention, he said:

"Besides that we have a special right. England made a treaty with the Sultan in 1878, and in that treaty he was bound to give effect to all those reforms in Armenia which, even if a small part of them had been accomplished, would have rendered impossible the occurrence of the dreadful case that is before us to-day, and that treaty was the treaty that gave to England the power, if she thought fit to exercise it, of taking upon herself the redress of these wrongs by requiring, in a way not to be mistaken, from the Turkish Government that they should be brought to an end. Let me remind you of this. The treaties which confer rights have another side to them. In conferring rights they impose duties."

True; but is not this whole paragraph a most complete vindication of Lord Beaconsfield's Asiatic policy, a reversal of all Mr. Gladstone's previous views regarding British intervention in Armenia, a contradiction in terms of his own resolution as presented to this very meeting? Is it not a practical denunciation of the policy which made the right of single intervention a dormant and useless one; which introduced in its place the vain European Concert; which failed to obtain, or re-assume, that influence "outside the Turkish Government" just declared by the speaker himself to be the only alternative to continued massacre?

Waiving consideration of questions of consistency or party politics, here, however, was Mr. Gladstone's opportunity to have made a great and practical step in the direction of helping the Armenians. "Let the dead past bury its dead." He might well have done this, and with all the prestige of his great name and career followed up his admission that circumstances had now made the Cyprus Convention a possible blessing in disguise; declared himself in favour of its revival at the hands of Lord Salisbury; and with the consent of the Liberal party—which, in this case, he might for the moment have led and represented—appealed to the heart and conscience of England to unite in the re-assumption of the protectorate over Asiatic Turkey. It would have been a bold step, and for the moment might have failed. European complications were many, and Great Britain's allies few. Turkey would have resisted, and France and Russia been antagonized and thrown into alliance with the Porte.

But who knows what force the picture of a union between the two historic parties of Great Britain might not have had upon divided Europe? A determined British sentiment along these lines, backing up the efforts which we may be sure Lord Salisbury would have personally enjoyed—as a national vindication of his old-time diplomacy—by the support of Lord Rosebery in Parliament and Mr. Gladstone in private life, might have done much. It would certainly have won sympathy, and perhaps even practical support, from the United States, and might, in that case, have averted the dangerous and unpleasant Venezuelan complications. It would perhaps have been hard to unite the Liberals upon it all at once, but the ensuing and still more ghastly horrors of 1895—to say nothing of the repeated and evident failures of the European Concert—might have greatly helped in creating a practically unanimous British opinion and action.

But the moment passed, and, to return to his speech, Mr. Gladstone merely went on to propose the appointment of a Commissioner in Armenia, who should govern in the name of the Sultan, but *under the auspices of the Powers*. He suggested, as a good man, Baron Von Kallay, the very excellent Austrian Governor of Bosnia and Herzegovina. This practically terminated the speech, so far as matters of permanent interest are concerned. It had been a great opportunity—amply lived up to in eloquence, and marvellous energy, and able denunciation. But the speech had failed to support any practical steps, or to in any way help the Government in its most difficult situation

While eulogizing and dwelling upon the nomina right possessed by England to intervene singly, Mr. Gladstone had refused to aid in urging the exercise of that right, and had supported and carried a resolution asking the Government to continue the long-tried and useless combined intervention of the Great Powers. And then, a few short months later, he had to admit, in a letter to the Rev. Dr. Clifford, which was read at a mass-meeting in London, December 17th, 1895, that :

" We witness at the present moment a strange spectacle. The six great Powers of Europe, which between them spend over £200,000,000 in each year upon what are termed defences, lie prostrate at the feet of the impotent Sultan of Turkey, who, with their cognizance, appears to prosecute massacres at his will from day to day. Presumably this is a condition of deep disgrace for us all ; presumably now, and, if it continues, then finally and irrevocably. Which Power or Powers are to blame, we know not. Our country is quite able to cope not only with Turkey, but with five or six Turkeys, and *she is under peculiar obligations*. But she is not omnipotent."

Here is a renewed admission of England's obligations under the Anglo-Turkish Convention, and also an admission, for the first time, of the failure of the European policy of concerted action. There is as yet, however, no defined expression of opinion as to future policy. The expected advantages of international pressure have proved fallacious, but there is no suggestion as to any superseding plan, although a week later Mr. Gladstone, in a letter to Murad Bey, of Constantinople, speaks of the Turk in more emphatic terms than ever. " There are degrees in suffering," he writes, " and degrees in baseness and villainy among men, and both seem to have reached their climax in the case of Armenia."

Shortly after this, a writer of unknown nationality, but author of a book entitled, "Under the Czar and Queen Victoria," inquired of Mr. Gladstone whether he had no word to say for the persecuted Christians in Russia, whom he declared to be "in even greater slavery than the Armenians." The aged statesman refused to fully answer the question, as he had a right to do, but denied that there was any really fair comparison between the two cases. He was, of course, quite correct in this, but, indirectly, the question throws light upon his own expression of doubt, in a letter just quoted, as to which of the Powers was mainly responsible for the failure of the European Concert. It was, indeed, Russia, with an entirely characteristic absence of honest sympathy toward the Christians of Turkey, and controlled entirely by selfish motives, which had checked the joint action of the Powers, and prevented England from achieving any useful end. This has since been proved by the British blue-books of 1896, on Turkish affairs, and must have been very sorrowful reading for the veteran statesman who has always regarded Russia as a misrepresented country, and a sincere friend to the Christians of the East.

These latter months of 1895, however, were the periods of the last and most widespread massacres in Armenia, and, though the more recent references by Mr. Gladstone to the question are anticipated a little in the time of this narrative, it is well perhaps to consider them consecutively. Those already dealt with come very closely to the heart of the question, as to why Great Britain has not more strongly intervened, and are important to any full and fair comprehension of the general problem. And, after the failure—the painful failure—of European threats and diplomacy, which came toward the end of the year, during the final slaughters in Armenia, Mr.

Gladstone wrote to Madame Novikoff—his old-time Russian friend—the following sorrowful and indignant words :

" I see in my mind that wretched Sultan, whom God has given as a curse to mankind, waving his flag in triumph, and the adversaries at his feet are Russia, France, and England. As to the division of the shame among them I care little. Enough that I hope my own country will (for its good) be made conscious and exhibited to the world for its own full share, whatever that may be. May God, in his mercy, send a speedy end to the governing Turk and all his doings ! "

This burst of anger and grief was natural, but, as may be gathered from preceding considerations, hardly just. It was not just to Lord Salisbury's difficulties, to the buried opportunities of the Anglo-Turkish Convention, to the prolonged Liberal policy of concerted action by the Powers, to Russian intrigues and hostility. But it none the less embodied the passionate indignation felt by millions of the English-speaking peoples, and further expressed by the same distinguished writer, in a letter to Mr. Chauncey M. Depew, of New York. He speaks hopefully in this epistle of the coming crash of an " impious and iniquitous " form of government, and declares his own reason for not taking active steps to be owing to " diminished strength, imperfect vision, and growing deafness."

Taken altogether, this brief survey of Mr. Gladstone's position regarding Armenia will show how easy it is for national leaders to take action in a diplomatic connection which a decade or two will render regrettable even to themselves ; how external events, absolutely beyond control, may reverse conditions, and make what once seemed unsafe and dangerous appear to be really useful and beneficial.

Through it all, however, Mr. Gladstone has proved himself a sturdy Englishman, anxious to do right, but with sympathies and dislikes which were sometimes too strong for great statesmanship. His detestation of the Turk in 1878 led him to minimize and overlook the possible value of the Asian protectorate, which in 1895 he had to recognize—when practically too late— as being a force and factor which might have saved the Armenians. His sympathy for Russia has led him to under-estimate its persistent policy of aggression, and to lay too much stress upon a religious sentiment which has only been used by the Czars whenever and wherever it might be capable of furthering national aims. All honour, however, must be accorded the great Liberal leader, in this connection and at this time, for an early knowledge and consistent denunciation of the real character of the Turk, and the atrocious nature of Turkish rule.

Interior of Armenian Coffee House in Erzeroum

Trebizond, one of the Scenes of Armenian Massacre.

CHAPTER XXII.

RENEWAL OF THE OUTRAGES.

Meanwhile a year had slowly passed since the massacre of Sassoun—a year of trembling terror amongst the Armenians; a year of vigorous and sympathetic exertion amongst a few earnest men in England and the States; a year of diplomatic doubts, delays, and futile declarations. But as the month of October, 1895, brought the annual Christmas celebration of "Peace on earth, and good will toward men," into the minds of the Christian world, reports came from Armenia of horror upon horror; of murder, misery, and the very madness of crime and cruelty. All the concentrated evils of Mahometanism, in its most barbarous and brutal mood, seemed to have been poured out upon the Christians of Armenia. The dark and wretched annals of the Turk appeared to have been ransacked for methods of maltreatment and the expression of a malignant hatred.

It was not for want of warning that the people of this beautiful land were now to be destroyed by thousands, with every accompaniment of pitiless ferocity. The records of Bulgaria and Greece, Crete and Syria, should have been sufficient to make the powers realize that the Turk never undertakes a work of massacre in any half-hearted way, and that the events in Sassoun were sure to be repeated in other and worse forms. As far back as February, 1878, Dr. Humphrey Sandwith, the well-known authority upon Asiatic Turkey, had protested against the giving back of

Armenia to the Turk, declaring it to be a crime, and one which showed that the English people did not understand what Turkish rule meant for the helpless populations who were subject to its tender mercies. How much more fierce would have been his denunciations had he known that the saving clause in the Berlin Treaty—the British protectorate over Asia Minor and its Christians—was to be abandoned by the succeeding English Government! But to him and others, who understood the evils of Moslem rule, Turkish occupation of these naturally lovely, fertile, and resourceful countries was not un'ike Shakespeare's "dragon in a cave of beauty"; a ravening wolf amongst sheep and lambs.

The massacres, which began early in October, and included Trebizond, Bitlis, Erzinjan, Marash, Kharput, Cæsarea, Orfah, Aintab, Erzeroum, Zeitoun, and a myriad minor places in their terrible scope, are, like those of Sassoun, indescribable in detail. Dr. E. J. Dillon, the Armenian correspondent of the *London Daily Telegraph*, writing from the spot, under his own signature, and in the responsible pages of the *Contemporary Review*, declared that butchery to have been "a divine mercy compared with the hellish deeds that are being done every week and every day of the year. The piteous moans of famishing children; the groans of old men who have lived to see what can never be embodied in words; the shrieks of mothers made childless by crimes compared with which murder would be a blessing; the screams, scarcely human, of women writhing under the lash; and all the vain voices of blood and agony that die away without having found a responsive echo on earth or in heaven, combine to throw Sassoun and all its horrors into the shade."

The occurrences at Trebizond are described by a *London Times* correspondent at Odessa, who obtained the facts from a reliable eye-witness on board a Russian vessel in the harbour. About ten o'clock in the morning a terrible noise was heard in the town, and then the report of firearms. Suddenly a number of Armenians appeared flying before a horde of Turks, who were shooting them down or stabbing them as they caught up. Upon reaching the shore the Christians were, of course, helpless, being without arms, and were butchered before the very eyes of the persons on the vessel. Some attempted to escape by swimming, but were pursued in boats and hacked to pieces in the water. Later on, the Armenians who had been hiding were driven out of the town in a body and massacred by hundreds. The neighbouring Armenian villages were set on fire at the same time that the murders in Trebizond commenced, and in these outlying places the same system of destruction took place Some 800 people, chiefly men, were killed in this neighbourhood. The troops and police—when they did not actually assist—looked on and approved the proceedings.

The scenes at Sivas were even worse. The outbreak of the Turks began on November 12, and was allowed to continue seven days, during which 1,200 Armenians were slaughtered. Suddenly, at noon on the date mentioned, and as if by a given signal, the Turkish labourers seized their tools, clubs, or whatever was at hand; the soldiers, Circassians, and police, took their arms; and all, under the command of officers, rushed into the market place and commenced the work of murder and pillage. No resistance was possible by the Armenians, who were killed in their offices, at their desks, and in their houses, with indiscriminate cruelty and outrage. In the Erzinjan district the Christians had sent some of their priests to the infamous Zekki Pasha, expressing their fears and asking for protection. On the morning of the day upon which the local massacres occurred an order came from the authorities to disarm any Armenians who might possess weapons of any sort. The latter thought that the order applied also to the Turks, and quietly gave up what was demanded. During the massacre which ensued in Erzinjan, and in surrounding villages, more than 1,000 men and women were killed, over 800 wounded or maltreated, and thousands rendered homeless.

The events at Erzeroum, where there are 10,000 Armenians and over 30,000 Mahometans—including a large body of Turkish troops—were still more atrocious. For some time there had been open threats of violence by the Turks, and, as the fatal day approached, it was generally rumoured and believed that the Government officials had given orders to the soldiers to soon begin killing. Preparations were commenced by the troops being placed in front of the various Consulates, in order to prevent any victims from finding refuge there. The English Consul stopped this in his vicinity by threatening some shooting on his own account. His "dragoman," who passed through the streets about this time, heard an officer of one of the bands of soldiers say to an unruly Turk: "Can't you keep quiet now? Wait until it begins, and then you can do what you like." It was in the market that, as usual, the massacre opened. There the troops fired steadily on the defenceless people, and the dragoman already mentioned saw one Armenian run up to a Turkish officer, throw his arms around his feet, and beseech him for protection. But the brute only pushed his suppliant away and shot him with his own hand.

In the afternoon of the day on which the massacre took place, the English and Italian Consuls, accompanied by Tewfik Bey, made a tour of the Armenian quarter. Hardened as the latter was, the surrounding ruin and misery affected even his equanimity and characteristic Turkish calm. The soldiers had fired volley after volley into the houses and then looted them, slaughtering any survivors—men, women, or children—who might be found cowering in the corners. In one home were seen two young brides who had been brutally murdered, lying on carpets saturated with their blood. Detailed description of the horrors perpetrated can hardly be given. " What I myself saw this Friday afternoon," writes a correspondent of the *Times*, " is forever engraven on my mind as the most terrible sight a man can see. I went to the Armenian cemetery. Along the walk on the north, in a row, lay 321 dead bodies of the massacred Armenians. Many were fearfully mangled and mutilated. Everybody seemed to have at least two wounds, and some a dozen." His estimate of the total killed in Erzeroum is 1,000, with possibilities running up to double that number. His concluding remarks are very pathetic :

" This Erzeroum slaughter was purely a massacre of innocent inhabitants by enraged Turks. The Armenians in this city kept quiet by the solicitation of foreigners living in the city, who said, ' Have patience ; England, France, and Russia will help you.' But as month after month rolled by, the Moslems became more rabid, until the helpless Armenians fell victims. Had it not been for the Consuls in this city, the British particularly, I believe things would have been far worse. Now, winter is before those penniless people, the bread-winners of the families are gone, and the misery will, I think, be terrible."

In the village and district of Kharput, a large number of Christians fell victims to the local massacre ; eight of the American missions in the village were burned down ; and great distress and desolation were caused in the surrounding district where thousands of the inhabitants were murdered, outraged, or deprived of even the barest means of subsistence. At Cæsarea, on Saturday, November 23rd, the Turks organized, and for three hours murdered, burned houses, and plundered, undisturbed by the local troops. Only a few houses immediately surrounding that of Reuter's correspondent—a schoolmaster —found immunity, and he, apparently by orders from Constantinople, was allowed to go unscathed, though sheltering upwards of a hundred refugees. He described the condition of the corpses as "literally hacked to pieces," and estimated the number killed as anywhere from several hundred to 1,000. Turks came from neighbouring villages to help, and many Christian women were maltreated or carried off. Some perished in the flames of their burning houses. At least one local preacher— Dr. Avedis—his wife and eldest son, were killed, while his two daughters were afterwards reported as "missing."

Another correspondent, who is described as entirely trustworthy, wrote from Cæsarea, that, "to judge from the wounded," all kinds of weapons must have been used, and he mentions axes, sickles, and daggers. "The first wounded person I took care of was an old man who had a large wound made by a meat-axe on the back of his neck. Besides this, there were seven or eight other wounds about his head and face. He lived fifteen days, and died in great agony. His wife and son also were wounded severely, and his two young daughters were maltreated." In another case which he refers to, Mr. Yeretzian, a medical man and preacher, his wife, son, and brother-in-law, were all ruthlessly butchered, and thrown into the flames of their burning home. A pathetic incident is also told of four young women whose house was attacked by the Turks. Two of them were carried off, and the marauders promised to return shortly for the others. Seeing that there was no hope, the latter filled the Oriental oven—dug in the floor of the kitchen—with fuel, and threw themselves into the flames.

Still another witness wrote to the *New York World* that the mob in this case had divided into four parts. The first plundered the Armenian stores, the second looted the houses, the third secured the young women, while the fourth, whom he describes as "fiends incarnate," attacked the public baths for women, killing some, dragging others through the streets by their feet, and maltreating all. " My hand almost fails me to write the awful particulars. It took three or four days to remove the bodies of the dead with forty carts. Add to this the want, the desolation!"

The massacres at Harpoot and surrounding villages were of a most horrible nature. The Rev. O. P. Allen wrote shortly after the event that they were hardly themselves aware of the full extent of the outside pillage and murder, and abduction of women and girls. But the pressure upon the people to become Mahometans was known to be terrible, and " large numbers have been instantly shot down or butchered who would not abjure their faith." He had already heard of the murder of thirteen of their native pastors and preachers. The story of one amongst the 176 villages which had been plundered or burned in this district is typical. About 400 Kurds surrounded it and commenced firing at random into the place. Thinking their object was plunder, the head men appeared and proffered £100 (Turkish) as ransom. This they took and then demanded all the watches in the village, then any weapons which might be there, then the grain, the oxen and the cattle. All of these they received, and then proceeded to go through the houses so as to take any other valuables which might be left. And after all this they drove the people out of the houses; stripped them—men, women, and children—of their clothing, and even shoes; burned down their homes, and killed the pastor because he would not change his religion. Finally, they took forty-five of the young men away in the night, and two by two offered them the choice of Islam or death. All but five, who managed to escape, were slaughtered because of their prompt refusal to deny Christianity.

In this Province of Harpoot an estimate of the massacres, published in February, 1896, gives the total number of men, women, and girls murdered as being about 29,000; persons burned to death in the fires as 1,300; ministers, preachers, and school teachers killed as 51; deaths from hunger and cold as 3,200; deaths from exposure in the mountains and snow as 4,000; the number wounded as 8,000; the number of persons forcibly circumcised and converted to Islam as 15,000; the number of violations as 5,500; the number of women forcibly taken in marriage by the Moslems as 1,500; the number of men, women, and children in destitute condition as 54,000. Of course, these figures are purely approximate, and could not in existing conditions be exactly verified, either then or afterwards. But they are probably as near the truth as it will ever be possible to get—Sultan's commissions and European official investigations of the future notwithstanding. And whether within or without the mark, they indicate the horrible nature of the crimes committed, as well as the wholesale and widespread character of a slaughter which covered not only this entire province, but a whole country.

At Marash the murders and outrages were much like those of Cæsarea and Erzeroum, and so many other places. But an especially full and authentic account is available from the pen of Miss Hess,* in a letter written

Toronto Globe, January 14th, 1896.

to a friend in Constantinople, and by her forwarded to Miss Barker, of Toronto. "For four weeks," she writes, "we have been having a reign of terror. Armenians were shot down at night in the streets, shops and houses were plundered, children disembowelled (I know of two), men's heads put on poles or used as balls in the streets, and every other horrible thing." The city was first filled with soldiers—estimated at 7,000—and then the Turks were let loose. Fire and murder and outrage soon filled the air with shrieks of pain and fear, and the hearts of the trembling girls in the Missionary College with more than terror. Miss Hess herself saw from its windows a band of ruffians seize two theological students of the neighbouring and now blazing Seminary, and beat them and shoot them over and over again.

Afterwards, when a guard of soldiers had been sent to the College—the presence of women of other nationalities alone saved its inmates from a horrible fate—these two wounded students were brought in, and the narrator describes them as being a perfect mass of wounds. Instances are given in which whole families were slaughtered; two churches were burned in which a large number of women and children had taken refuge, and Miss Hess adds pathetically that "they were all lost, of course." She heard an estimate of 4,700 as the total number killed, and describes the plunder as being something tremendous. From the victims everything was taken, "dishes, clothes, provisions—every single thing." The letter concludes with an appeal for aid; the statement that ten cents a week will keep body and soul together amongst these people; and the charge that "we have every reason to think that the order (for the massacres) came from the Capital."

The events at Anitab took place three weeks after those at Marash, and were commenced in the markets by a mixed mass of Turks and soldiers, armed with either axes or clubs, or stones, or knives, or guns, or pistols, rushing through the city in a storm of plunder and murder. After the massacre Dr. Caroline T. Hamilton declared that : " It was a sight to sicken the bravest. Most of the wounds were made with axes and large knives, and little children, women, and old men, as well as the young and strong, had been attacked as they fled. Covered with blood which had dried on head and hands and clothing, weak from lack of food and the pitiless cold, frightened so that several were wildly insane, one could not endure the sight of the survivors. Efforts are being made to provide food and clothing. Industry is paralyzed, and there are multitudes to be cared for."

The slaughter which took place at Orfah on the 28th and 29th of December included some five thousand victims and a peculiarly awful scene in the Armenian church. Like a similar building at Batak, in Bulgaria, some twenty years before, it proved too strong for the party of Moslems which sought to enter it and massacre the three thousand people within, or to burn it to the ground. The result was that they climbed upon the roof, got down to the galleries surrounding the interior of the church, and there poured thirty cases of petroleum oil upon the writhing mass below. Into the midst of them they then threw lighted torches, and hardly a hundred escaped from the ensuing hell of fire and murder. The Kurds, who in this case were the criminals, afterwards cast one hundred and fifty wounded Armenians down a well, and the correspondent of the London *Times* adds the almost incredible statement—incredible regarding any but Kurds or fanatical Turks—that they poured petroleum over this mass of living human beings and set it on fire. Terrible as this slaughter was, it had been in some measure anticipated, and several days before it occurred the Armenian clergy of Orfah—most of whom were afterwards killed—sent out a secret message and warning. It was a most pathetic document, and the following passages deserve respect and consideration:

"We are doomed to die. Everywhere it is whispered that the Armenians of Orfah have but the fearful alternative of 'Islam or the sword.' Before this reaches you we may have joined these who have gone before to the city of God. The attitude of relentless hostility in the Sultan and the ferocious aspect of our Moslem neighbours has not abated. We are as sheep waiting to be slaughtered, and, while waiting with bleeding hearts for the last act in this tragedy, we desire to send a farewell message to our fellow-men.

"To our sovereign, the Sultan, Abdul-Hamid, we say: For such as you this destruction of a whole people is, no doubt, an easy task, and in accomplishing it you will perhaps win from your admirers the proud title of 'The Victorious.' For ourselves, we can only make our last solemn protest that we are not, and never have been, rebels, and we regret that your energy and valour, and that of your soldiers, should have been displayed, not against the enemies of your Empire, but in the massacre and plunder of your unarmed and loyal subjects.

"To our Moslem fellow-countrymen our message is: Our complaints and appeals have been based solely on the sentiment of humanity, and the common rights of men. It was Britain who arranged the 'Scheme of Reforms' and urged it upon our Sultan, till he was irritated to the extent that he seems to have adopted the plan of ridding himself finally of this annoyance by exterminating our nation. . . . With some of you humanity has been stronger than passion and prejudice, and for this we honour and thank you.

"To the Christians of the United States of America, we say: Farewell! We have been strenuously opposed to your mission work among us, on the ground that it was divisive and subversive of our national Church traditions, but these bloody days have shown us that some of our Protestant brethren have been staunch defenders of our honour and our faith. You have laboured to promote among us Christian intelligence and purity; it is not your fault that one result of your teaching and example has been to excite our masters against us."

This remarkable letter contains more than one subject for thought. It shows the general belief entertained by intelligent Armenians that their extermination was, in reality, the policy of the Government; it reveals the horror of the situation during the weary months of waiting between Sassoun and its dreadful aftermath; it indicates one of the chief difficulties encountered by all missionaries in these Turkish countries—the popular knowledge that their faith is peculiarly obnoxious to the Porte. Meantime other massacres were steadily taking place. At Biredjik the British Vice-Consul—Mr. Fitzmaurice—telegraphed that 150 Christians had been killed, and 1,500 persons compelled to embrace Islam in order to avoid its deadly sword. Other despatches indicate that terrible cruelties were practised here in order to force conversion. In one case the Turks found twenty people in a cave, and murdered the men and boys on their refusing to profess Mahometanism. They put live coals upon the body of one old man, and, as he lay writhing in torture, held a Bible before his face and taunted him.

Near Baibourt a body of 500 Mahometan soldiers of an irregular type attacked several small villages, set fire to the houses, schools, and sheds, and drove the people back into the flames of their blazing homes when they endeavoured to escape. Some young men and women are said by the *Times* correspondent to have been here burned alive at stakes. And the Governor of Baibourt refused to send protection when appealed to. At Diarbekr the number of victims was estimated to be at least 5,000, and a traveller who arrived at Trebizond shortly afterwards reported that he had encountered 300 women near the city who fell on their knees before him, saying that their husbands were killed, and imploring his protection in the name of God. In the village of Akhissar the Armenians were attacked on October 9th, and twenty dead bodies were afterwards recovered from a well, and buried by the Bishop of Ismid.

Between the Persian borders and the city of Van more than fifty villages were destroyed by Hamidieh cavalry, large numbers of Christians killed with every kind of barbarity, and crwods of women carried off by these Kurdish "soldiers" to their mountains. Many Armenians, here as elsewhere, were compelled to embrace Islam—and it must be remembered that under the laws of the Koran, and the principles of the Turk, any one relapsing from such a profession of faith is doomed to death. The Rev. Mr. Chambers, in a letter to Principal Grant, of Kingston, tells how dreadfully these "converts" to Mahometanism felt their fate. They wrote asking him not to blame them, and described their situation in words like these: " We were, and are, ready to undergo torture and submit to death for the sake of our religion, but (God forgive us) we could not hand over our wives and children to the Turkish soldiers."

Around Bitlis, some 4,300 forced Moslem conversions were effected after the massacres had been completed. In one case, however, fifteen Armenian families of Tchabakeiour retracted their profession and returned to Christianity. They were promptly murdered by the Kurds. But the list of massacres need not be further extended. Fully 50,000 Armenian Christians during two

IMAGE EVALUATION
TEST TARGET (MT-3)

Photographic
Sciences
Corporation

23 WEST MAIN STREET
WEBSTER, N.Y. 14580
(716) 872-4503

months had been put to death, in ways of such awful cruelty as even the instances recorded in these pages can only indicate. To quote the Stamboul correspondent of the London *Speaker*: "The destruction of the Armenian communities has been completed amid scenes of fiendish barbarity which no pen can describe. Those left alive are left without anything." And if 50,000 were massacred during the special days devoted to that occupation by the Turks and Kurds, at least as many more died of starvation, of wounds, or, in the case of many women, from heart-broken misery at the loss of everything which made life worth living, or prevented it from becoming utterly unbearable.

Meantime, the craze for slaughter had been early aroused in Constantinople, if, indeed, it was not originally created there and in Armenia by orders from its government. During one of the first days in October, about 3,000 Armenians had assembled in the Karum Kapou Cathedral for religious purposes. At the conclusion of the service, some kind of petition was presented to the Patriarch, asking him to lead a Christian procession or deputation to the Sultan in favour of reforms in Armenia. He refused to do so, and urged his people not to attempt any demonstration at that particular time. But he was unfortunately unheeded, and the congregation seems to have streamed into the street with a vague intention of marching to the Palace.

Of course, the idea was never realized. Such things as peaceful popular movements are not understood in Stamboul, and the ever-convenient soldiers at once intervened. Just how the massacre started can only be guessed at, but pistol shots were fired, and in the ensuing mêlée some Turks, as well as Armenians, were killed. The opportunity, however, was quite sufficient, and during the next two days the "rioting," as it was called, continued. It was presently ended by the interference of the Ambassadors, and the Armenians, who had meanwhile crowded into the churches for protection—as a rule, of course, they were without arms—gradually obtained confidence and liberty. But some hundreds had been slaughtered, and many of the bodies afterwards recovered were most terribly wounded. One corpse had twenty knife cuts, and others were fearfully battered with clubs. Numerous victims were thrown into the sea and the bodies never recovered. The *Times* correspondent says, that:

"At some points veritable man-hunts took place, and several Armenians who became the quarry of the ferocious bands were cruelly ill-treated and bludgeoned to death. Thus, shortly before noon on Tuesday, two Armenian porters passing down the street through which the tramway runs to Galata were set upon, and, in the presence of a number of spectators, cudgelled to death with indescribable ferocity. . . . No police were present, and the assassins, after completing their work of butchery, withdrew unmolested."

So in other cases. And it must not be forgotten that these disturbances arose under the very shadow of the Sublime Porte—almost within sight of the absolute ruler of these people in both a religious and national sense. Yet the murderers did not fear his displeasure, and certainly went unpunished, while the jails became literally filled with innocent Armenians, who in many instances were bastinadoed, and in others, according to general belief, were tortured. If such things could occur in the capital of Turkey, while the gunboats of foreign Powers were patrolling neighbouring seas, and foreign ambassadors were daily going through the farce of demanding reforms and protection for the Christians of the empire, what might not—and did not—occur in distant Asiatic provinces?

During the succeeding months, and well into 1896, murder and outrage continued, though not upon the wholesale plan. In Armenia it has indeed been going on even while British and American relief funds are being distributed; and, in Constantinople, the correspondent of the *Speaker*, already quoted from, declared late in December that "every day numbers of Armenians disappear, and what becomes of them no one knows." This is really typical of all these horrible events. Open massacre when there was no fear of immediate external force; prolonged murder and outrage where there was no power of individual defence or concerted local resistance; secret assassination where there was a possibility of international interference. The Sassoun massacres had deserved Christian intervention at the point of the bayonet; the horrors of the succeeding year merited the annihilation of Turkish power and the overthrow of the Ottoman race. But destiny—and Russia—decreed that nothing should be done, and no present punishment be inflicted.

The Marquess of Dufferin and Ava.

Rt. Hon. Sir Philip Currie, G.C.B.
British Ambassador at Constantinople

CHAPTER XXIII.

THE CHRISTIAN POWERS AND THE MOSLEM.

One of the greatest crimes of this or any other century had now been consummated. Amid the despairing appeals of the Armenians to Christian Europe the massacres had continued to the end, while the sympathies of Christians had been absolutely wasted through the haggling jealousies of the chief Powers, and the absence of that spirit of Christian enthusiasm which made the Crusaders great even in their divisions, and distinguished even in their final defeat and dispersion. It was not sentiment that the Armenians wanted; it was practical intervention. It was not protest or promised reform that they needed; it was the compelling of just laws from the Porte, and their enforcement under the shadow of a Christian sword. And it was not so much the lack of action on the part of the great Powers that they had to complain of as the absence of any practical result. The hypocritical falseness of Turkey, combined with the hatred of Russia towards England, prevented any possible good from coming out of mere diplomatic interference.

The position of Great Britain was a difficult one. Her sympathies were all with the unfortunate Christians, her consuls everywhere did their best, her rich men gave abundantly in aid of the sufferers, her diplomats toiled night and day to produce some good out of the tangle of evil which exists in Stamboul. But to declare war upon the Turk, under existing circumstances, meant a struggle with Russia also, to say nothing of trouble at the hands of the loyal Mahometans of India, who had hitherto formed the very backbone of British power in that great empire. France was hostile, and merely awaiting her chance to force England out of Egypt as soon as she might be even partially exhausted in a struggle such as that indicated, while Germany showed its hand, a little later, with more than lurid distinctness. And, as if to cap the climax, Great Britain found herself threatened by her most natural ally—the United States—at a moment when all Europe seemed thus bent upon her humiliation.

No wonder, therefore, that Lord Salisbury, in the midst of all this "splendid isolation," did not care to resort to steel and cannon—even in a cause so just. Had the Anglo-Turkish Convention been sustained and maintained, he might have moved without such danger; but then the massacres would not have occurred. To resume the practice of an obsolete clause in a treaty eighteen years old would have been a new departure, and one which Russia would never have permitted short of the last arbitrament of war. And it must be remembered that while powers such as France, and Germany, and Austria, are nominally Christian, their foreign policy can hardly be termed Christian in either form or purpose. It is essentially selfish. So, to a certain extent, is that of Great Britain. But in the latter case there are other influences at work, and public opinion has now a controlling power over even the secret labours of the diplomat. In a free and absolutely self-governed community no policy of selfish autocracy or diplomatic despotism is possible, as it still is upon the continent of Europe.

What could be done was done. At the time of the Sassoun troubles the British Government had urged reform upon the Porte with an energy which, in almost any other country, would have produced some result. The co-operation of France and Russia, Germany and Austria, was obtained, and the farcical concert of Europe was persisted in through all the weary months of diplomacy which followed. While the foreign guard-ships were stationed at Therapia, and doubled after prolonged dispute; while massacres were staining the soil of Armenia, and even the streets of Stamboul, red with the blood of the Christians; while despairing cries for aid were echoing through Europe and America, the great Powers continued to "act together."

So far as England was concerned, the attitude of the Rosebery and Salisbury Governments toward the Porte and the other Powers interested had been very much the same during this entire period. Both pressed for reforms; both tried to keep up the European Concert. Mr. Bryce, a member of the first-named administration, speaking on January 21st, 1896, stated that after the Sassoun massacres:

" Lord Rosebery's Government spoke in the strongest terms to the Sultan, pressing on him the need for immediate and sweeping reforms, and endeavoured to get Russia and France, as the Powers most directly interested, to join with them. The Turks resisted, while Russia and France gave a *somewhat qualified support*—hesitating to adopt so drastic a scheme as we thought necessary. We were still arguing with them and pressing the Sultan when we quitted office in June last."

Such was the line of action inherited by Lord Salisbury, and at once carried on by him in accordance with what Mr. Chamberlain, in a speech some days later than the above, termed "a policy based upon the Concert of Europe, which Mr. Gladstone insisted upon as absolutely essential to any intervention by this country in the East, and which Lord Rosebery equally pursued." Meantime the Commission of Inquiry into the Sassoun iniquities had met, and investigated, and dissolved, without substantial result, while during the four months which passed from the time of Lord Salisbury's accession to power the same round of weary efforts to obtain reforms from the Sultan was steadily pursued. In the middle of October an Imperial Iradé was finally issued at Constantinople, approving of certain changes which were, in official language, to promote the progress, well-being, and tranquillity of the Sultan's subjects, in harmony with his well-known wishes and the policy of his illustrious predecessors! Like the measures of similar nature and interest in previous years, these absolutely worthless engagements were drawn up in most satisfactory terms—as might have been expected from the product of half a year's gestation at the hands of the Sultan, and the English, French, and Russian ambassadors.

They comprised reforms in the communal administrative districts, the inspection of prisons by six judicial inspectors, the formation of a mixed body of police and gendarme in each village, and the appointment of a sufficient number of rural policemen. It might be asked, in passing, what in the name of common sense and justice was the value of new officials who would all alike be corrupt and so many more instruments of oppression, or of new police and soldiers, when the existing ones were the prime sources of disorder and crime? Other provisions were as follows:

I. The inhabitants and the local landed proprietors will be protected by gendarmes and troops when they visit their pasture lands in the mountains. The inhabitants will thus be able to conform to the laws regarding the carriage of arms.

II. The nomadic tribes will be settled on lands granted by the Government.

III. Special regulations will be drawn up by the Minister of War for the regiments of Hamidieh cavalry.

IV. A committee of four members will be formed in each village and sandjak, in order to examine and verify all titles to property.

V. Four officials will be sent each year from Constantinople to inquire into any abuses on the part of the new administration.

VI. The collection of taxes is to be entrusted to mukhtars, and to taxgatherers elected by the inhabitants.

VII. The sale of tithes will take place separately in each village.

VIII. The *Corvee* (or forced labour upon Government works) system will continue abolished.

IX. The sale of land or cattle necessary for the subsistence of persons imprisoned for public or private debts is forbidden.

The Kurds were also to be escorted by a military force whenever emigrating from one place to another, were to be subject to the law about wearing arms; and were to have all their nomads settled forthwith on Government lands. Nothing in the document provided for the carrying out of all these proposals, but in communicating them to the Ambassadors the Sultan informed the latter that a Commission would be appointed composed of Mahometans and Christians in equal proportions—with a Moslem official as president.

In any ordinary civilized community under Christian rule, such pledges would have been of some value. But in a country where, despite numerous previous promises and irades, no Christian oath is yet worth anything; where Christians converted by force or otherwise to Islam, and recanting, still suffer death, despite the Porte's pledges and assurances to the contrary; where officials, and soldiers, and police, and governors, and judges are all alike Moslems, and bound by religious fanaticism to give neither consideration nor justice to an "infidel"; where corruption permeates everything Turkish, whether it be high or low in position and condition—of what earthly use were such regulations? Protection from Turkish soldiers and police was shown at its true value in Sassoun, and painted in the most awful colours upon the rest of Armenian soil within a week of the issuance of these very reforms! The idea of Turkish control over the Hamidieh cavalry in the interests of law and order was simply a screaming farce. The committees on land titles and the four officials to be sent from Constantinople would have been so many more centres of corruption and robbery, while an election of tax-collectors in a Turkish-Armenian village would have simply presented an interesting study in electoral intimidation. Indeed, the very idea of a contest between a Turk and an Armenian for office in Asiatic Turkey was enough to make all Europe and America laugh.

On paper, these reforms were, of course, excellent. But their enforcement was not relegated to a governor of high character and strong hand, as was absolutely essential to the making of even a commencement. It was not to be placed under the official control of the Ambassadors through a representative of the Powers being appointed to supervise the changes. It was to be handed over to a Turkish commission composed, in part, of Christians. Such a plan was farcical on the face of it. The "Christians" might be purchased Greeks of the baser sort—who already acted as cruel tax-gatherers and relentless officials in European Turkey. They would not be

Armenians in all probability, and in any case their suggestions on the commission would have never been accepted; their advice would have been continually disregarded; their influence in the provinces would have been as small as it was on the commission; and their resignation might have been forced at any time convenient to the Porte in its varied diplomatic affiliations.

The reforms did not, however, get as far as the stage of experiment. In fact, they do not seem to have been even published in official form in the provinces concerned, and before the ambassadors had been able to do more than accept the empty compliment conveyed in this final recognition of their labours the Sassoun massacres had been repeated in a far wider sphere, and the vilayets, which were to have been blessed by these beautiful paper theories, had been turned into what an American missionary has termed " one vast flaming hell." And the massacre in Constantinople itself soon gave them a little object-lesson in Turkish methods which should have been useful. In fact, they had to make immediate representation to the Porte that, almost within their own sight, private persons, after being arrested, had been beaten and killed with the tacit approval of the police; that orderly private persons had been attacked and wounded; and that wounded Christians taken to courts, police stations, and prisons, had been killed in cold blood after reaching their destination.

The weeks and months which followed will be a disgrace to Christian diplomacy for all time to come. And the central mark for condemnation will be Russia. The British blue-books upon Armenian affairs prove the attitude of that country, from the time of the Sassoun massacre until the surrender of starving Zeitoun, to have been a prolonged and systematic effort to hamper reforms, to encourage Turkey in its defiance of England, to hold France back from any effectual joint action, and to prevent punishment for the Turkish murderers in Armenia. To quote the official documents themselves is the best way of indicating the truth of this charge. As far back as May 30th, 1895, the Russian ambassador informed Lord Kimberley, then Foreign Minister, that Russia would refuse to associate herself with any proposal " to have recourse to measures of constraint," should Turkey refuse justice and reform in connection with the events of Sassoun. A little later, Prince Lobanoff, Russian Minister of Foreign Affairs, denounced any plan or talk of " the creation, in Asia Minor, of another Bulgaria," or independent Armenian kingdom. Not long afterwards this representative of the country which had invaded Turkey a dozen times, with no other cause than ruthless ambition, announced that "the idea of the employment of force was personally repugnant to the Emperor, and that employment of force by *any one of the three Powers* would be equally distasteful to the Russian Government."

In a certain peculiar way, the situation was not unlike that at the time of the Crimean war. But it was in reversed order. England now stood alone in defence of the Christians of Armenia, as Russia had then been alone in its determination to break up the Turkish Empire. Lord Palmerston, in those old days, was able to point to the sympathy of France and the neutrality of Germany; Prince Lobanoff was now able to claim the admitted alliance of France, the neutrality of Germany, and the practical dependence of the Porte. Finally, on January 25th, 1896, after the Sultan's schemes in Asia had been consummated, and " reform " rendered impossible through the wholesale massacre of the people and the aroused spirit of Turkish fanaticism—without armed European intervention—he informs Lord Salisbury that the renewed British proposal for coercive action was " a direct interference in the internal affairs of Turkey," a violation of the Treaties of Paris and Berlin, and " an infringement of European public law." He added the willingness of Russia to participate in giving the Sultan " friendly and well-meaning advice," and the expectation of that Power that assistance would be given the Turkish ruler in his " arduous task," so as "to increase his authority and prestige."

Of course, this sort of language simply meant that attempted coercion by England alone would be met by the combined force of Russia and Turkey—with France probably thrown in. This situation has been further illustrated and explained to those who understand Eastern diplomacy, by the fact that after these communications had passed, together with many others not quoted, the Ambassadors at Stamboul agreed early in February, 1896, that ordinary representations connected with Armenia should in future be presented to the Sultan through M. de Nelidoff, the Russian Ambassador. It is almost a wonder that the shade of Stratford de Redcliffe did not appear in protest. A few weeks later the Czar sent a pair of superb Japan vases for presentation to his Imperial brother, and in the succeeding month permitted Prince Lobanoff and M. de Nelidoff to accept from the Turkish Sultan his highest possible decoration. At this evidence of the fraternal relationship of the Power which had just concluded its horrible labours in Armenia, and the Empire which so often professes Christianity and practises paganism, even Mr. Gladstone—with all his old-time friendship for Russia—had to raise a voice of protest. This action alone was indeed sufficient proof of Russia's attitude in the question, had the afterwards published official despatches never appeared.

But what else was to be expected ? The talk which is sometimes heard regarding Russian sympathy for Christians and general benevolence of disposition is the veriest nonsense. The fact is that, in spite of the ameliorating influence of its Church, Russia is still a barbarous nation, with a policy naturally more in harmony with barbarian Turkey than with Christian England. And this, aside from its diplomatic, historical, and geographical hatred and rivalry in all questions connected with the latter country. To quote Lord Lyndhurst, the veteran orator and statesman, as far back as June 19th, 1854:

"The history of Russia, from the establishment of the Empire down to the present moment, is a history of fraud, duplicity, trickery, artifice, and violence. The present Emperor has proclaimed himself protector of the Greek Church in Turkey, just as the Empress Catharine declared herself protector of the Greek Church in Poland. By means of that protectorate she fermented dissensions and stirred up strife in the country. She then marched into Poland under the pretence of allaying troubles, and stripped the kingdom of its fairest provinces. We know the ultimate result."

This same policy was pursued in Turkey during the last two centuries. It was the policy of Nesselode in and before the Crimean war ; it was the policy of Gortchakoff in 1876; it was the policy of De Giers in the Balkan States ; and it has been for the moment reversed by Lobanoff, simply because British efforts in favour of Armenian reform have diplomatically, and naturally, driven the Porte into the arms of Russia. This present Prime Minister of the Czar is a remarkable man. He has had a prolonged political record, and has been ambassador at the Courts of Stamboul and London and Vienna. He is understood to hate England with more than mere historic sentiment, and has recently devoted his great ability to efforts at outwitting her diplomats wherever possible. In China he has been successful, but the British have held Japan. In Turkey he has certainly won the day, and seems to have also made successful efforts in Persia and Bulgaria.

It is perhaps not necessary to say more of the Russian policy which has thus prevented action regarding Sassoun, paved the way for the ensuing massacres, prevented forcible intervention during their continuance, and fitting punishment after their completion. Mr. Gladstone, writing while all was yet vague and shadowy, called down the vengeance of Heaven upon the Power, or Powers, which had hindered action during this crisis. Let the condemnation of the world also fall where it is so justly merited. And while any real sympathy in Russia with the Armenians should not perhaps have been expected, its Government might, in the sacred name of humanity, have at least desisted from its threat of applying force to any other Power which tried to save those wretched people. When it is borne in mind, however, that this Russian Government has closed up Roman Catholic churches, Jewish synagogues, and Baptist meeting-houses, to say nothing of having banished preachers and hounded Jews, its action will not seem altogether surprising. But condemnation of its policy is none the less deserved, and may even be enhanced, by remembering Prince Lobanoff's contention in the very midst of the massacres, and during the corresponding negotiations with the Sultan, that "ample time" should be given so as to allow the excitement to subside, and that the Powers ought to "await patiently" the result of the Sultan's "efforts to tranquillize the disturbed districts."

The attitude of other Powers was not so aggressively opposed to the British policy; but it was equally discreditable to them as Christian nations. Facts seem to prove that many even of the massacres might have been stopped by stern and immediate action. For instance, at Diarbekr, when the slaughter had been going on for three days, M. Cambon, the French Ambassador, heard that his Consulate there was in danger, and—according to a despatch in the London *Times*—sent word after midnight to Kiamil, the Grand Vizier, that " if any mischief befell his Consul, he would require the head of the Vali (governor), and would hold Alexandretta with a French squadron until he got it. Straightway, Kiamil sent this to the Sultan at Yildiz, and two hours later Diarbekr was tranquil." Of course, this was the voice of France speaking on behalf of a French citizen. Had some English Consul been threatened or murdered, it might have served the unfortunate Armenians well ; but the shrewd Government, whose responsibility is so clearly illustrated in this incident, knew better than to allow such a mistake.

This seems, however, to prove that something might easily have been done if the shadow of Russia had not practically stood behind the holder of the sword of Islam. Germany, all through these events, did nothing except give occasional advice. Austria, unfortunately, seems to have become impressed with the possibilities of an awful European war, and through its Minister, Count Goluchowski, went so far as to say that the adoption of coercion amid existing elements of conflict would have " infinitely more calamitous results to humanity than even the savageries now being perpetrated on this wretched people." Under the circumstances indicated by these various facts, and the dark evidence of the British bluebooks, it can hardly be considered surprising that Lord

Salisbury did not forcibly interfere, and had finally to admit to Sir Philip Currie that the threatened conflict between the Powers " would far outweigh any advantage that could possibly be expected from isolated action." And just before these documents were published the British Premier spoke at length upon the subject in the House of Lords, February 11th, 1896. After a reference to England's great naval strength, but comparative military weakness, he went on :

" When the noble Lord (Rosebery) reads the papers to-morrow he will at once see that the other Powers of Europe were by no means inclined either to encourage or to help or to tolerate a military occupation on our part. Russia has stated, in the clearest terms, that the Emperor objects and has the strongest repugnance to the use of force on the part of Russia, and an equally strong repugnance to the use of force on the part of any other Power. In order, therefore, to satisfy the demands of the noble Lord, we should have had, in the first instance, to undertake a military occupation without the military power of doing so. In the second place, we should have had to push that military occupation against some 300,000 Turkish soldiers. In the third place, we should have had to meet the danger I do not wish to define more closely, the danger involved in the disapproval of the European Powers."

This is a clear and concise statement, and, read between the lines of a necessarily diplomatic speech, means that England pushed her intervention to the point of war, and then, finding nothing but enemies in Europe, with, unfortunately, a fresh and unexpected antagonist in America, drew back. It would have been a gallant and chivalric deed to have gone to war; but the plunging of a world-wide Empire into such a stupendous struggle, for a people entirely outside its limits and practical interests, was a responsibility from which the British Government naturally shrank. And Lord Salisbury had to consider the difficulties connected with 50,000,000 Mahometans in India, to say nothing of the effect of letting loose French cruisers and Russian war-ships upon the commerce of nearly 400,000,000 people scattered over the globe. The British navy is powerful enough, and British resources in men and money and armament great enough, to have ultimately crushed the united forces of Russia, France, and Turkey.

But meanwhile, the whole Christian population of Turkey might have been slaughtered and at least endangered; the Mahometans in India would have been unquestionably seriously disturbed, although their loyalty is extreme; the Germans might very probably have realized the fruit of their intrigues in South Africa; the United States might have taken unfair advantage of the situation —although it may be fairly believed that Christianity and a common English-speaking civilization would have prevented hostile action; and the whole world would have been in a turmoil. It was too much to expect of the England of to-day—the much burdened and weary Titan of the age. What responsibility she had rested upon the reversal of the policy of a great statesman, when, in 1880, Mr. Gladstone and the electorate of the nation repudiated the British protectorate over Asia Minor. And in the European crisis concerning Armenia, to quote Mr. Bryce again—as a consistent opponent of the Salisbury Government—it could hardly have been supposed possible that the Powers would have refused to allow Great Britain to herself apply the necessary coercion. "If they do refuse —if, that is to say, they will neither help us to stop the massacres nor permit us to stop them, they will make themselves responsible for the present horrors, and our hands will be clean."

Meanwhile, Kiamil Pasha had lost his post in one of those sudden palace "revolutions" for which Turkey is noted, and Said Pasha had succeeded him as Grand Vizier. Within a few months the latter was fleeing for his life to the British Embassy from a similar plot, and Kiamil again came into favour. And through all the varied events of these months the Sultan kept on in his even, determined, bigoted, and miserable path. Neither diplomatic storms, nor rivers of blood, nor cries of agony, nor the execration and contempt of individual Christendom, seemed to disturb the outward equanimity of this typical Turk and Commander of the Faithful. What his inward feelings and fears may have been, the world in general can never know. They must have been bitter, indeed, before he finally determined to imitate Mahmoud II., in similar national difficulties, and throw himself into the spider-like web of Russian protection.

He knew, however, that by prolonged failure to do justice to the Christians of Turkey he had forfeited all claim to defence or support from England. By ready acceptance of Lord Beaconsfield's policy in 1879, he might have saved the situation and made such reforms in Asia Minor as would have prevented the succeeding reversal of that policy of British alliance, defence, and Christian protection. But his refusal to accept the opportunity was deliberate, and, despite Lord Salisbury's expressed belief and hope to the contrary, history will say that the Sultan's responsibility for what followed in Armenia is far greater than that of Abdul-Aziz for the Bulgarian massacres. In fact, it is proved as clearly as such a horrible incident of barbarian government can ever be. And, as the reforms promised under the Cyprus Convention were, from various causes, never carried out, Mr. Goschen very properly stated in the House of Commons on February 13th, amid loud Liberal cheers, that "we are relieved of any engagement under that Convention to defend the integrity of the Sultan's dominions in Asia Minor."

After a careful review of the many and complicated considerations connected with this whole miserable episode in European diplomacy, it may therefore be fairly claimed that England comes out of it with honour. The present impression existing in many quarters to the contrary will pass away in time, as the disgraceful attitude of Russia and the other Powers become understood and appreciated. And when the Duke of Argyle, a devoted friend of the Armenian cause, admits that a study of the blue-books has convinced him that the Government's action is not open to attack; when Mr. Bryce declares England to be practically free from responsibility; when Mr. Gladstone and Lord Rosebery are seen to have declined making the issue, in any sense, a political question; when the immensity of the war resulting from direct intervention is apprehended; when the sorrow and sympathy of the moment with the wretched victims of Islam becomes merged in historic retrospect; it will be felt that neither Lord Salisbury nor the Mother Country of the English-speaking race have in this connection forfeited public respect or Christian esteem and admiration.

Gervont Shishmanian.

The Armenian Patriarch.

CHAPTER XXIV.

THE INTERESTS AND DUTY OF THE UNITED STATES.

American interests in the Turkish Empire are very considerable. American sympathies with the Eastern Christians are embodied in the contributions of countless individuals towards the work of Turkish missions. American feeling for the Armenians vibrates through myriad resolutions of Christian bodies, newspaper letters and editorials, mass meetings, and the voice of Congress itself. And American public opinion, as a whole, is well embodied in the following extract from a letter written by Mr. Chauncey A. Depew:

"Much as I believe in peace and its blessings, much as I detest war and its horrors, much as I feel that great provocations and the most imminent dangers in the liberty or the existence of the territories, or the safety of the citizens of the country, will justify an appeal to the arbitrament of arms, nevertheless, I do feel that by a concert of action of Christian nations, of which the United States should be one, such a presentation should be made to the Sultan and his advisers as would stop these horrors and save our Christian brethren."

But the concert of Europe is a useless farce, and a positive danger to the peoples whom it affects to aid. Its divisions make the Sultan laugh; its antagonisms make him absolute master of the situation. For the United States to join such a "concert" would be the subject of infinite regret, and the cause of still more diplomatic chaos. What is needed is an alliance between

Great Britain and the United States—the combined might of the great Christian empire and republic directed towards the settlement of the Eastern Question in the interest of Eastern Christians and the world at large.

After all, the interests of England and the United States are identical in Turkey. They both desire the better government of the Christian populations. They both devote immense sums of money to missions, and send many devoted men and women to labour amongst the Mahometans. They both want peace and opportunities to develop trade, or to utilize the vast and now unproductive richness of these gardens of the East. They have a common—though hardly recognized—interest in checking the onward march of Russian autocracy and despotic strength. They should both aim at the development of the Christian states of Turkey, apart from the dominance of either Czar or Sultan. They have a common sympathy with the suffering Armenian, as eighteen years ago they had with the crushed and tortured Bulgarian.

American mission organizations in the Turkish Empire are indeed very numerous. The Boston Board of Missions does much work in Bulgaria and Asiatic Turkey. The New York Presbyterian Board of Foreign Missions labours in Syria, and the United Presbyterian Mission Board in Egypt. The Mission Boards of the New York Reformed Episcopal Church, the Methodist Episcopal Church, the Church of the Disciples, and the Baptist Church, have large interests in Bulgaria, Syria, and Constantinople respectively. The Constantinople Bible House, the Syrian Protestant College of Beyrout, and the Robert College at Constantinople, are American institutions. The latter has done an especially valuable work in the direction of Christian education. Many of the devoted young men who helped to free Bulgaria from Turkish rule in 1877, and who are now struggling amid almost equal difficulties to train its people in self-government and keep them free from Russian intrigues, were scholars of Robert College. Nine years ago the Hon. S. S. Cox, then United States Minister in Turkey, gave the following figures of the work done by the above societies:

Cities, towns, and villages occupied..	394
American citizens engaged in the work	254
Turkish subjects assisting	1,049
Number of high schools and colleges	35
" girls' boarding schools....	27
" common schools............	508
Pupils under instruction...............	25,171
Preaching places (about)	400
Average attendance at each service..	50,000
Organized churches	138
Average annual sale of Scripture or parts of the Bible	50,000
Average annual sale of religious books and tracts	100,000
Number of newspapers..................	13
Value of real estate, books, printing machinery, etc.......................	$1,000,000
Estimated sum sent out and expended annually in Turkey...............	$360,000

These figures may be taken as immensely increased at the present time, and Dr. Talmage, in a recent speech, declared that the American missions had charge of 27,000 students in their day schools and 35,000 in their Sabbath schools. In Asiatic Turkey alone, there are now 152 American missionaries, with 800 native helpers, 101 churches, 12,000 communicants, 47,000 adherents, 48 colleges and high schools for girls, and 350 common schools. These local Christian agencies raise $60,000 a year for expenses, and the Rev. Dr. Evans, of Montreal, lately a missionary in Turkey, states that at least $10,000,000 has been expended by the people of the United States in the evangelization of the Ottoman Empire, while through their agency some seven million of Bibles and other Christian books have been circulated since operations began in 1820.

It was in this latter year that the Rev. Levi Parsons commenced the first American mission in Jerusalem. Ten years afterwards a number of others came to Constantinople, and, in 1837, the now veteran Dr. Cyrus Hamlin appeared as an agent of the American Board of Foreign Missions. Their vicissitudes were many, but, as an American Minister at Stamboul has admitted, the Capitulations, or British treaty arrangements with the Porte, were of "special service." And a study of Lord Stratford's life and work shows how much he did for missionaries from the States, as well as for native Christians living in any and every part of the Turkish dominions. Within a few years the result of these labours became apparent, and missions had been established in Smyrna and Broussa, in Trebizond, Erzeroum, Aintab, and throughout Asia Minor and Armenia. As time passed it was found necessary, in 1847, to organize the greatly enlarged mission communities into a Protestant Church, and to obtain the formal recognition of the Sultan. Later on, the wide Turkish field, instead of being managed entirely from Constantinople, was divided into the Western mission, which included the Capital, Broussa, Smyrna, Trebizond, Marsovan, Sivas, and Cæsarea; the Central mission, including Aintab and Marash as its chief stations; the Eastern mission, with Van, Erzeroum, Harpoot, Mardin, and Bitlis; and the European mission, chiefly in Bulgaria.

It will be seen by the names of these places that American missionaries have been in the very heart of the storm of massacre; and the nobility with which they have stood their ground, fought the fight of mercy and alleviation, and faced the fiends of murder and outrage, is not only proof of their Christian zeal and courage, but a strong practical appeal to the aid of American leaders and the American people. Financially, that assistance has been given in unstinting abundance. It is probable that $200,000, at least, have been forwarded to the relief of the starving thousands in the stricken districts, of some of whom the British Consul Graves reported, in September, 1895, from Dalvorig, that:

"There are about 860 of these houseless wanderers now living in the woods and mountains, in caves and hollow trees, half-naked, and some, indeed, entirely without covering. Bread they have not tasted for months, and curdled milk they only dream of, living, as they do, upon grains and the leaves of trees. There are two varieties of grains which are preferred, but these are disappearing, as they wither at this season. Living on such food, they have become sickly; their skin has turned yellow, their strength is gone, their bodies are swollen, and fever is rife among them."

Such terrible distress as this and a myriad other descriptions exhibit aroused sympathetic and immediate action, and caused the formation of the Armenian Relief Committee of New York. Then came the last terrible massacres, and the despatch from Rev. Henry O. Dwight, of Constantinople: " Armenia is at her last gasp. The work of extermination continues. The number of people massacred reaches 100,000, and half a million survivors have taken refuge in forests and mountains, where they are feeding on herbs and roots. In the name of humanity and Christianity, save us!" The response was as prompt as it had been in England, where the Duke of Westminster's exertions, and subscriptions in Manchester, Dublin, Bradford, Salisbury, and other places—headed by himself with £1,000—soon despatched many other thousands to the relief of the suffering Christians. Meetings were held in many parts of the United States, and vigorous protests passed against the lurid crimes of the Ottoman administration. In Chickering Hall, New York, a great gathering on November 21st, 1895, declared that the ruler of Turkey had plundered Armenia, burnt its towns, destroyed its people, and that in its opinion :

"The Sultan of Turkey has forfeited all right to rule over the Armenian peoples; that we respectfully urge our Government to make every possible effort to induce the governments of Christendom to rouse themselves from their apathy and put an end to this intolerable state of affairs, which threatens with extermination thousands and thousands of innocent fellow-Christians; that we urge our Government also to do everything in its power to preserve the fruits of American missionary toil; that we express our ardent sympathy with the unutterable sufferings of this persecuted race; and that we call upon all the people of Christendom to insist that these unutterable sufferings shall cease."

On October 10th, the General Convention of the Protestant Episcopal Church passed a very similar resolution, urging succour and contributions, and asking the authorities of the Church of England, in England, "to take such action as will fitly commend the cause of the Armenian Church to the whole English-speaking world." A little later the National Council of the Congregational Churches of the United States resolved, by a standing vote, that, "in our judgment, the time has come when the Government of the United States should take such measures in co-operation with the other great Powers as will not only effectually protect all American citizens, missionaries, and others in Turkish dominions, but in the name of our common humanity, will present a determined protest against these barbarities, and that our Government should give moral support to the movement of European Powers to cause the outrages to cease, to the extent, if necessary, of the abolition of the Turkish Government."

The House of Bishops of the Anglican Church also issued a pastoral calling upon its people to " remember in your prayers and with your prompt and liberal help the long-suffering and down-trodden people of the ancient and faithful Church of Armenia." So, with a mass meeting in Detroit, presided over by the well-known politician, General R. A. Alger, which sent a cabled appeal to Her Majesty the Queen, and urged that, in the name of humanity, she should use her great power to stop without delay the slaughter in Armenia. "We believe," declared the resolution, " that it is the supreme duty of the hour, for all civilized nations, including the United States, to intervene and end this outrage upon humanity and modern civilization by that barbarous and despotic Government. We have also appealed to our own Government to co-operate in every practical effort to end these atrocities and assure security to the Armenians." Finally, on January 22nd, 1896, the sentiment of these and very many similar resolutions was embodied in the passage of a concurrent motion through the Senate and the House of Representatives of the United States. It recapitulated the terms of the Berlin Treaty, denounced the outrages in Armenia, and then declared:

"That it is an imperative duty, in the interests of humanity, to express the earnest hope that the European Concert, brought about by the treaty referred to, may speedily be given its just effects in such decisive measures as shall stay the hand of fanaticism and lawless violence, and as shall secure to the unoffending Christians of the Turkish Empire all the rights belonging to them, both as men and as Christians, and as beneficiaries of the explicit provisions of the treaty above recited.

"That the President be requested to communicate these resolutions to the Governments of Great Britain, Germany, Austria, France, Italy, and Russia."

Unfortunately, nothing came of the resolutions. They were passed, and then shelved by the President, in whose hands the ultimate action remained. And in them, as in the expressions of opinion at mass meetings and in the American press, one fatal defect was visible—the absence of any offer to Great Britain of practical national co-operation and alliance. There were three reasons for this. The first was the traditional lack of sympathy with England, and the growth of a more aggressive spirit of hostility owing to the Venezuelan affair. The second was a very considerable and natural ignorance concerning the history of England's relations with Turkey; her struggles for reform; her position under the Berlin and Anglo-Turkish treaties; and her relations with Russia. The third was a somewhat vague and ill-defined, but still fairly strong, sentiment of friendship towards Russia, and failure, of course, to appreciate the unutterably selfish attitude of that country toward Turkey and its subject Christian races.

Aside from the old historic prejudice against Great Britain, which it may be hoped mutual knowledge and increased intercourse were gradually dissipating; the unfortunate message of President Cleveland regarding Venezuela, and the ensuing outburst of spread-eagleism in the Republic, undoubtedly did have a most injurious effect upon British influence and the question of British interference in Armenia. The incident came at a most unfortunate moment, and the claim made by the New York

Tribune, and endorsed by most of the United States papers, that it had no influence upon the negotiations then going on, serves either to minimize, to a very fine point, the weight of American threats of war and expressions of hostility then current, or to deny the absolute proof to the contrary afforded by the history of British policy and the growth of Russian determination, shown in the blue-books published during February, 1896.

The President's message was sent to Congress on December 17th, and during the succeeding week occurred the outburst of anger against England which to European Powers seemed a most complete evidence of national antagonism, and an indication of probable war between the two countries. The negotiations between Great Britain and the other Powers were then in full swing, and Lord Salisbury was straining every diplomatic possibility in order to obtain joint intervention, or else the right of isolated action. It was on the 19th of December, *two days after the message*, and while the European press teemed with the chances of an Anglo-American conflict, that Sir Philip Currie cabled his Government that the situation in Armenia was such as to "call for interference on the part of the Treaty Powers, in order to obtain the restoration of order and to prevent further disturbances."

It was after that date that the British Government pressed its proposals as far as was possible without war with Russia and Turkey, and probably France. It was after that date that Austria finally refused to join England in active intervention. It was after that date that Russia made up its mind definitely not to permit any British single intervention short of war, and boldly declared even the proposal to be "an infringement of European international law." It was after that event that British diplomacy in Constantinople received its final blow in this connection by the almost complete surrender of Turkish foreign policy into the hands of Russia. So much for the *Tribune's* contention that there was "no reason outside of Bedlam for supposing Mr. Cleveland's message was in the remotest degree responsible."

Of course, no European statesman or British leader could publicly state such to be the case. But every one knows that the delicate chords of diplomacy, in a case where the tiniest thread may influence the strength of a whole chain, are terribly affected by the possibilities of war in some new and unexpected quarter. Amongst themselves the European Powers know each other's exact military and naval strength; the force of existing or probable alliances; the contingencies which may at any moment arise and overthrow their most careful arrangements. And into this carefully calculated situation, at a moment when Russia had succeeded in isolating England through the latter's eager efforts to befriend the Armenians; had brought Turkey for the same reason into her net of dangerous friendship; had obtained the alliance of France, and made sure of the indifference of Germany and the neutrality of Austria; at this juncture, to the delight of Russia and Turkey, the United States appears with what seemed to the careful, minute, and practised diplomacy of Europe to be almost a declaration of war.

This, therefore, was the situation, and it is one which still exists in part, and seems to warrant a strong appeal for better relations between England and the States in the interests of common humanity, the cause of a common Christianity, and the honour of a whole great race. Just how far this unfortunate incident prevented justice, and mercy, and reform in Armenia can never be accurately told. It can only be guessed at from current international relations. Mr. H. M. Stanley declared, in a published letter, that it was probable the British Government—in view of the intense public indignation at home—would have "dared the resentment" of the Powers had not "the miserable Venezuelan squabble intruded itself so inopportunely." The London *Spectator* went further—too far, indeed—and alleged the President's message to have been "the death warrant of Armenia."

Of that factor in American public life which includes lack of accurate knowledge concerning England's relations with Turkey and its tributary States, and with Russia, it is not necessary to say much. Time would have cured the evil—one which some English leaders and papers themselves seemed to share. And the official evidence of the negotiations concerning Armenia might have done much to lift this cloud. The sentimental regard for Russia which undoubtedly exists in the Republic is a more curious factor, but one which can hardly last. Especially is this the case when such a picture is presented to us as that referred to by the New York *Tribune*, February 5th, 1896, where "the great white Czar swears a blood-brotherhood with the Turk, so that the knout may fall upon those whom the scimitar has spared."

There never has been any real or substantial basis for this friendship. It could only be logically founded upon mutual antagonism to Great Britain, and surely in this age of the world, with the conscience, and heart, and wisdom of the best elements of the two great English-speaking empires in favour of harmony, and alliance, and co-operation, such a reason can hardly prevail. There is no other common ground—either in constitution, or liberty, or toleration, or commerce, or religion, or law. One nation is a pure despotism, controlled by a personal power which is based upon Siberian methods and the subjugation and ignorance of the peasantry; modified by an Eastern form of Christianity which may be struggling towards the fuller light, but is still far from it; founded upon the ruins of Poland, the crushing of the smaller peoples of Central Asia, and a policy of steady, ruthless ambition; practising at times a system of far-reaching persecution toward the Jews and minor religious sects. The other is a great Republic, founded upon the principles of popular government and living in the blaze of a democracy which scoffs at autocratic administration, and in many cases believes even the free Parliamentary system of England to be almost despotic in its nature.

The policy of the United States and Great Britain in this Turkish world-wide crisis should have been one of common and united action. There were many reasons calling for it. American missions, American Christians, American sympathy, American money, American interests, were all concerned. The missionary buildings at Marash and Kharput which were pillaged and burned had to be replaced, and the Minister of the United States at Stamboul—Mr. Terrell—promptly demanded $100,000 indemnity. His influence during the latter part of this period seems to have been considerable, though it was unfortunately due to the national expressions of hostility against England. And, more important still, the United States was not a signatory to the Treaty of Paris, and did not therefore consider the Dardanelles to be closed to its ships of war.

It was a great opportunity for united action. Had the powerful American Republic consented to a joint intervention, Russia would not have dared to oppose such a combination by threats of war or hostile action; the European Concert—really a Concert against England—would have been broken up; the Powers would have retired beaten from the diplomatic field; the Porte would have been compelled to allow British and American war-ships in the Bosphorus, whilst a force of United States and British troops could have been despatched to Armenia, and have reached there in time to save the miserable Christians from an immensity of further suffering. The expedition need not have been a large one—the prestige of the two countries would have easily ensured the peaceful establishment of a reformed government, under efficient and strong control. French and English troops achieved a similar end in part of Syria during 1860, and the Mountains of the Lebanon have had a myriad of reasons since then to bless their intervention, and the system—incomplete as it necessarily was—established through its means upon the recommendations of Lord Dufferin.

Moreover, such joint action would have made Great Britain more than willing to discuss all questions concerning the Monroe doctrine in a fair, broad, and friendly manner, and would have greatly facilitated a settlement of the various problems involved. The two Powers can indeed work together in so many and such beneficial directions that it is a marvel the fact has not been long since recognized and acted upon. Away back in 1823, President Monroe expressed, and Congress confirmed, the national sympathy with struggling Greece—on whose behalf England laboured so long and earnestly. About the same time the United States and the United Kingdom—Canning and Monroe—formulated the famous Monroe doctrine, which was then intended to help the battling Republics of South America, and to warn Spain and the Holy Alliance off American soil. In 1849, President Taylor expressed—though Congress would not endorse the national sentiment of both England and the States in favour of Kossuth and the Hungarians, in their great struggle with the armies of Austria and Russia. It might well have been, therefore, that these two great English-speaking peoples, while uniting in a common cause, should have promoted not only the lasting good, and earned the everlasting blessing of the Armenians and Christians of the East, but have also advanced each other's welfare and unity and peaceful co-operation in mutually useful directions. To quote the striking words of Mr. Chamberlain on January 26th :

"Would it were possible that, instead of wasting breath in a petty South American boundary dispute, we could count on the powerful support of the United States in enforcing the representations which hitherto we have fruitlessly made in behalf of those who are suffering from Turkish tyranny and Turkish fanaticism."

CHAPTER XXV.

THE ATTITUDE OF CANADA.

While Great Britain and the United States were thus stirred to the heart with sympathy and sorrow for the Armenians, Canada was not behindhand in either sentiment or practical support. Through the energetic labours of Dr. Walter B. Geikie, the Honorary Treasurer of the Dominion Fund, something over $8000 was forwarded from Toronto up to the 1st of May, 1896. A similar sum was sent from Montreal, mainly through the action of the Montreal *Witness* and Mr. J. R. Dougall, its proprietor, and Treasurer of the local fund, who was also strongly supported by other local papers. Halifax and St. John followed suit, with the aid of Bishop Courtney and Sir Leonard Tilley, while the small contributions which came from all parts of the country to swell the general total showed how the feeling had permeated the masses of the people, and stirred up the poorest as well as the richest to the presentation of their mite.

Meantime, however, Canada was adding to the strength of Great Britain by its loyal allegiance and offers of help in the event of war, both before and after the unfortunate Venezuelan complications. And in so doing she was helping the Armenians in a most powerful, though indirect manner, whilst the United States was regrettably adding to the burdens and complications of the only European Power which cared one iota whether the Armenian people lived or died. It is an unpleasant statement to make, but a true and necessary one. The ensuing difficulties, however, brought out not only strong Canadian expressions of sympathy with the motherland, but very many and earnest wishes that the United States would forego its spirit of momentary antagonism, and the soreness aroused by its prevailing newspaper war, and unite with England in the relief of Eastern Christendom. Perhaps Principal Grant, of Kingston, voiced public opinion upon the wide issues of the moment as clearly as was possible, in the following extract from a letter dated March 4th:

"Never before did I feel more keenly that we have no voice, because we have never asked for it, in directing the policy of the British Government. But I do wonder that a strong man does not rise in the (Imperial) House of Commons and urge the Government to open negotiations with the United States with the object of taking conjoint action. Surely the heart of a people who have been trying so long to spread the light in Turkey would respond to such an overture. They have made no answer to the public addresses in which Mr. Balfour and Mr. Chamberlain urged this on them, but a formal proposal should be made. Even were that refused, our hearts would glow if Britain decided to dare all risks and act alone! We have no right to ask or even to suggest it. We are apparently content that Britain shall bear all the burdens of the empire."

There can be no doubt that for a time Canadians shared the American feeling that England should have intervened at all hazards. And the former were willing to take their share of the possible responsibility, although unaware of the real diplomatic situation in the East, or how far the mother country had really gone toward the point of war. But the trouble with the United States, and the outburst of German hatred and intrigue in South Africa, helped to throw light upon the general situation, and while deeply regretting the attitude of the Republic, and freely condemning that of Germany, the people of Canada began to appreciate the difficulties under which the British Titan laboured; which their own Minister of Finance, Mr. G. E. Foster, had voiced in his famous phrase of "splendid isolation"; and which has been so expressively embodied in the words of an unknown poet:

> "Dim shapeless shadows pass like ghosts;
> Along the trembling earth they feel
> The distant tramp of marching hosts,
> And hear the smothered clash of steel;
> Till, reaching out for friendly hands
> To guide them through the gloom, they press
> To where one silent figure stands
> Serene in lofty loneliness."

That isolation can, of course, never be complete while the Colonies stand by the heart of their Empire, but this miserable Turkish question was one which tested local loyalty, and required a really earnest belief in the high motives of British statecraft, on account of the varied grounds for possible misapprehension and unjust condemnation. And no matter how strong an advocate of closer Imperial unity one may be, it is perhaps a little difficult to see just how Canadian representation in the British Imperial Parliament could have affected this question. It was one of diplomacy, alliances, and readiness for war. By standing side by side with England in a common cause, Canada was doing more for the Armenians than she could have known, while by blazing up into what we may hope was a state of temporary hostility, the United States did more harm to the Eastern Christians than all their beneficent contributions and noble missionary labours could undo in a prolonged period.

Meanwhile Canadian sympathy was being expressed in many directions. The Metropolitan of the Church of

England in Canada—Archbishop Lewis—issued a letter of appeal for help to the Armenians; the Archbishop of Canterbury issued a short prayer for use in the Dominion, as well as in Great Britain; the House of Bishops passed a resolution of strong sympathy; the Diocesan Synod of Montreal denounced the atrocities amid a most affecting scene, and declared "the sufferings of this ancient branch of the Church Catholic" to deserve every possible financial amelioration; the Montreal branch of the Evangelical Alliance issued a strong appeal for aid signed by its President, Mr. T. M. Dewey, and its Secretary-Treasurer, Mr. W. J. Smyth; whilst the Toronto branch of the same Alliance passed fervent resolutions, issued an appeal to "the Christian Churches and people of Ontario," and appointed a Committee of which Dr. Geikie was Treasurer, and Principal Caven, Mr. S. H. Blake, Q.C., Mr. J. J. Maclaren, Q.C., Professor Rand, and Mr. N. W. Hoyles, Q.C., were active members.

On March 25th, 1896, a meeting was held in St. John, New Brunswick, presided over by Sir Leonard Tilley, and addressed by a number of clergymen and citizens. One of the speakers—Mr. H. A. McKeown—declared that the only solution of existing difficulties was for "the Anglo-Saxon civilization of the world to step in. The British Empire and the United States together need not fear Islamism and Europe combined." Resolutions were passed denouncing the Sultan and the jealousies of the Christian Powers; promising aid in practical contributions; and forwarding a memorial to the World's Evangelical Alliance in London, which urged the action of Christendom in stopping the fiendish work of the Turk and Kurd. About the same time a gathering met under the auspices of the local Council of Women, which was presided over by

Lady Tilley, passed a brief resolution, and then collected $150 on the spot.

Some time before this a meeting had been held in Halifax under the auspices of the Evangelical Alliance, with Rev. Dr. Lathern in the chair. There was a marked tendency amongst the speakers to rebuke the attitude and action of the United States in this connection, and to urge a more sympathetic and less hostile relationship with England, in the common cause of Armenia and the Christian world. But the central event of the evening was an eloquent speech from Dr. Courtney, the Bishop of Nova Scotia,* and the passage of his resolution in favour of "the policy of treaty intervention." It must be admitted in this connection that in all these resolutions and the accompanying speeches there were no demands for British intervention at the point of the sword, and in the teeth of Europe. There was, in spite of natural and intense indignation at the attitude of the Powers— amongst whom it was as yet impossible to apportion the responsibility—a general feeling that British policy would be found

*The following extracts from a letter received by the Author from Bishop Courtney—dated March 21st, 1896—are of general interest :

"As to the effect of joint action by England and the United States I have no manner of doubt. Could these two countries be so joined together in action as practically to be one, they would probably be invincible, but the difficulty is to get them to act. That difficulty is, I suppose, a double one. England is, by treaties and otherwise, enmeshed with all the leading countries of the world, and therefore is not free to be completely conjoined with the United States in offensive and defensive actions ; and the United States could only undertake such a conjunction with England by becoming a party to some, at least, of the engagements which bind England and her actions with other European Powers ; and they would have to alter the chief distinguishing features of American national policy, which is to keep out of entangling alliances.

"Could you succeed in suggesting a practicable mode of bringing about an offensive and defensive alliance between England and America, the first work of which should be intervention on behalf of Armenia, you would not only bring relief and protection to that wretched people, but bring sensibly nearer the advent of universal peace.

" I remain, yours truly,
" F. NOVA SCOTIA."

in the end to have been honourable, strong, and pronounced.

It was seen that both parties were apparently united in England upon the question, and, although the respective responsibility of these parties under the Anglo-Turkish or Cyprus Convention was hardly understood, it could not but be felt, however vaguely, that the diplomatic situation in Europe must have been very serious when neither Mr. Gladstone nor Lord Rosebery would attempt to embarrass the Government by using this most terrible of weapons for stirring up indignation and popular passion. And there was, besides, the general wish embodied in Principal Grant's letter—and once more declared in the resolution of a meeting of Toronto citizens held on March 24th—that the United States would join with England in the final settlement of the question. The following extract from the motion, as proposed by Principal Caven, of Knox College, and seconded by the Rev. Dr. Potts, speaks for itself:

"Among the nations of the world there are none upon whom the obligation more surely rests to represent the cause of righteousness and humanity, and to afford succour (as may be in their power) to the oppressed and persecuted, than upon Great Britain and the United States of America. These nations have been signally endowed by Providence with abundant resources, with the largest measure of ordered freedom, and their position in many respects amongst the nations of the earth makes these Anglo-Saxon communities influential in every worthy cause, especially when they act in concert. Whatever be the political complications of the Armenian problem there is surely reasonable ground for hope that something might be done on behalf of a people threatened with extermination, should Britain and the United States agree to act together in doing whatever may be possible to befriend Armenia and stay the hand of the ruthless persecutor."

Such, in brief, has been the action and attitude of Canada in connection with this wide-reaching subject. And, if the sympathetic interest aroused in Armenia does nothing more than send some $20,000 to the relief of the distressed, it will have done very good service. But Canada has before now led the Empire in many things, and it will be a great additional benefit to humanity should it be able to in some way impel international consideration to the point of united action between the English-speaking peoples on behalf of Eastern Christians. Lying half-way between the United Kingdom and the United States, it is admirably adapted in many ways to further such a policy of international co-operation, and to suggest future action of the kind—even apart from the immediate Armenian situation of starvation and suffering.

There is, of course, the fact that Canadian relations with the American Republic have always been delicate, sometimes unpleasant, sometimes hostile. But any practicable proposal which would add the United States to the strength of England in the East; which would promote the friendship of the two great Powers, and ensure the maintenance of that peace and harmony so essential to the development of the Dominion; which might facilitate the formation of an Anglo-American Board of Arbitration; which could be operated without involving the ever-vexed question of tariffs and commercial interchange; would be sure of cordial support from all parties and portions of Canada. The Dominion, it must be remembered, has very considerable interests at stake in the East. Great Britain's quarrel is hers also. When the motherland is involved in some great war, the safety of Canadian commerce, the security of Canadian coasts, the stability of Canadian credit, will be as much concerned in the result, comparatively, as will the local interests of Great Britain h rself. Upon the ability of the British navy to guard the countries and coast cities and merchant vessels of the Empire will depend Canadian prosperity and immunity from invasion. And the Canadian Pacific Railway constitutes a very pronounced factor in this connection. It will afford—and has already done so, by way of experiment—a British passage over British soil for troops and munitions of war going from England to the East. It is an alternative route to the much-talked of Suez Canal, and a decidedly safer one.

And this may be said despite Mr. Goldwin Smith's recent remarkable statement that the United State *would not allow* it to be used for such a purpose. The Republic could not prevent such a use without first declaring war, and it may be presumed, and hoped, that a conflict will not take place upon issues of this nature. But if there is serious danger of a struggle—as the Venezuelan affair certainly indicated—it becomes all the more desirable that a basis should be found for united friendly action in some point of the external policy of the Empire and the Republic. Once that is discovered and utilized, the growth of friendship will be steady, and the sympathy of natural relationship be given an opportunity to develop. To quote Senator Wolcott, in one of the few great and honourable speeches heard at Washington along these lines in recent years: " Blood is thicker than water, and until a just quarrel divides us—which Heaven forbid!—may these two great nations, of the same speech, lineage, and traditions, stand as brothers—shoulder to shoulder, in the interests of humanity—by a union compelling peace."

And this Turkish question is one which may well prove a foundation for some such union. But, so far as Canada is concerned, the matter should be freed from all connection with the talk of annexation to the United

States, of which so much is heard in the American Congress, in American political speeches, in American Commissions upon railway matters—and of which so little is ever heard in Canada. The Dominion would like, above all things in an international sense, to contribute to the co-operation of England and the States in bringing peace to the Christians of the East and strength to the civilizing arm of Anglo-Saxon power. The wish, however, is born of loyalty to the Empire, as well as of the desire to be upon most friendly terms with the Republic.

There is no annexation sentiment to speak of in the Dominion, and such as there is hardly dares to show itself. If in the general elections of 1891 Sir John Macdonald formulated what became first a party motto, and was then accepted as embodying a national principle, in the famous words, "A British subject I was born, a British subject I will die"; the face 'of the Opposition leader in that campaign and in the fight of 1896—Mr. Laurier—may be seen over the length and breadth of the country in party placards with a coloured Union Jack on either side. The same party has apparently given up its policy of discrimination in trade matters against Great Britain, just as the Conservative party has declared itself for discrimination in favour of Great Britain. But, aside from fiscal affairs, which, like questions of finance in a man's household, may be said to constitute the personal part of a nation's policy and action, all Canadian parties are a positive unit in support of the friendliest and closest relations between the Empire and the United States.

There are many reasons for this. Common Christianity and the influence of the pulpit is one. Mutual interest in missions is another. At the present moment eighty per cent. öf the world's Christian workers in foreign lands is Anglo-Saxon, and eighty-eight per cent. of the funds used in mission fields is British and American. When the General Conference of Foreign Missions was held in London during 1888, 121 out of 139 delegates were found to be of Anglo-Saxon origin or nationality. Personal friendships, intercourse, and intermarriage are also factors of considerable importance. Opposed to them is the undoubted hostility of the American press as a whole; the pride of the British press and people, which is thus naturally aroused in return; the effect of an educational system in the United States which is based upon an old-time and historic prejudice against England; the result of American ignorance concerning the general attitude of Canada and the condition of Canadian public opinion.

These are all capable of practical amelioration or removal, under the soothing influences of joint international action. So far as Canada is concerned, it is perhaps regrettable that Mr. John Charlton did not succeed in passing some resolution of sympathy with Armenia during the last session of the Parliament which died in April, 1896. To be effective along the lines indicated, it should have been so worded as to obtain the support of both parties; and if the next Parliament takes action in the matter at all, it might well urge the final settlement of the Turkish question at the hands of England and the United States, together with the hope that such an alliance might be arranged as would prevent further massacres in the future, and ensure the peace and prosperity of Eastern Christendom under the guardianship of the two great Christian empires of the West.

Canadian public opinion would most strongly endorse such a step, and the horror universally felt throughout the country would find some alleviation in realizing the fact that Canada has stood side by side with Great

Britain, and shared its "splendid isolation" during the diplomatic struggle for relief to Armenia; has contributed sums, not large in amount, but remarkable in the wide distribution and great number of their donors; and has made practical suggestions for the future welfare of Eastern Christians, and the saving of other bodies and sections of that religion from similar atrocities. The expression of sympathy in the press of Canada has very well voiced this general feeling, and perhaps the following denunciation of the Powers in the Toronto *Globe* of February 3rd best illustrates the popular sentiment:

"The vocabulary of the awful has been exhausted in writing of Armenia. The world has paused to find new qualitatives each morning as further details of the brutal carnival have come in, and has then gone on calmly eating its breakfast. The *laissez-faire* policy the nations have pursued, viewed from self-interest alone, has been simply suicidal. The edge of feeling has been blunted, the clock of progress turned back, and the very foundations of civilization threatened. Words of sympathy and encouragement must be now a by-word and a hissing in the ears of the Armenians. Two courses alone have ever been possible to the European Powers—to rescue them from their tormentors or to abandon them. Indecision has but added to the agony."

That this indecision was simply fear of a European war; that it turned upon Russian objection to any action whatever; that it has resulted in an alliance between the Sultan and the Czar; that it has become a concert of the great Powers against England as the champion of Armenia, instead of against the Turk as the instrument of slaughter and outrage; are all reasons for greater Canadian sympathy with the Armenians, and more pronounced good will towards Great Britain, as well as for deeper regret at the American feeling and action which so weakened British influence at a critical moment.

CHAPTER XXVI.

WHAT OF THE FUTURE?

The tottering empire of the Turk still holds within its wracked and enfeebled frame the seeds of much future misery and possible devastation. How to prevent the development of these germs of trouble has constituted the Eastern Question of the past hundred years. How to kill them outright and replace the Turk by a brighter and better régime is the Eastern Question of the future. How to bring about this change without war between some of the great rival powers of Europe is the question of the immediate present.

Coupled with all the varied complications of the time in connection with Egypt and Syria, Armenia and Bulgaria, Greece and Roumania, is the well-defined and reasonable fear that the final collapse of the Turk will be preceded by an internal convulsion more terrible than anything which has yet occurred, and accompanied by a dying struggle which will revive the worst memories of Mahometan warfare and fanaticism. It may be true that the Turk is only encamped in Europe, and that his institutions, religion, and government have obtained no permanent foothold. But it is also true that there are more than a million pure Ottoman Turks in Europe, and from four to seven millions of Mahometans, while in Asiatic Turkey there must be at least ten millions more. Figures are so varied upon this point that exactitude is almost impossible, but those mentioned embody the lowest estimate.

Here, then, is a mass of ignorant, fanatical, and once warlike people to deal with. Corruption has eaten into every form and phase of their national life; immorality has undermined the individual strength of the people; disorganization has destroyed the discipline of the army; decay has brought the once great navy down to the point of a solitary and unworkable ironclad; the provinces have dropped away or been torn from the empire one by one; the prestige of the conquering Moslem has absolutely gone. Yet there are in the Turk unpleasant possibilities of revived fanaticism and military passion. Many of the poorer and peasant class are still uncontaminated by the prevailing moral degradation. Pride of possession, and memories of past dominance, are still struggling in the breasts of thousands with the feeling of fatalism which says that everything was given by Allah, and if it be his will to take it away—well and good. The sacred standard of Mahomet still rests in the Mosque of St. Sophia, and may be brought forth at any time to command all the faithful to battle and arouse the myriad wandering Dervishes to outbursts of wild fanaticism. And back of all this are the potential possibilities of a hundred million Mahometans spread through Asia and Africa, and owning, in the main, some sort of spiritual allegiance to the Caliph at Constantinople.

To Great Britain this is a very vital consideration. The safety of her Indian Empire in 1857 owed much to the loyalty of its Moslem population; the Queen is, at the present time, the greatest of Mahometan sovereigns, and rules three times as many adherents of that faith as does the Sultan himself; the people of Egypt, which may now almost be termed British territory, are bigoted devotees of Islam; the religion itself is a growing one throughout Africa, and the subject of intense and widespread fanati cism. Finally, the Sultan is, outside of Persia, the recognized religious head of the Moslem world, and it is absolutely impossible to estimate how much influence the unfurling of the Sacred Standard of the Prophet at Stamboul might have upon the vast mass of Britain's Mahometan subjects. Some faint indication may be found in the resolution passed during November, 1895, by the Anjuman-i-Islam—a body of Indian Mahometans in London—declaring, that after having:

" For several months past urged upon the British public and Her Majesty's Government the importance of taking into consideration the religious feelings and sentiments of the Moslems in India in their dealings with Turkey . . . they hope that in any future development of the Turkish question the British Government, following the traditional policy of England, will maintain the integrity and independence of the dominions of His Imperial Majesty the Sultan, the Commander of the Faithful, and the Guardian of the Kaaba."

A holy war proclaimed by the Sultan is something which England has never had to encounter. The Prophet's standard is a green banner, now torn almost into shreds, and preserved in a golden case in the Imperial Treasury at Constantinople. Originally, it was given by Mahomet on his deathbed to his lieutenants, with the words, "Take this standard and march forward!" And although never used except in cases of great emergency—the last occasion was the Sultan Mahmoud's conflict with the Janizaries—it still retains the inherent religious right to call every Moslem into the field. Just how far that right could be realized is one of the questions of the day.

There can be no doubt of the present fealty and friendship of the Indian Mahometan. His princes are towers of strength to British rule, and not the less so for being consistent and conspicuous enemies of Russia.

They have given large sums to the Vice-regal Government for use in frontier defence, and have offered still larger amounts. They are as superior to the Hindoos, who in far greater number of millions cover the soil of Hindustan, as the English people are, in enterprise and intellect, to the Boers in South Africa. But there can be equally little doubt of their religious loyalty to Mahomet, and Sir Richard Temple, speaking from prolonged experience of India, declares that Christianity can make no headway whatever amongst them. And, up till this present period, with a few trivial exceptions, Great Britain has appeared in their eyes as a sort of permanent protector of the Turkish Empire against Russian aggression.

It is well to remember that while the better classes of the Moslems are more or less educated into a comprehension of existing conditions, and the value of British rule to the peace and prosperity of all the varied races of India, the masses are as greatly influenced by religious prejudice as are the Turks of Asia Minor, or the Hindoos themselves. They are prone to sudden conflict with their neighbours of Buddhist belief, and if the strong hand of England were removed, for even a moment, the streets of Indian cities and the highways of Indian territory would stream with the blood of Hindoo and Mahometan. But though ignorant, they are of a better type than the low-class Turk, whose ranks are yearly showing fewer men of honesty and moral cleanness.

They can fight, and have frequently proved their bravery; and it is a question whether the Mahometan of India, taken as a whole, is much changed in character from the days when the local rulers defied, and fought, and conquered the Hindoo Rajahs; or when some really great man, such as Akbar the Magnificent, governed an Indian empire upon the ordinary Mahometan bases of despotism, pillage, and the strong hand of military might. Since the inauguration of the *Pax Britannicus* amidst this myriad mass of people, the votaries of Mahomet have been preserved from much of the corruption, the enervating immorality, and cruelty of fanaticism, which circumstances have fostered amongst the Turks. But, d(; the fact that they embody the best elements of thei. eligion, the upper classes are none the less as proud as any Turk can be—and that is saying much; while the masses are more devoted to the active exercise of their religious forms than are those of Turkey. The one class will not lower itself to seek employment at the hands of the Government or work for a living if it can possibly be avoided; and the result is that some years ago, out of a population of 9,400,000 Mahometans in the Northwest Provinces and Oudh, there were only six of that religion employed in the various departments of the Government. as compared with 140 Hindoos. The other class send' ousands of pilgrims yearly to the sacred shrine of Me

Taking these facts into consideration, it is therefore impossible to do more than surmise the result in this connection of any great British war against Turkey, as one of two or more hostile Powers. It may, however, be concluded that the chief danger would not take the form of an open rebellion in India, but rather of secret subsidies to the Sultan; the private enlistment of many armed individuals in his forces; and a certain amount of paralysis in the military system by which the Empire would have to be guarded from Russian invasion. Of course, these are only possibilities, and perhaps pessimistic ones, but they are of a nature which none the less require to be mentioned.

This, then, is one very important point in considering the future. Another is the attitude of Russia. Its hostility to England and its ambition need not be more than mentioned here. Its antagonism to reform in Turkey is based upon opposition to any policy or action which might strengthen the lion still lying along its path to Stamboul. Upon this subject, Dr. Cyrus Hamlin—writing as an American, and a life-long missionary and divine in Turkey —declares that " Russia has always opposed every reform which England has inaugurated. Lord Stratford de Redcliffe was more than a match for her, but with that one exception England's attempts to strengthen Turkey have been notorious failures. Russia's efforts to weaken her have been a notorious success." Moreover, the idea prevalent in some quarters that the Russians desire, and should be allowed, to intervene in Turkey on behalf of the Armenian population is entirely erroneous. They might desire to do so, if there was any chance of their being left in permanent possession of that gateway to Asia Minor and the Bosphorus, but not for any reasons connected with such a very disinterested idea as the betterment of conditions amongst its Christian population. Upon this latter poin. Hobart Pasha, the ex-officer of the British army who so greatly aided the Turks in the war of 1877, declared in the *Nineteenth Century* of April, 1885, that:

" The aims of Russian ambition extend like the arms of an octopus throughout Asia Minor. Having once bagged Armenia, she will try to push her conquest further south, so as to threaten the coveted goal of Constantinople from the Asiatic side, and thus avoid a conflict with Austria, as well as a dispute with her jealous German neighbours, should Turkish European conquests be attempted. . . . Once in Diarbekr (the extreme end of Turkish Armenia), it is not necessary to be a prophet to predict that the Russians would not forget their old claim to a protectorate of the Holy Places in Jerusalem. Nothing could be more popular than this pretension with the mass of Russian peasants. Like everything done by Russia, this, too, would be disguised under the name of religion."

Russian treatment of Christian countries in the Balkan Peninsula are cases in point. Upon one occasion (1812) she made peace with the Porte, and handed back the Christians of Moldavia, Wallachia, and Servia to the Turks in return for the cession of Bessarabia. Cunibert, the Servian historian, says that the vagueness of the terms of this treaty showed utter indifference to the fate of her Servian allies, and was probably intentional. "Such conduct" he adds, "might promote the ulterior designs of Russia in the East; but it showed little justice and little generosity to Servia."

But this in passing. To return to the Armenian situation. While the whole Christian world was denouncing the Powers for not taking definite action; while Mr. Gladstone was calling down the vengeance of Heaven upon them—jointly or singly; while the Duke of Westminster was declaring that "they ought to know how it was that England had been thwarted in her strenuous endeavours to put a stop to the red-handed villainy of the Sultan, and what and where had been the influence which had enabled and almost encouraged that monster in human shape to destroy some 50,000 unoffending Christians, and to ruin thousands more with perfect impunity"; the Russian Government was steadily backing up the Porte against the other Powers, and refusing to permit any foreign intervention in Armenia, while taking no sort of sympathetic action itself—rather the reverse. Upon this point, Mr. Balfour was sufficiently explicit in his speech at Bristol, on February 3rd, when he declared that Russia is not willing, and has not been willing, to take upon herself this duty. We have not prevented her from doing what she has never desired to do—what she would certainly refuse to do."

The future attitude of the Turk is, of course, an all-important matter. What the Sultan has allowed to-day can happen again to-morrow, and his responsibility for the situation in Armenia is undoubted. This branch of the Eastern Question is therefore no more settled than is the problem of who shall eventually possess Constantinople. One thing, however, may be taken for granted. The "Young Turkey" party, the alleged section in favour of reform and progress, is almost as mythical as were the miserable Turkish fabrications about Armenian sedition and rebellion. There is some natural and seething discontent among the Turks, as there was, and is, amongst the Christians of Asia Minor. But its only possible achievement—if it ever came to anything at all—would be the murder of Abdul-Hamid and the characteristic Ottoman revolution which consists in a violent change of rulers.

There is, no doubt, this element of organized Turkish discontent in the country, but it is small, and without real influence, except in the very useful direction of pointing out the need of reforms, and the abuses of despotic power, to the foreign press and the foreign representatives. A true Turk is a thorough Mohometan, and no follower of Islam—no true believer—can be a " Reformer." The two things are as incompatible as oil and water. Hence any such party must consist, in the main, of men whose faith in the Prophet is somewhat loosened by contact with Europeans—and they would be without influence over their fellows; or else of Christians, who are all naturally anxious for reforms, but cannot, of course, be termed Turks. The genuine Turk is never converted to Christianity. But there is always the possibility of a "revival" amongst

Moslems. This is illustrated in the history of the Wahabites of Arabia, who in the end of the eighteenth century swept over that country with what they claimed to be a reformed, and refreshened, and invigorated Islam. It was, in fact, a revival, pure and simple, of Mahomet's aggressive religion, and proved too much for both Sultans and Pashas, until the power of Mehemet Ali, of Egypt, finally crushed the sect in 1818.

The rise of El Mahdi in the Soudan, and of Arabi Pasha in Egypt, together with the successful career of Osman Digna, illustrate the modern and immediate force of this principle in other local applications. The possibility of its ever being applied to the Turk is one, therefore, which must be considered. The chances are certainly against it. Turkish character is so indolent, fatalistic, and debauched by its normal surroundings that there is no longer room for any wide capabilities of hot and eager action. The Bedouin of the deserts of Arabia, or the fierce slave-hunter of the Soudan, have natures which can easily be blown upon by the fierce breath of fanaticism. But even a threatened invasion of his territory would hardly arouse the old fighting spirit in the modern Turk, except to the point of massacring helpless Christians and neighbours.

There would, of course, be many exceptions to this rule, and a fair-sized army of good material could, no doubt, be got together. The Dervishes—not the natives of the Soudan, who for some inscrutable reason have been given that name in press despatches—would be on hand, throughout the Turkish dominions, to arouse fanaticism with all those wild freaks of action and manner which Asiatics often consider an evidence of holy priesthood; and they would spread themselves throughout the East, and India, and Africa. But in any short, sharp campaign the Turks would be overpowered before aid from these quarters could reach them. And, if we may judge from the story of the siege of Zeitoun, even the long-crushed Armenians showed in that isolated case of a successful resistance during long months of surrounding murder and outrage a bravery which the Turks certainly did not exhibit. Says one account :

"Once the Zeitounlis collected a great flock of mountain goats—a few men secreted themselves amongst them —and came down close upon the Turks. There was a mist, and the Zeitounlis fired a few shots. The Turks, thinking surely a great army was upon them, turned and fled. Even at a quarter of a mile distant it is hard to distinguish between goats and men. The goats keep in almost perfect ranks, are black with white faces, and walk almost as fast as soldiers walk."

The whole record of this siege is, indeed, a distinct evidence of what the Christian populations of the East can really do when firm, determined, and united. And it also shows what the Turk can not do. Seeing the sufferings of their co-religionists everywhere, the Armenians here decided that they would not quietly submit to the same fate. The first step for safety was, of course, to get possession of the town fort, and this they did by pouring sand and kerosene oil into the water supply. After enduring this for three days the Turks came out, and, after fifty-six hours' fighting, surrendered—to the number of 250 men. Later on, when the Turkish reinforcements arrived to recapture the place, and these prisoners made an effort to escape while the Armenian men were struggling with their foes upon the walls, the armed women of the town anticipated and averted a similar fate for every Christian soul in Zeitoun by themselves slaughtering the Turks, and throwing their bodies over the cliff.

The terms then offered the gallant inhabitants by their surrounding enemies were immediate surrender, to be followed by the execution of twenty per cent. of the population. "Wait one day," they declared, "and we will have the life of every man, woman, and child." But for many months they had to wait, and then, by the intervention of the Powers, the Christians were eventually saved through the granting of an amnesty. It was their own heroism, however, which, in reality, preserved them from the most fearful fate, and not the long-delayed action of the Russianized concert against England. And it is typical of the modern and cowardly character of the Turks that, after being unable to capture the place by force of arms, they got possession by deceitful pledges to the Powers, which were promptly broken. One was the promise of a Christian governor; the result was the appointment of a Mahometan shortly after the surrender.

The future of Turkey, therefore, is complicated, from any present standpoint, by the fact that the Sultan holds in his hand the religious fanaticism of Mahometan peoples—an utterly unknown, but all the more dreaded influence; by the fact that Russia now controls the diplomatic situation at Constantinople, and appears to have enmeshed the Porte in some such arrangement as that of Unkiar Skelessi; by the fact that owing to the absolute ruin of the Ottoman navy the Black Sea now lies open for the transportation of Russian troops to the Bosphorus—when they have hitherto had to fight their way over the Balkans—and thus enables the million men comprising the Russian active army to join with comparative ease the armies of the Turk. The latter are estimated by themselves at 1,100,000 men, but probably do not amount to more than half that number, or indeed a quarter of it. Moreover, the absence of money or means of equipment, the influence of endless corruption, the constant and increasing demoralization of Turkish character and physique, would still further diminish even this low estimate.

And, in the event of war, there are many possibilities to predicate. A British fleet might force its way through the Dardanelles, and prevent any juncture between Russian and Turkish troops, while the British armies, small as they would be in comparison with the five millions which Russia claims to have upon a war basis, ought to obtain much support from the Greeks, the Bulgarians, the Servians, and the Roumanians, as against their traditional enemy, the Turk. Much, of course, would depend upon which of these ambitious States was given precedence in the race for Constantinople, or how they might be previously organized. Combined, they could, under serious pressure, put perhaps 400,000 men in the field; separated by mutual rivalries, the force might be comparatively small. England could also draw to some extent upon the 2,000,000 men comprising the Italian army on its war establishment, though with present complications in Africa that country might find its hands pretty full. And from the States of the British Empire a formidable contingent would be obtained in time of need. Of course, the enormous money power of Great Britain would be a vital factor in the contest, enabling her to obtain and spend one thousand million dollars—according to Sir M. E. Hicks-Beach, the present Chancellor of the Exchequer—without imposing a single cent of additional taxation.

This would mean a tremendous lever for organizing armies—one which makes the almost bankrupt nations of Europe, with all their huge armaments, look far from startling. Such a consideration of the military situation would turn, however, upon the somewhat uncertain chances of France and Germany being kept neutral by their own rivalries and hatreds. And it is subject to absolute change by any combination in which the United States might take a hand with Great Britain. At present, intervention in Asiatic Turkey means for England a single-handed war with the Turkish and Russian Powers, and probably with France.

It is, in fact, very likely that the French Republic would be thus involved, because her most dangerous neighbour—Germany—in its recently aroused and displayed antagonism to England, might bide its time as to Alsace-Lorraine, in the hope that after Great Britain had been more or less weakened in the struggle she would then be able to take her own way in South Africa. This is, of course, all pure speculation; but the whole great issue could be peaceably settled in comparatively short order by an arrangement between Great Britain and the United States along some such lines as these:

I. Abandonment by the United States of that principle in the Monroe doctrine which is supposed to exclude interference in international politics—a principle which has really been given up by Congress in connection with Cuba and Armenia, and is not practised by the people, the press, or the political leaders.

II. An arrangement with England for the re-assumption, under joint auspices, of the protectorate over Asia Minor, still legally inherent in the treaties between Turkey and England.

III. Acceptance by Great Britain of the Monroe doctrine, so far as American control over the foreign policy of the South American continent and Central American States is concerned, with a mutual agreement as to the settlement of the existing boundaries to British

American territories, and the acknowledgment of existing British rights, property, and treaty privileges.

IV. An understanding between the two Governments that both will aid in the eventual driving of the Turk out of Europe, and the establishment of Constantinople as either the capital of a Grecian or a Bulgarian Christian kingdom; or the head of a Confederation of Christian States stretching from the Balkans to the Bosphorus, and from the Black Sea to the shores of the Adriatic.

V. The establishment of an Anglo-American Council of Arbitration and Advice, appointed by the British and American Governments in equal numbers, and including amongst the former a representative from Australia, one from Canada, and one each from India and South Africa. Its functions to be the consideration of appeals upon international issues between the two central governments, and the finding of some reasonable solution satisfactory to the Legislatures concerned.

These suggestions may at first sight appear chimerical, but a study of the situation will show them to be a legitimate, beneficial, and not impossible outcome. As to the first, the United States may be said to have long since abrogated what has never been established, if such a phrase can be used. The policy of non-intervention for a small American people, scattered over a very wide territory, was eminently wise. But for a great nation of nearly seventy millions, with growing naval strength and spreading commerce; with interests in many lands, and subjects scattered from the Transvaal to Armenia; with a press, a pulpit, and a platform dealing in the fiercest denunciation of other countries and the policy of foreign States; such a policy is not only impossible, but is actually non-existent.

It hardly required Congressional resolutions which aroused the Spaniard about Cuba, or the Turk about Armenia, to emphasize this plain international fact. Similar action regarding the Turks in Greece and the French in Mexico, or concerning Samoa, Hayti, and Hawaii, had already proved it sufficiently. As to the recent crisis in Turkey, the American press has surely been plain-spoken enough, to say nothing about its treatment of the Venezuelan question. It rang with news of possible and impossible war preparations, first against the Turk, then against the British, and then against the Spaniard. Redress was demanded from the Sultan for outrages upon American missionaries and the destruction of American property. At one time the Dardanelles was to be entered by an American fleet; in one case the Smyrna Custom House was to be seized and held; and in another the Island of Crete was to be occupied. In other connections Cuba was to be held for the local insurgents, and Canada invaded and captured in the early morning.

Of course, much of this was effervescent nonsense, but its spirit none the less indicates that restless feeling which makes a foreign policy, in spite of theoretical Monroe doctrines and the possibility of a genuine war. Looked at in the correct light, it shows difficulties past, present, and future, in which the alliance of Great Britain would have been, is, and will be, of immense value, while it also clearly demonstrates the absence of any real obstacle to negotiations along that line—aside from recently aroused antagonisms and the educated prejudices of a past period. But the Americans are emphatically a business-like people, though an occasional streak of sentiment—as also in the British—may scatter almost any carefully devised calculation. An arrangement, however, which would, to take their point of view first, give them a recognized sphere of influence over the broad American continent—apart from Canada and present British possessions—and enable them to join their own vast home strength to the immense foreign and naval power of England in all European complications, and coming continental difficulties, could not but be worth some sacrifice of prejudice or of ill-defined phantasms such as " non-intervention."

American difficulties at home and abroad are by no means few. There is a French Guiana as well as a British Guiana; there are German interests in Brazil— and a hundred thousand Germans—as well as Italians in New York, and Irish everywhere; there are British boundary questions elsewhere than in Venezuela, and British citizens from Nicaragua to the Argentine. A friendly arrangement with Great Britain would prevent even the possibility of any other nation troubling the Americas; would remove the basis now existing for innumerable opportunities of struggle in South America between two countries which must, by the nature of inherent character and similar pursuits, be great rivals or great allies; and would replace that bugbear of the American politician—the Irish vote—by a strong, united, and vigorous British vote.

It would do more than this. By the removal of the cause in South America of present ill-feeling, and the restriction of reasons for future war in other complications of a similar nature, much good would accrue to American business, American investments, and American credit. The recent panic in Wall Street, created by the withdrawal of British money, showed abundantly how the financial interests of the United States are bound up in friendly relations with England. It indicated also the great disasters which would follow any war between the two countries, and proved that although American fast cruisers might injure British commerce, and American soldiers cause the Canadian people much of suffering, the unpleasant results to the Republic would not be limited to the loss of a market for its products or the bombardment of some of its seaports. Hence the practical value of an alliance which would not only prevent war —that fatal injury to international material interests; but the threat and danger of war—an almost equally hurtful thing to the financial welfare of a people or country.

It should also be remembered that England is not an aggressive country in the ordinary sense of the word. Defence, not defiance, is her practical platform. The British wars of this century have, as a whole, been primarily connected with the protection of her possessions, the guarding of her commerce, or the complications arising out of a Colonial Empire spread all over the world. For this reason she is a natural ally of the United States, which, above most things, needs peace, and, above all other matters of external policy, needs it with England. The one sends most of its agricultural products to the other, and Great Britain would find it difficult, though not impossible, to do without American food, while the United States could neither eat nor sell its wheat and pork, if temporarily deprived by war of the British market. And surely an alliance with England would be not only an advantage to the great daughterland, but an honour as well. To quote Mr. John Morley in an eloquent and scholarly speech delivered during the month of January:

"Our Empire extends over vast zones of the surface of the earth. It extends over races of every colour, of every kind of history, and every creed. It rests not alone on our unrivalled material and money resources. It rests not on the sword alone; it rests not on the mighty battle-ship alone; it rests not even alone on the undaunted spirit of the people of these isles. No; it rests upon the conviction and the belief—and, on the whole, a justified conviction and belief—that in the inmost mind of the governing people of these islands our flag waves not as a token of dominion, but as a token that our councils are animated by a spirit of inflexible equity, that we will not suffer our rights to be invaded just because we will not invade the rights of others."

The British point of view is a simple one. An alliance of this kind would so strengthen its hands that half the complications of the day would disappear. Prestige, in these modern times of trouble, is much, and when Europe was convulsed in 1878, and peace with honour obtained at Berlin, chiefly through Lord Beaconsfield's daring policy of bringing Indian troops to Malta and thus revealing the possibilities of using a million Asiatic soldiers in case of war; when the press of the world regarded the sending of a few Australian and Canadian volunteers to the Soudan in 1884 as a sign of significant and hitherto dormant strength in the British Empire; what would the great Powers not feel concerning England's prestige when they saw her power united with the vast resources and population of the United States?

What could the pauperized nations of Europe, with all the admitted greatness of their historic past, and the mighty armaments of the present, do in conflict with the money and men of the Anglo-Saxon race? Such an alliance would mean the peaceful settlement of African questions; the stretching of the red line of British territory from the Cape to Cairo; the realization of Cecil Rhodes' dream of a great British African Empire, and railway and telegraph lines connecting Cape Town with Khartoum, and Khartoum with Cairo. It would indirectly remove danger from Russian ambition on the borders of Afghanistan and

Turkey, and settle the questions connected with France and Egypt, and France and Newfoundland. It would throw open the disordered and undeveloped States of South America to the trade and enterprise of the United States. It would bring appreciably nearer the period when civilization shall mean peace instead of preparation for war, and Christianity represent the principles of harmony instead of discord.

But in this connection the union of these countries means much for the Christians of the East—how much no pen can tell. There are now several possibilities before them and the world, if they be not first exterminated in Asia Minor as a sort of last desperate product of Turkish fanaticism. Invasion and conquest by Russia is one, and would prove preliminary to a prolonged and devastating European war, and the addition of one more link to the chain of endless battles which connects the past and present of these historic lands. Such an occupation might be carried out with Turkish consent, but it could never be allowed by Great Britain. The general result would be doubtful, so far as the Christian populations were concerned, and would be dependent upon a multitude of European international considerations.

The second alternative is an agreement amongst the Powers to let Austria occupy Constantinople and administer it in friendly relation—which she has always fairly maintained—with the various Christian States of Turkey, while letting Russia occupy Asia Minor. But this solution would be only temporary, and would bring neither comfort to the Christians of Asiatic der the selfish despotism of the Czar' permanent peace to Europe. It xt(Russian territory and expand Russ. stre n fo. the final struggle over Constantinople. The nird alternative is the interference of England with power enough behind her to ensure success, and to avert a general war. This can only come through her combination with the United States in joint, harmonious action.

Their policy would naturally be a revival of the Anglo-Turkish agreement—with or without Russian consent—and the occupation of Asia Minor, together with a steady development of friendly relations with Austria and the Balkan States. After a few years of administration in Asiatic Turkey it should be possible to present such an object-lesson in Christian government and such a picture of material progress as would surprise the East, and promote harmony, by pure force of example, amongst the rival States of European Turkey. The influence of Austria, the withdrawal of the disorganizing pressure of Russian intrigue, and the weight of mutual racial affiliation, should also help in drawing Servia, Bulgaria, Bosnia, Herzegovina, and Montenegro into some sort of friendly relationship, and a position in which the patriotic dream of centuries might be accomplished, and a Confederation of the Slavonic Balkan States be finally realized. With the accession of Roumania—different in race, but similar in its interests—and the giving of Albania and the lower part of Macedonia to Greece, the partition of the Ottoman Empire could be safely accomplished, and Stamboul once more echo to the tread of Christian rulers, and for the first time in its stormy annals become the head of a really peaceful Christian Confederacy.

But whether this Confederation were accomplished or not, the city and surrounding country could be given to either Bulgaria or Greece, in trust for Christendom, and as an assurance that it would not be acquired for aggressive military and naval purposes by the great Power to the north. Thus, under the joint and powerful operation of the two chief Christian nations of the world, peace and a chance of prosperity would be brought to all these more or less unhappy Eastern lands; the future of Armenia and the Armenians could be assured under some local ruler of their own; the Eastern Question in its central form would be peaceably and beneficially settled. And the four thousand years of conflict and invasion, struggle and conquest, persecution and massacre, to which suffering Armenia has been subjected, would give way to a brighter, better, but certainly not nobler era—one in which the cherished cultivation of the fertile soil could be pursued in peace; the genius of the people for trade and business be developed in full; and the homes of the nation be made happy in religious quiet and surrounding comfort.

The removal of the Turk from amongst the Powers of the world would thus be accomplished—gradually, and without any great international change or terrible European conflict. Under this steady pressure of two great Powers in its Asiatic territory, and the environment of hostile and growing Christian States around and within its European possessions, the Porte would be slowly but surely squeezed out of national existence; and the once all-conquering Ottoman forced into subjection by a combination of circumstances, and by that logic of necessity which the fatalism inherent in his religion, and now dominant in his enervated character, would render such an all-powerful factor in compelling his submission to the decrees of Kismet.

It would be a great relief to Christendom. During its aggressive days Turkey was a burden and menace to Europe, and the cause of an enormous amount of suffering and ruthless bloodshed. During its decline the power of the Sultans has been a curse to humanity. Two hundred years ago Ahmed Kiuprili—the greatest of Ottoman statesmen—spoke of the Sword as "that keen and decisive judge," and of God, "who hath poised upon nothing heaven and earth, by whose aid Islamism has for a thousand years triumphed over its foes." But the time has nearly come for the crushing of a Power which first used its false religion for the attempted coercion of the world, and has since developed the evil inherent in that creed into a system of corrupt misgovernment, cruel oppression, and individual immorality, probably unequalled in the history of mankind. For a long period this system has been disgracing Europe, and, despite the efforts of British statesmen for its betterment, has been getting worse year by year. It is nearly half a century now since Lord Aberdeen, Prime Minister of England, declared that:

"Notwithstanding the favourable opinion of many, it is difficult to believe in the improvement of the Turks. It is true that under the pressure of the moment benevolent decrees may be issued; but these, except under the eye of some Foreign Minister, are entirely neglected. Their whole system is radically vicious and inhuman. I do not refer to fables which may be invented at St. Petersburg or Vienna, but to numerous despatches of Lord Stratford himself, and of our own Consuls, who describe a frightful picture of lawless oppression and cruelty."

But the difference between the past and present is only one of degree. The brilliance and glamour of conquest has gone from the history of the Turk, and been replaced by dependence and treachery. All the evil which once exhibited itself in the Ottoman character has been preserved, and increased by the elimination of the little that was good and the enhancement of whatever was bad. During his five hundred years in Europe he has benefited no one, and injured every people that he has come in contact with. Liberty died under the torch of Islam, as personified in the Turk; progress became retrogression; independence was turned into bondage; religion became the instrument of endless cruelty; fertility of soil and beauty of scenery were transformed into deserts and regions of utter wildness; and in fact, as well as in proverb, "Wherever the Sultan's horse-hoof trod, grass never grew again."

The Turk, in short, can show no memorials of cultivation, of development, of improvement he can only show memorials of destruction, of sorrow, of suffering, and of crime. To quote Mr. E. A. Freeman: "This dominion is, perhaps, the only case in history of a lasting and settled dominion, as distinguished from mere passing inroads, which has been purely evil, without any one redeeming feature." But the day of retribution is near, and whether by European war and renewed desolation to these historic lands, or by the beneficent intervention of Britain and America, as here suggested, the Turk must surely be crushed. And when that event occurs, to quote words once applied to Venice in its days of decadence, the Christian world can truly say:

> "Mourn not for Turkey—though her fall
> Be awful as if ocean's wave
> Swept o'er her—she deserves it all,
> And Justice triumphs o'er her grave.
>
> Thus perish every King and State
> That run the guilty race she ran,
> Strong but in fear, and only great
> By outrage against God and man."

Of course, the policy thus outlined is very great and far-reaching, but certainly not more so than the population, wealth, resources, and power of the Empire and the Republic. It would, to sum up, involve permanent peace and co-operation between them in the interest of Christendom. It would give the United States a noble ideal and a worthy foreign policy. It would add the vast naval strength of England, her enormous Indian facilities for Eastern warfare, and her immense monetary strength, to the unequalled fighting possibilities of the United States. It would ensure the peaceful development of the British Empire, whilst enabling the United States to expand at will amid the varied resources and possibilities of South America. And, finally, it would not only give to all English-speaking people an alliance so strong as to compel external peace, and so great as to help their own mutual prosperity, but it would have forced the Turk of Asia Minor into subjection to the beneficent reforms of the new protectorate; would make that garden of the East blossom under new conditions, as it was originally fitted by nature and Providence to do; would drive back the pressing weight of Russian despotism from the Christian States of the Balkan Peninsula, and eventually replace Constantinople in its old historic position as a Christian capital.

INDEX

Abdul-Aziz.................41, 68, 78, 82, 290
Abdul-Medjid.....................64, 68, 78
Abdul-Hamid II........................69, 83
Abd-el-Kadir.......................... 256
Aberdeen, Lord....................... 445
Adrianople, Treaty of...........63, 177, 221
Ahmed Kiuprili 33, 445
Alaeddin............................. 21
Albanians, The......................127, 167
Alexander, King of Servia..........171, 275
Ali Pasha of Janina.................60, 81, 139
America, South....................... 436
Amurath II........................... 31
Anglicanism and the Armenian Church 241
Anglo-Turkish Convention. 330, 335, 337, 347
Appeal of Armenian Clergy........... 373
Arbitration.......................... 437
Armenia.21, 67, 69, 74, 122, 124, 157, 190, 200
    209, 212-228, 239-244, 247-259, 285, 293
    294, 325, 329, 333, 340, 349, 366, 370-
    378, 380-396, 403, 409, 412, 419.
Armenian Independence............... 217
Armenian Churches Abroad........... 227
Armenian Relief Committees......... 320
Armenians in War.................... 433
Argyll, Duke of 314, 320, 333, 350, 351
Avsood, Atrocities at................. 306

Bajaset II............................ 25
Bagdad, Capture of................... 43
Balractar Pasha...................... 58
Balfour, Mr.......................430, 431
Balkan States and Confederation...... 444
Berlin, Treaty of...127, 143, 179, 190, 291,
    327, 405.
Bessara................................94, 283
Beaconsfield, Lord..160, 177, 190, 291, 326,
    330, 331, 355.
Bitlis...................224, 298, 304, 316, 375
Blake, Hon. S. H..................... 416

Bosnia..23, 97, 126, 156, 167, 184-192,
    296, 356.
Britain and the Turk..56, 60, 90, 96, 98, 99,
    101, 141, 143, 148, 160, 200, 206, 278,
    293, 326-342, 379.
British Interests in Egypt............. 209
British Consul's Report in 1896....... 322
Bryce, Mr., on British Policy........ 383
Bucharest, Treaty of.................. 97
Bulgaria..97, 129, 131, 135, 147, 149-166, 190,
    193, 238, 279, 284, 290, 291, 323, 329, 347
    23, 105, 109, 110.

Canada's Help to Armenia........... 413
Canadian Attitude................... 419
Caven, Principal.................... 416
Cause of the Recent Massacres....... 314
Charlton, Mr. John.................. 422
Chamberlain, Mr., on United States
    Co-operation.................... 412
Character of the Turk.
    Relations of the Sexes........... 83
    National Attachment to......... 200
    Religious Pride................. 264
    The Element of Fatalism,....... 269
    Its General Result.............. 274
Chester, Public Meeting at.......... 351
Christian Rising, Rumoured......... 322
Constantinople, Taking of........... 27
Constantinople, Slaughter in 376
Corruptions of Turkish Rule 270
Cox, Hon. S. S. 75, 241, 401
Crusaders, Moslem Struggle with..... 43
Cyprus, The Session of.............. 331

Deputation to Hawarden............. 349
Dervishes, The...................... 432
Dewey, Mr. T. M.................... 416
Diarbekr............................ 223
Dougall, Mr. J. R. 413

INDEX. 449

Druses, The.................... 230
Dufferin, Lord......... 76, 207, 284, 292, 411

Eastern Question, The.....282, 290, 313, 330-
  342, 431, 439-441, 447.
Egypt and Turkish Rule............196-209
Elliot, Sir Henry..,.............76, 159, 160
England and Turkey..............434-436
English Minister to Turkey, First.... 280
Ertoghrul........................... 21
Erzeroum, City of............223, 313, 366
European Powers and Armenia....... 329
Eutychian Heresy, The........... 236

Farcical Nature of Reforms.......... 386
First Christian Church in Armenia.... 231
Foster, Hon. G. E................... 415
Freeman, E. A..................... 446
Funds Raised in Canada............ 413
Future of Armenia.................. 444
Future of Turkey................... 434

Geikie, Dr. W. B.................. 413
Genghiz Khan 43, 199
Gladstone, Mr....125, 148, 160, 177, 190, 191,
  288, 331, 333, 340, 345·360, 389, 394, 396
Grant, Principal, Letter to 375
  "   "   Views of........... 413
Great Britain's Helplessness 393
Greek War of Independence...60, 63, 134, 148
Greek Influence on Armenia......... 232
Greece and Christianity 104-115
Gulhané, Hatti-Scheriff of........... 65

Halifax, N.S., Meeting............. 417
Harpoot, Butchery of............... 369
Hatti-Scheriff of Gulhané........... 65
Herzegovina..........156, 164-193, 290, 356
Hess, Evidence of Miss............. 370
Hierarchy, The Armenian........... 238
Hobart Pasha..................... 429
Hoyles, Mr. N. W.................. 416

Ibrahim Pasha......61, 63, 139, 196, 202, 205
Immorality of the Turk............ 273
India, Safety of................... 426
  "   Religious Loyalty of.......... 426
  "   Mahometans in........427, 428
Intervention, The Policy of......... 379
Iradé, The Turkish................ 384
Ismail, Khedive of Egypt........... 206

Jassey, Peace of................... 96

Janizaries, The.35, 36, 56, 57, 58, 60, 144, 170,
  186, 197.
Kara Mustapha.................... 3
Kainardji, Treaty of................94, 95
Kharput Massacre................. 367
Kinglake, Mr...................... 173
Kingdom of Armenia............... 214
Koran, The....................... 267
Kurds, The..247, 250, 297, 302, 305, 316, 341,
  '385.

Lathern, Rev. Dr................... 417
Laurier, Hon. Wilfrid.............. 421
Layard, Sir Austin Henry.......76, 248, 292
Lewis, Archbishop................. 416
Lobanoff, Prince, and England....... 390

Maclaren, Mr. J. J................ 416
Magna Charta of Turkey............ 65
Mahomet II., Conquests of.......... 24
  "   IV., Reign of........ ....32, 81
Mahomet the Prophet...............42, 426
Mahmoud II..................50, 78, 98
Mahometan courage................ 198
Mamelukes, The.....60, 63, 94, 197, 199, 201
McKeown, Mr. H. A................ 416
Meeting at St. John, N.B............ 416
Mehemet Ali.................200-202, 249
Mesrob 232
Midhat Pasha 67, 69, 83
Migrations of Armenians............ 219
Military Strength of Turkey ...425, 432-434
Mohammed Kiuprili 33
Moldavia 63, 94, 97, 156, 280
Montenegro.......95, 118, 127, 185, 193, 329
Morley, John, on the British Empire 440, 441
Moussa Pasha..................... 57
Mustapha IV...................... 57

Nova Scotia, Bishop of............413, 417
Novikoff, Madame................. 359

Œcumenical Councils and Armenia... 235
Opinion of Toronto Globe 423
Orfah 223, 373
Origin of Armenian Christianity...... 215
Ottoman Empire, Rise of the........ 22

Palmerston, Lord.....65, 67, 68, 69, 170, 177,
  288, 335, 388.
Persian Attack on Armenia 220, 233
Population of Armenia............. 227

INDEX

Queen Victoria..............287, 358, 405

Rahim Pasha........................... 305
Rand, Professor....................... 416
Reforms of Lord Granville............. 338
" in Egypt, Present............ 207
Religion of the Turk..^s............... 40
    Compared with Others.......... 41
    Doctrines of the Koran......... 41
    Mahomet's Life.................42, 43
    Acknowledged by Persia....... 43
    The Military Element..........44, 49
    The Immoral Element........... 45
    Influence of the Koran......... 45
    Taught in the Schools.......... 46
    Worship of One God............ 47
    The Moslem Paradise........... 61
Reschid Pasha...................67, 69, 271
Rosebery, Lord...208, 314, 335, 340, 347, 396
Roman Catholicism and Armenia...... 239
Roumania....218, 256, 269-281, 282, 301, 329
Roumelia.......................95, 126, 163
Russia, Duplicity of.................. 387
   " and Armenia..............429, 430
   " and Servia.................... 430
Russian Conquest of Armenia......... 220
   " Ambition..................... 428
   " Relations with Turkey........63, 73,
    88-101, 140, 153, 163, 329-339.

San Stefano, Treaty of..99, 172, 179, 291, 301, 329.
Saracens in Spain, The............... 43
Salisbury, Lord..160, 164, 177, 292, 322, 326, 331, 335, 353, 389, 392, 395.
Said Pasha........................206, 395
Sale's Translation of the Koran....... 48
Selim I........................25, 196
Selim II............................ 30
Selim III.......................36, 36, 138
Servia..23, 118, 120, 124, 129, 141, 149, 169-181, 185, 186, 193, 285, 329.
Smith, Mr. Goldwin..........284-286, 420
Smythe, Mr. W. J.................... 416
Solyman the Magnificent..............26, 45
St. John, Knights of................. 27
St. Gothard, Battle of............... 34

Stratford de Redcliffe, Lord..64, 66, 67, 76, 98, 123, 141, 142, 207, 265, 282, 285, 289, 290, 291, 389.

Tiflis............................. 240
Tilley, Sir Leonard..............413, 416
Times on the Massacres.............. 314
Trebizond.....................225, 256, 259
Turk, Conquests of the................ 22
    Attack on Vienna............. 28
    Mediterranean Campaign...... 29
    In the Eastern Seas.......... 43
    Trebizond Over-run........... 24
    First War on Armenia......... 219
    Massacre of Races............ 252
    Removal of the............... 444
Turkish Reform...................... 431

Unkiar Skelessi, Treaty of...........63, 98
United States Citizens Attacked...... 67
   " Interests in Turkey........ 397
   " Policy towards Christians.. 398
   " Mission Organizations..... 398
   " First Missionaries......... 402
   " Protests against Outrages.. 404
   " President's Inaction........ 405
   " Alliance with Britain Advocated..............410, 436
   " And War with England.437-8, 440
   " And Eastern Question....438, 439

Van, City of....................224, 298
Venezuelan Affair, The............406, 438-9
Von Kallay, Baron.................... 356

Wahabites.........................63, 431
Wallachia............63, 94, 97, 152, 156, 280
War, a Holy......................... 426
Westminster, Duke of......314, 320, 351, 404
Women, Treatment of ....192, 234, 300, 317, 328, 368, 370.
Writers on the Turkish Question...... 272

Yeretzian, Murder of................. 368

Zeitoun........................387, 433
Zohrab's Evidence, Consul........... 297

www.ingramcontent.com/pod-product-compliance
Lightning Source LLC
Chambersburg PA
CBHW032007300426
44117CB00008B/929